TIME LIFE ® BOOKS

Other Publications:

PLANET EARTH
COLLECTOR'S LIBRARY OF THE CIVIL WAR
LIBRARY OF HEALTH
CLASSICS OF THE OLD WEST
THE EPIC OF FLIGHT
THE SEAFARERS
THE ENCYCLOPEDIA OF COLLECTIBLES
THE GREAT CITIES
WORLD WAR II
HOME REPAIR AND IMPROVEMENT
THE WORLD'S WILD PLACES
THE TIME-LIFE LIBRARY OF BOATING
HUMAN BEHAVIOR
THE ART OF SEWING
THE OLD WEST
THE EMERGENCE OF MAN
THE AMERICAN WILDERNESS
THE TIME-LIFE ENCYCLOPEDIA OF GARDENING
LIFE LIBRARY OF PHOTOGRAPHY
THIS FABULOUS CENTURY
FOODS OF THE WORLD
TIME-LIFE LIBRARY OF AMERICA
TIME-LIFE LIBRARY OF ART
GREAT AGES OF MAN
LIFE SCIENCE LIBRARY
THE LIFE HISTORY OF THE UNITED STATES
TIME READING PROGRAM
LIFE NATURE LIBRARY
LIFE WORLD LIBRARY
FAMILY LIBRARY:
   HOW THINGS WORK IN YOUR HOME
   THE TIME-LIFE BOOK OF THE FAMILY CAR
   THE TIME-LIFE FAMILY LEGAL GUIDE
   THE TIME-LIFE BOOK OF FAMILY FINANCE

*This volume is one of a series that explains and demonstrates
how to prepare various types of food, and that offers in each
book an international anthology of great recipes.*

Cookies & Crackers

BY
THE EDITORS OF TIME-LIFE BOOKS

TIME-LIFE BOOKS/ALEXANDRIA, VIRGINIA

Cover: A chocolate-frosted cookie—formed by shaping creamed dough with a cookie press *(pages 22-23)*—is lifted from a plate that displays seven examples of the cookie baker's art. Clockwise from the right are pressed rosettes, garnished with apricot jam and pistachios; ring-topped sandwiches *(page 18)*, filled with raspberry jam and dusted with confectioners' sugar; pressed cookies, garnished with candied green cherries and almonds; spicy Linzer-cookie cups, filled with raspberry jam *(recipe, page 139)*; and meringue-based cinnamon stars *(page 60)*. At center are hand-molded almond crescents *(pages 58-59)*.

Time-Life Books Inc.
is a wholly owned subsidiary of
TIME INCORPORATED

Founder: Henry R. Luce 1898-1967

Editor-in-Chief: Henry Anatole Grunwald
President: J. Richard Munro
Chairman of the Board: Ralph P. Davidson
Executive Vice President: Clifford J. Grum
Chairman, Executive Committee: James R. Shepley
Editorial Director: Ralph Graves
Group Vice President, Books: Joan D. Manley
Vice Chairman: Arthur Temple

TIME-LIFE BOOKS INC.

Editor: George Constable. *Executive Editor:* George Daniels. *Board of Editors:* Dale M. Brown, Thomas H. Flaherty Jr., William Frankel, Thomas A. Lewis, Martin Mann, John Paul Porter, Gerry Schremp, Gerald Simons, Kit van Tulleken. *Director of Administration:* David L. Harrison. *Director of Research:* Carolyn L. Sackett. *Director of Photography:* Dolores Allen Littles. *Production Director:* Feliciano Madrid; *Assistant:* Peter A. Inchauteguiz. *Copy Processing:* Gordon E. Buck. *Quality Control Director:* Robert L. Young; *Assistant:* James J. Cox; *Associates:* Daniel J. McSweeney, Michael G. Wight. *Art Coordinator:* Anne B. Landry. *Copy Room Director:* Susan Galloway Goldberg; *Assistants:* Celia Beattie, Ricki Tarlow

President: Carl G. Jaeger. *Executive Vice Presidents:* John Steven Maxwell, David J. Walsh. *Vice Presidents:* George Artandi, Stephen L. Bair, Peter G. Barnes, Nicholas Benton, John L. Canova, Beatrice T. Dobie, James L. Mercer

THE GOOD COOK

The original version of this book was created in London for Time-Life Books B.V.
European Editor: Kit van Tulleken; *Design Director:* Louis Klein; *Photography Director:* Pamela Marke; *Planning Director:* Alan Lothian; *Chief of Research:* Vanessa Kramer; *Chief Sub-Editor:* Ilse Gray; *Chief of Editorial Production:* Ellen Brush; *Quality Control:* Douglas Whitworth

Staff for *Cookies & Crackers: Series Editor:* Ellen Galford; *Series Coordinator:* Liz Timothy; *Text Editor:* Margot Levy; *Anthology Editors:* Markie Benet, Anne Jackson; *Staff Writers:* Tim Fraser, Thom Henvey, Alexandra Carlier, Sally Crawford; *Researchers:* Margaret Hall, Deborah Litton; *Designer:* Michael Morey; *Sub-Editors:* Sally Rowland, Charles Boyle, Kate Cann, Frances Dixon; *Design Assistant:* David Mackersey; *Editorial Department:* Steve Ayckbourn, Sarah Dawson, Debra Dick, Judith Heaton, Theresa John, Lesley Kinahan, Stephanie Lee, Debra Lelliott, Linda Mallett, Molly Sutherland, Julia West, Helen Whitehorn, Sylvia Wilson

U.S. Staff for *Cookies & Crackers: Editor:* Gerry Schremp; *Senior Editor:* Ellen Phillips; *Designer:* Ellen Robling; *Chief Researchers:* Barbara Fleming, Barbara Levitt; *Picture Editor:* Christine Schuyler; *Text Editor:* Sarah Brash; *Writers:* Patricia Fanning, Leslie Marshall; *Researchers:* Robert Carmack, Ann Ready (techniques), Fran Moshos (anthology); *Assistant Designer:* Peg Schreiber; *Copy Coordinators:* Nancy Berman, Tonna Gibert, Katherine F. Rosen; *Art Assistant:* Mary L. Orr; *Picture Coordinator:* Alvin Ferrell; *Editorial Assistants:* Carolyn Bounds, Brenda Harwell, Patricia Whiteford

CHIEF SERIES CONSULTANT

Richard Olney, an American, has lived and worked for some three decades in France, where he is highly regarded as an authority on food and wine. Author of *The French Menu Cookbook* and of the award-winning *Simple French Food,* he has also contributed to numerous gastronomic magazines in France and the United States, including the influential journals *Cuisine et Vins de France* and *La Revue du Vin de France.* He has directed cooking courses in France and the United States and is a member of several distinguished gastronomic and oenological societies, including L'Académie Internationale du Vin, La Confrérie des Chevaliers du Tastevin and La Commanderie du Bontemps de Médoc et des Graves. Working in London with the series editorial staff, he has been basically responsible for the planning of this volume, and has supervised the final selection of recipes submitted by other consultants. The United States edition of The Good Cook has been revised by the Editors of Time-Life Books to bring it into complete accord with American customs and usage.

CHIEF AMERICAN CONSULTANT
Carol Cutler is the author of a number of cookbooks, including the award-winning *The Six-Minute Soufflé and Other Culinary Delights.* During the 12 years she lived in France, she studied at the Cordon Bleu and the École des Trois Gourmandes, and with private chefs. She is a member of the Cercle des Gourmettes, a long-established French food society limited to just 50 members, and is also a charter member of Les Dames d'Escoffier, Washington Chapter.

SPECIAL CONSULTANTS
Pat Alburey, a member of the Association of Home Economists of Great Britain, has wide experience in preparing foods for photography, teaching cookery and creating recipes. She was responsible for a majority of the step-by-step demonstrations.
Joyce Dodson Piotrowski studied cooking while traveling and living around the world. A teacher, chef, caterer, food writer and consultant, she also demonstrated step-by-step techniques for this volume.

PHOTOGRAPHERS
John Elliott, based in London, trained at the Regent Street Polytechnic. He has extensive experience in advertising and magazine photography, as well as in his special interest, food photography.
Tom Belshaw was born near London and started his working career in films. He now has his own studio in London. He specializes in food and still-life photography, undertaking both editorial and advertising assignments.

INTERNATIONAL CONSULTANTS
GREAT BRITAIN: *Jane Grigson* has written a number of books about food and has been a cookery correspondent for the London *Observer* since 1968. *Alan Davidson* is the author of several cookbooks and the founder of Prospect Books, which specializes in scholarly publications about food and cookery. FRANCE: *Michel Lemonnier,* the cofounder and vice president of Les Amitiés Gastronomiques Internationales, is a frequent lecturer on wine and vineyards. GERMANY: *Jochen Kuchenbecker* trained as a chef, but worked for 10 years as a food photographer in several European countries before opening his own restaurant in Hamburg. *Anne Brakemeier* is the co-author of a number of cookbooks. ITALY: *Massimo Alberini* is a well-known food writer and journalist, with a particular interest in culinary history. His many books include *Storia del Pranzo all'Italiana, 4000 Anni a Tavola* and *100 Ricette Storiche.* THE NETHERLANDS: *Hugh Jans* has published cookbooks and his recipes appear in several Dutch magazines. THE UNITED STATES: *Judith Olney,* author of *Comforting Food* and *Summer Food,* received her culinary training in England and France. In addition to conducting cooking classes, she regularly contributes articles to gastronomic magazines.

Correspondents: Elisabeth Kraemer (Bonn); Margot Hapgood, Dorothy Bacon (London); Susan Jonas, Lucy T. Voulgaris (New York); Maria Vincenza Aloisi, Josephine du Brusle (Paris); Ann Natanson (Rome).
Valuable assistance was also provided by: Janny Hovinga (Amsterdam); Bona Schmid (Milan); Mimi Murphy (Rome).

For information about any Time-Life book, please write:
Reader Information, Time-Life Books
541 North Fairbanks Court, Chicago, Illinois 60611

Library of Congress CIP data, page 176.

CONTENTS

INTRODUCTION 5 — Small delights / Embellishments sweet and savory / Finishes for grace and flavor / Uncooked butter icing / Confectioners' sugar glaze / A diversity of fillings / A paste of dried fruit / Praline: A powdered amalgam of sugared nuts / The selection and preparation of baking sheets

CREAMED-BUTTER BASES 15

1 — Opportunities for improvisation / A basic formula for firm cookies / Frameworks for fillings / A trio of tools for shaping / Refrigerator dough: A medium for molding / Spirals from layered sheets / Drop cookies: Quick and easy favorites / A soft batter for delicate disks / The molding of just-baked cookies

PASTRY DOUGHS 37

2 — A repertoire of simple techniques / Rich results from a rubbed dough / Forming a disk of crumbly shortbread / Kneading to develop pliability / A spiced wrapper for a nut log / Short-crust spirals with a cinnamon glaze / Shaping a many-layered puff dough / A strong dough for deep frying

EGG-WHITE CONFECTIONS 55

3 — Textures from dense to airy / Macaroons: Chewy cookies from a granular nut paste / Almond crescents with a crunchy coating / Meringues: A range of effects / Dense dough from a foamy base / A hot syrup to stabilize foam

SPONGE FOUNDATIONS 65

4 — Capturing lightness in beaten eggs / Embossed shapes with a sugary crust / Snowy domes scattered with anise seeds / Madeleines: Molded cookies with a cakelike texture / Ladyfingers with a beaded surface

SYRUP-FLAVORED MIXTURES 73

5 — Melting in sweetness / A generous use of syrup for spicy lebkuchen / Scope for inventive shaping / Golden brown nuggets from a sticky dough / A blueprint for a gingerbread house / A molten binding for fruit and nuts / Brownies: Traditional favorites

CRACKERS 85

6 — Crisp and tasty treats / Cooking a flatbread on a griddle / Puffy biscuits from a rubbed dough / Firm deep-fried wafers / Old-fashioned soda crackers made at home / A cheese coating for crunchy straws

ANTHOLOGY OF RECIPES 93 — Drop cookies 94 / Bar cookies 103 / Rolled cookies 112 / Refrigerator cookies 126 / Molded and hand-shaped cookies 129 / Pressed and piped cookies 144 / Meringues and macaroons 148 / Fried cookies 152 / Crackers 155 / Standard preparations 164

RECIPE INDEX 168

GENERAL INDEX / GLOSSARY 170

RECIPE CREDITS 173

ACKNOWLEDGMENTS AND PICTURE CREDITS 176

Small Delights

The art of making cookies and crackers is that of turning simple ingredients into wonderful things. It takes only a peaceful hour or two to transform the most common kitchen staples into raisin-flecked oatmeal cookies, savory cheese twists, delicate ladyfingers or dark and fragrant gingerbread men. The techniques required differ little from those used in cake and pastry making because cookies and crackers are, in effect, miniature cakes and pastries. And, like cakes and pastries, cookies and crackers are the descendants of the earliest food cooked by man—grain-and-water pastes baked on hot stones by Neolithic farmers 10,000 years ago. The development of cookies and crackers from these primitive beginnings is a history of refinements inspired by two different impulses—one plain and practical, the other luxurious and pleasure-loving.

Savory crackers represent the practical and may well have been the first convenience foods: A flour paste, cooked once, then cooked again to dry it thoroughly, becomes a hard, portable victual with an extraordinarily long storage life—perfect for traveling. These rudimentary crackers had little of the culinary charm of their modern descendants, but what they lacked in interest they made up for in utility. For centuries, no ship left port without enough bone-hard, twice-cooked ship's biscuit—the word biscuit comes from the Old French *biscoit,* meaning "twice-cooked"—to last for months, or even years.

While sailors and other travelers chewed their way through unyielding biscuits, cooks of the ancient civilizations of the Middle East explored the culinary possibilities of sweetness and richness. These cooks lightened and enriched the paste mixtures with eggs, butter and cream and sweetened them with fruit, honey and finally—when the food became widely available in the late Middle Ages—with sugar. They added a panoply of other flavors with flower waters and with spices—ginger, cardamom, cloves, nutmeg, cinnamon, allspice and anise seeds.

Luxurious cakes and pastries in large and small versions were well known in the Persian empire of the Seventh Century A.D. With the Muslim invasion of Spain, then the Crusades and the developing spice trade, the cooking techniques and ingredients of Arabia spread into Northern Europe. There the word cookies, distinguishing small confections, appeared: The word comes from the Dutch *koeptje,* meaning "small cake."

By the 14th Century, one could buy little filled wafers on the streets of Paris; as reported in the *Menagier de Paris,* a household manual of the period, these were made by pressing batter between two hot irons. Renaissance cookbooks were rich in cookie recipes, and by the 17th Century, cookies were commonplace. Any reasonably prosperous household was capable of producing little slabs of sugared puff pastry, iced cookies shaped like lover's knots, or wafers made with cream and rose water, such as those recommended in the 1604 English cookbook, *Delights for Ladies.*

Like most foods filled with the rare and sweet, cookies have been associated since time immemorial with festivals and celebrations. And unlike cakes, cookies have a special and easily exploited virtue: The various doughs and batters can easily be shaped into images from the everyday world. This is reflected in the charming and often whimsical names found throughout recipe books: There are cookies called cats' tongues and cookies called dead men's bones; there are roof tiles and wood shavings, parson's hats and little horns, butterflies and cocoons. For special occasions, there are specially shaped cookies. Scottish shortbread *(pages 38-39),* traditionally served on New Year's Eve, is cooked as a large disk whose notched edges are said to symbolize the Celtic sun god. And the cheerful Christmas cookies of Northern Europe—Scandinavia, the Netherlands and Germany—have from medieval times been legion. Many are shaped with the aid of wooden molds, as are Germany's springerle *(pages 66-67),* pale, sugary plaques embossed with fruits, animals and other figures. From Germany, too, comes lebkuchen, the ancestor of gingerbread men *(pages 76-77).*

The mechanics of shaping cookies depend on the texture of the raw material. Some mixtures are firm enough to stamp out with cutters or twist into looped pretzels *(page 27).* Others, such as that for madeleines *(pages 68-69)* are so soft they must be baked in molds. Some thin mixtures, such as creamy egg-white batters, are baked into thin wafers that, when hot, are flexible enough to shape around rolling pins *(pages 34-35).*

This book explains how to mix and shape virtually any cookie—and cracker—dough or batter. The introductory section provides a guide to garnishes, icings and fillings. This is followed by five chapters that demonstrate the use of basic cookie mixtures—creamed doughs based on butter and sugar, pastry doughs, meringues formed from egg whites, sponge bases aerated by whole eggs, and mixtures incorporating syrups such as molasses and honey. A sixth chapter shows how to apply techniques learned throughout the book to savory crackers.

The second half of the book is an anthology chosen from among the world's best cookie and cracker recipes. These come from many different ancient and modern sources; they include 19th Century recipes preserved as treasured heirlooms, as well as new ideas from leading cooks of the present day.

Embellishments Sweet and Savory

Bits of nuts, chocolate and candied or dried fruits ornament and enliven cookies whether sprinkled on top or mixed with the dough. Grated cheese, chopped herbs, coarse salt or savory seeds perform similar roles for crackers.

Such small, solid elements may demand little, if any, advance preparation—or a good deal. Nuts, for example, need to be shelled, and often are peeled and cut up as well: Only fresh nuts prepared at home will ensure high-quality cookies. A coconut requires the most effort: Two of the three soft indentations, or eyes, in the husk must be pierced with a skewer or screwdriver; the liquid must be drained out and the shell cracked with a mallet. Only then can the white flesh be pried out, peeled, and chopped or grated.

Smaller nuts can be opened with a nutcracker. If the pressure is applied along the seams in their shells, even the irregularly shaped meats of walnuts or pecans can often be extracted whole or in halves. Because their thin, inner skins darken dough, small nuts are often peeled.

Nuts with relatively loose skins, such as pistachios or the almonds shown here, are parboiled *(top, right)* to soften their skins for peeling—a process known as blanching. However, the softened skins dry and harden as they cool, so these nuts must be blanched in small batches that can be peeled while still warm. Nuts with tighter skins, such as Brazil nuts or hazelnuts, are first baked for 10 minutes, then rolled in a towel to remove their parched skins *(top, opposite)*. Only the size of the baking pan limits the number of nuts that can be peeled at one time.

Depending on the texture you desire, small nuts can be left whole or halved, chopped with a knife, pounded in a mortar or ground in a processor.

By contrast, raisins or dried currants can be used straight from the box, as can coarse salt and whole seeds. Cheese, of course, needs grating, and herbs, chopping. Large dried fruits such as apricots should be cut into small pieces. So should chocolate *(bottom, right)*. And candied citrus peel or angelica will be easier to handle if it is briefly parboiled to reduce its stickiness *(bottom, opposite)*; you can then chop these ingredients successfully, or cut them into attractive shapes.

Blanching Nuts to Free Loose Skins

1 **Blanching nuts.** Drop shelled nuts—in this case, almonds—into boiling water. After two minutes, remove a nut with a skimmer or perforated spoon. If the skin slips off easily, lift out the remaining nuts or drain them in a colander.

2 **Removing the skins.** Let the nuts cool briefly. While still warm, squeeze each one with your fingers to pop it from its skin. To dry the nuts thoroughly, spread them on a baking sheet and—stirring occasionally—bake them at 350° F. [180° C.] for five minutes. To toast the nuts, bake them for 10 minutes.

Cutting Chocolate Chips

Chopping chocolate. Refrigerate bar chocolate—here, semisweet—for 15 minutes to firm it. With a sharp knife, slice the bar into slivers about ¼ inch [6 mm.] wide *(above, left)*. The chocolate will fragment as you cut it. Heap the chocolate pieces together. Holding the knife blade over the pile, steady the knife tip with your free hand. Using the tip as a pivot, rock the blade up and down as you move it back and forth in an arc *(right)*. Continue chopping until the pieces are the size required. Transfer the pieces to a sieve and shake them free of dusty particles.

Baking Nuts to Parch Tight Skins

1 **Baking nuts.** Spread nuts— hazelnuts are shown here—in a single layer on a baking sheet. Stirring occasionally, bake the nuts in a preheated 350° F. [180° C.] oven until the skins shrivel—about 10 minutes. Lay a cloth towel on a work surface and spill the nuts onto one half of the towel.

2 **Peeling the nuts.** Fold half of the towel over the nuts. Rub your hands lightly back and forth to roll the nuts in the towel; after one or two minutes, most nuts will have shed their skins.

3 **Removing stubborn skins.** Rub partly peeled or unpeeled nuts between your fingers to remove the clinging skins. Reserve any nuts that still have not shed their skins for purposes in which appearance is not important.

Chopping Nuts by Hand

Chopping nuts. Heap nuts— pistachios are shown—on a chopping board. Position the cutting edge of a heavy, sharp knife across the nuts. Holding the knife tip steady with one hand, use your other hand to rock the blade up and down in a side-to-side arc across the pile of nuts.

Preparing Candied Fruit and Peel

1 **Softening.** Bring a pan of water to a boil. Drop pieces of candied citrus peel and angelica into the pan and boil them for one to two minutes until they are soft. Remove the peel and angelica with a skimmer or perforated spoon.

2 **Cutting.** Place the angelica and peel on a chopping board. Slice the angelica into matchstick-sized strips *(background)*. Using a small, sharp knife or, as here, an aspic cutter, cut out geometric shapes from the peel.

Finishes for Grace and Flavor

Icings and glazes both can be used—by themselves or in combination with garnish elements—to embellish otherwise plain cookies. An icing, being opaque, provides a contrast in color and texture whether it coats cookies completely or merely forms decorations *(pages 20-21)*. By contrast, a glaze may be either transparent or opaque and its chief purpose is to give cookies a sheen.

The best icings for cookies are delicate ones that set quickly. The simplest of these is prepared by melting sweet chocolate in a bowl placed over simmering water *(page 82, Step 1)*. More versatile, and almost as easy to make, are the uncooked butter and royal icings shown at top right *(recipes, page 164)*. Both icings are based on confectioners' sugar, which dissolves without cooking to ensure a smooth result. Either icing can be flavored with extracts, spirits such as rum or liqueur, or a few drops of strong black coffee; either can be tinted with food coloring.

Of the two, uncooked butter icing is the richer. Its butter-and-cream base keeps it soft for spreading or piping. However, the icing does not dry on standing, so it is best for cookies that will be eaten within a day or so—and served without being stacked. Royal icing, by contrast, is based on egg white and sets into such a firm, long-lasting coat that the thick version shown here can cement the components of a gingerbread house *(pages 78-79)*.

While icings are applied only to baked cookies, glazes may—depending on their nature—be spread onto either unbaked or baked ones. Many glazes are based on eggs, which firm while the cookies bake. Lightly beaten egg whites give a colorless shine; whole eggs or yolks, thinned with water, set to a lustrous gold.

Glazes also can double as flavoring elements. Melted jelly or granulated sugar dissolved in warm milk, for example, can be painted onto cookies just out of the oven to give them a subtly sweet gloss. Baked cookies will have a shiny white finish when spread with confectioners' sugar glaze *(right, bottom)*, flavored to taste with extract, spirits or citrus juice. Boiling granulated sugar and water to a caramel *(opposite, bottom)* forms an amber syrup that, when mixed with egg yolks, will create a reddish brown glaze.

Uncooked Butter Icing

1 **Combining butter and sugar.** In a heavy bowl, beat softened butter with a wooden spoon until it is light and creamy. Stirring constantly, add sifted confectioners' sugar by the spoonful and continue to stir until the sugar and butter become a smooth paste.

2 **Incorporating cream.** Stir liquid flavoring—in this case, vanilla extract—into the sugar-and-butter mixture. Then gradually beat in enough cream to give the mixture a soft spreading consistency. The icing can be used immediately or covered and kept refrigerated for as long as a week.

Confectioners' Sugar Glaze

1 **Adding rum.** Sift confectioners' sugar into a bowl and make a well in the center of the sugar. Add a spoonful of warm water, and stir it in. Gradually mix in more water to make a thick paste. Pour a spoonful of rum into the mixture.

2 **Checking the consistency.** Mix the rum into the glaze. Then lift the spoon; the glaze should coat the back of the spoon. Adjust the consistency if necessary, stirring in more water to thin the glaze, or adding more sugar to thicken it. Use the glaze at once.

Royal Icing Based on Egg Whites

1 **Adding confectioners' sugar.** Crack an egg and separate it over a mixing bowl, letting the white fall into the bowl and setting the yolk aside. Separate the remaining eggs in the same way. Add a few spoonfuls of sifted confectioners' sugar to the whites *(above, left)*. Pour in liquid flavoring—lemon juice is used here. With a wooden spoon, stir the sugar and flavorings into the whites and beat the mixture until smooth. Add the rest of the sugar, a little at a time *(right)*, beating well after each addition.

2 **Finishing the icing.** When all of the sugar has been incorporated, continue beating the mixture until it is stiff. The icing can be used immediately, or set aside, covered with a damp cloth, for 30 minutes; if it is kept longer, the icing will begin to set.

Egg-Yolk Glaze Enriched with Caramel

1 **Preparing ingredients.** Break up egg yolks with a fork; set aside. Combine sugar and water in a heavy saucepan and stir over medium heat until the sugar dissolves. Wipe the sides of the pan with a brush dipped in hot water, to remove any sugar that might make the syrup crystallize. Bring to a boil.

2 **Thinning caramel.** Maintaining a steady boil, cook the syrup without stirring until it turns a rich, red brown—about 350° F. [180° C.] on a candy thermometer. Remove the caramel from the heat immediately, lest it burn. Stir a little hot water into the caramel to thin it and prevent setting. Let the mixture cool to room temperature.

3 **Mixing eggs and caramel.** Pour a little of the caramel mixture into the beaten egg yolks, stirring as you pour. Gradually add enough caramel to turn the glaze a deep golden brown color. Use the glaze immediately.

A Diversity of Fillings

Fillings are indispensable elements in cookie assemblies. They create a core of contrasting flavor and texture when they are wrapped in dough before it is baked *(pages 18-19 and 42-43)*. And they contribute color as well when used to sandwich two flat cookies together or to fill the hollows of shaped cookies such as cigarettes *(pages 19 and 34-35)*.

The consistency of a filling dictates how it should be used. For example, a soft pastelike filling based on confectioners' sugar, melted butter and liquid flavoring will become runny if placed inside unbaked cookies, but is ideal for sandwiching baked ones together. The paste can be flavored with the juice and peel of oranges or, as shown at top, lemons *(recipe, page 164)*. Alternatively, it can be enlivened with a few sieved fresh currants or blackberries, strong black coffee or a dash of brandy, rum or fruit liqueur.

Fruit jam that has been strained for smoothness also can be used to cement cookie sandwiches. Left unstrained and, perhaps, mixed with a few nuts to give it rougher texture, it can be spooned into hollow cookies.

Dried fruits—including prunes, apricots and the figs shown at right, center *(recipe, page 165)*—can be chopped and cooked to form a paste stiff enough for stuffing unbaked cookies or for filling hollows. As another option, such fruits can be ground in a food grinder or processor, then bound with a little honey to form a thick, uncooked paste.

Fillings based on nuts are usually too dry to adhere to a baked cookie, so it is best to shape the uncooked dough around them. This applies to smooth, firm blends such as nut paste—a stiff mixture of finely ground nuts and sugar bound with egg *(opposite, below; recipe, page 165)*—as well as to looser mixtures of coarsely chopped nuts. A combination of walnuts, sugar and rose water is shown here *(below; recipe, page 165)* but you could also use hazelnuts or pistachios, and a different liquid—orange juice, maple syrup or sweet wine such as Marsala or sherry—for a similar effect.

Softened butter, beaten until fluffy, provides a particularly rich base for a filling that will be appropriate for sandwiches or for filling hollow cookies. The butter can be flavored with puréed dried or fresh fruit, cocoa powder or melted chocolate, or with praline—a powdered mixture of caramelized nuts *(page 12; recipe, page 165)*. To make the praline, nuts and sugar are cooked together. This toasts the nuts, intensifying their flavor, and also melts the sugar to a rich, dark caramel. As the caramel cools, it encases the nuts in a hard, brittle sheet that can be easily ground into a fine powder—either in a mortar or a food processor.

A Tangy Lemon Blend

1 **Assembling ingredients.** Melt butter in a small pan. Sift confectioners' sugar into a bowl; grate in lemon peel. Squeeze the lemon juice and add it

A Paste of Dried Fruit

1 **Preparing fruit.** Simmer dried fruit—here, figs—in water for 10 minutes, until the fruit is soft. Drain it, reserving the water. Remove any stems.

Chopped Nuts Moistened with Rose Water

1 **Adding sugar to nuts.** Coarsely chop nuts—here, walnuts. Place them in a bowl with an equal quantity of superfine sugar. Mix the nuts and sugar.

2 **Moistening the filling.** Pour in a spoonful of rose water *(above, left)*. Stir the rose water into the nut and sugar mixture. If necessary, add a few more drops of rose water to give the filling the consistency of coarse crumbs *(right)*.

2 **Stirring.** Add the butter. Set the bowl over a pan of boiling water and stir the mixture until smooth. Let it stand off the heat for 10 minutes; stir occasionally.

3 **Beating the filling.** Remove the bowl from the pan and beat the warm mixture with a wooden spoon *(above, left)*. As it cools, continue beating the lemon filling until it develops a thick, spreading consistency *(right)*.

2 **Chopping.** Heap the fruit on a board. Place a heavy knife over the fruit and steady its tip as you rock the blade to chop the fruit coarse.

3 **Cooking.** Place the chopped fruit, reserved water and sugar in a heavy pan. Stir the mixture over medium heat until the sugar dissolves *(above, left)*. Bring to a boil, then simmer for 10 minutes, until the filling is thick *(right)*.

Ground Nuts Bound with Eggs

1 **Mixing nuts and sugar.** Peel nuts— almonds, here—and grind them fine in a processor. In a bowl, combine the nuts, sugar and grated lemon peel.

2 **Adding eggs.** Beat eggs with a fork until blended. Stir a little beaten egg into the nut mixture. Add more egg, a little at a time, until the mixture coheres.

3 **Kneading the paste.** When the mixture holds together, gather it into a ball with your hands. In the bowl, knead the paste briefly until it is smooth.

Praline: A Powdered Amalgam of Sugared Nuts

1 **Mixing nuts and sugar.** Oil or butter a baking sheet; set it aside. Place nuts—here, blanched and peeled almonds are used—and sugar in a heavy saucepan. With a wooden spoon, stir the mixture over low heat until the sugar melts to an amber caramel—about three minutes.

2 **Cooling the praline.** Tip the pan over the prepared baking sheet. With the spoon, push the mixture of nuts and caramel onto the sheet and spread it into a thin layer. Let the praline cool to room temperature.

3 **Pounding the caramel.** Break the cooled and hardened praline into pieces and place the pieces in a sturdy plastic bag. Holding the end of the bag to prevent the contents from spilling out, pound the mixture with a rolling pin or wooden mallet. Alternatively, grind the pieces of praline in a food processor operated in short bursts.

4 **Sifting the praline.** When most of the praline has been reduced to a powder, tip it into a sieve held over a bowl. Stir the praline with your hand to separate the powder from any remaining lumps. Return the lumps to the bag or processor and repeat the pounding and sifting until all of the praline is reduced to powder.

5 **Mixing butter and praline.** In a bowl, let butter soften at room temperature. Beat the butter with a clean wooden spoon until it is pale and fluffy. Add some of the praline powder to the butter and stir it in.

6 **Beating the praline butter.** Beat the praline powder and butter until the mixture forms a smooth paste. Gradually incorporate more praline, beating well after each addition. When it is finished, the praline butter will be airy and light.

The Selection and Preparation of Baking Sheets

The most important piece of equipment for making just about any sort of cookie or cracker is the baking sheet. A heavy-duty baking sheet, properly greased or lined, can spell the difference between success and failure.

The baker's first consideration is the metal from which the sheet is made. Sheets made from shiny aluminum and tin-plated steel will deflect heat and tend to produce cookies or crackers with soft bottom crusts. Sheets of dark-surfaced carbon steel absorb heat and yield crispier, more deeply browned crusts.

Moreover, some metals impose special requirements. A tin-plated steel sheet cannot be used for recipes that specify very high temperatures: Tin melts at 425° F. [220° C.]. Because carbon steel is prone to rust, its porous surfaces must be impregnated with oil, or seasoned, before the sheet is used for the first time (below, left) and thereafter the sheet must be dried as soon as it is washed.

The thickness of the metal, as indicated by gauge, is equally important. A gauge of 1 to 1½ millimeters ensures uniform heat distribution—and browning. Because thinner sheets heat unevenly, part of a batch of cookies or crackers may burn. And thin sheets buckle when they get hot, thus spreading any unbaked batter or dislodging partially baked morsels.

All baking sheets have one or more raised sides to grasp when guiding them into or out of the oven. If a sheet has four raised sides, these should be lower than ½ inch [1 cm.] to permit air to circulate freely over the surface and to facilitate removing the cookies or crackers. Optimum size is determined by the size of your oven: For even heating, allow at least 1 inch [2½ cm.] of space all around the sides of the baking sheet.

For most cookies and crackers, the baking sheet should be greased to prevent sticking (below, right). Butter is preferred because of its flavor, but lard or mild-tasting vegetable oils such as corn oil or safflower oil are also suitable.

Whatever fat or oil you choose, wipe the sheet clean, let it cool, and grease it again before cooking each batch. This process may seem time-consuming, but is necessary to prevent the dough or batter from spreading excessively.

An alternative to greasing—and an essential strategy for sticky meringue-based cookies—is lining the sheet with parchment paper or aluminum foil. The best choice is silicone-treated parchment paper, which can be wiped clean with a paper towel between batches; sheets of untreated parchment paper or foil need to be replaced every time.

To shape the lining to fit, turn the baking sheet upside down on a cutting board and align two of its sides with two edges of the paper or foil. Run a sharp knife along the remaining sides of the sheet to cut the paper or foil. To hold the lining in place, dab all four corners with dough or batter, invert the paper or foil onto the sheet and press the corners down tight.

If you like, you may lay cut pieces of paper on a work surface and arrange the cookies or crackers on them so that the liner will be ready to lift onto the baking sheet as soon as it is cool. In this case, the weight of the dough will keep the liner tight against the sheet.

Seasoning Carbon Steel

Coating with oil. Scour a new carbon-steel baking sheet with soap and water, using a brush with plastic or natural bristles; metal bristles would scratch the sheet. Dry it well and spread a spoonful of flavorless vegetable oil over the baking surface with a paper towel. Oil the underside in the same way. Place the baking sheet in a preheated 375° F. [190° C.] oven. After 10 minutes, turn the heat off and let the sheet cool in the oven.

Brushing On Butter

Brushing with butter. Let solid fat—in this case, butter—soften at room temperature. Dip a pastry brush into the butter and stroke the fat onto the sheet in a thin layer. Use just enough butter to cover evenly all of the baking sheet's surface—an excess will cause the cookies or crackers to spread too much.

1
Creamed-Butter Bases
Opportunities for Improvisation

Capturing air in butter and sugar
Three ways to use fillings
Making a paper piping bag
Devices for shaping
The advantages of chilling dough

These golden cookies, decorated with raisins, derive their brilliant sheen from being glazed twice—first with a coating of sieved apricot jam, then with a thin confectioners' sugar glaze flavored with rum. The cookies, made from a creamed dough thinned with a large number of eggs *(page 31)*, have a tender, spongelike interior.

Of all the formulations in the cookie maker's repertoire, creamed dough is the most versatile. It takes its name from creaming, the process of beating butter and sugar so that air bubbles are forced into the butter. The aerated mixture is then moistened with egg, which is 74 per cent water, and blended with flour. The flour gives body to the dough and, when it becomes moist, the gluten proteins it contains form a microscopic mesh that unites the ingredients. If the dough is not overworked—this would strengthen the gluten too much and toughen the dough—a few minutes' baking will turn creamed dough into crisp, tender cookies.

The unassertive flavor of creamed dough makes it an ideal vehicle for solid confections such as nuts, chocolate bits, raisins, dried currants or candied fruit *(pages 6-7)*. The dough can be assembled with a sweet filling before or after baking *(pages 10-11 and 12)*, and the finished cookies enhanced with any of the icings or glazes described on pages 8-9.

Depending on the proportions of the basic ingredients, creamed doughs provide many opportunities for imaginative shaping. The basic dough made with a minimum of egg and a good deal of flour is firm enough to be molded into balls or rolled out and cut into any design: Circles—plain or fluted—hearts, crescents, rosettes and daisies are among the many cookie cutters available. When a little more egg is added, the dough becomes sufficiently malleable to shape with a tool such as a piping bag, a mechanical cookie press or even a sieve *(page 22)*. If refrigerated to harden it slightly, the dough can be rolled and molded into patterned, parti-colored cookies *(page 26)* or twisted into pretzels *(page 27)*. With still more egg, the dough becomes soft enough to be dropped from a spoon to produce irregular rounds.

Drastically changing the amount of liquid in creamed dough turns it into a batter with further potential for variation. For example, adding one part whole eggs to one and one half parts of dry ingredients will produce a delicate, runny batter that bakes into a cakelike cookie *(opposite and page 31)*. And forming an even thinner mixture with egg whites rather than whole eggs yields a batter that will spread paper-thin when baked, forming light, dry wafers *(pages 34-35)*. The wafers are brittle when cold, but while still warm they can be wrapped around a wooden spoon handle to create decorative containers for creamy fillings.

A Basic Formula for Firm Cookies

In a creamed cookie dough, butter provides lightness as well as richness. To form an airy base for other ingredients, the butter is first softened at room temperature just enough to become malleable; if allowed to melt, it would be too oily to contain air. The butter then is creamed by being beaten vigorously against the sides of a bowl with a spoon until it is light and blends readily with sugar.

As the sugar that sweetens the dough, and gives the sugar cookies their name, is beaten in, the edges of its crystals create tiny pockets for air. With further creaming, these pockets increase until the mixture almost doubles in volume and becomes fluffy and almost white.

The consistency of the dough depends on the amount of flour and egg added to the creamed base. To create a firm dough suitable for rolled cookies, as shown here, butter and sugar are used in roughly the same amounts and the amount of flour approximates their total. Only enough egg is used to moisten the dough and make it cohere (recipe, page 166).

Just as vigorousness is the rule for creaming butter and sugar, so gentleness is the watchword when adding the egg, flour and flavorings. The egg must be blended in quickly, but thoroughly, and the flour sifted, then added a little at a time. Stirring too long or too vigorously will break down the air bubbles in the creamed base, causing the cookies to be dense, and will strengthen the gluten in the flour, making them tough.

Liquid flavoring—vanilla and almond extract are both suitable—can be added with the egg to minimize stirring. Light solid flavorings, such as ground spices or grated orange peel, are incorporated with the flour; more substantial ones, such as chopped nuts or the candied fruit here, are mixed in separately.

The dough can be rolled and cut into cookies as soon as it is assembled. At this stage, too, handling should be gentle to preserve the air bubbles, which will expand when the cookies bake to lighten their texture, ensuring that while they crisp outside they remain tender inside.

As with all rolled dough, scraps may be rerolled and more shapes stamped out—but only one time. After that the dough becomes tough and should be discarded.

1 Creaming butter. Place the butter in a large, heavy bowl and let it stand at room temperature until it is soft enough to be worked easily. Set the bowl on a damp cloth to prevent it from slipping. With the back of a wooden spoon, mash the butter against the sides of the bowl. Then beat it with the spoon or—for speed—an electric mixer until it becomes pale.

2 Blending butter and sugar. Pour sugar into the creamed butter in the bowl. With the spoon or electric mixer, beat the butter and sugar until the mixture becomes fluffy and almost white—about five minutes. To ensure that all the sugar is blended in, scrape the sides of the bowl with the spoon or a rubber spatula from time to time.

6 Mixing in fruit. Finely chop candied fruit—about 1½ cups [375 ml.] of fruit is used here. Mix the fruit into the dough with your hand to distribute it evenly.

7 Rolling the dough. Gather the dough into a ball and place it on a lightly floured work surface. Sprinkle a little flour over the top of the dough to prevent the rolling pin from sticking. With quick, light strokes, roll out the dough to a thickness of about ¼ inch [6 mm.].

3 **Adding an egg.** Break a whole egg into the bowl. Pour in the extract if you are using it. Working quickly, stir the egg and extract into the creamed butter and sugar until the mixture is smooth.

4 **Stirring in flour.** Sift flour and salt onto a piece of wax paper or into another bowl. Shake a little flour into the mixing bowl and use a spoon—not an electric mixer—to stir it into the mixture gently but evenly.

5 **Adding flour by hand.** Shake the rest of the flour into the mixture, a little at a time. When the dough becomes too stiff to stir, gently incorporate the remaining flour with your hand.

8 **Cutting the cookies.** Using a cutter —here, a round fluted one—stamp out as many sugar cookies as possible. Press the cutter firmly into the dough each time to ensure a clean cut. With a metal spatula, transfer the cookies to buttered baking sheets *(page 13)*. Gather the scraps of dough into a ball, roll it and cut more cookies.

9 **Baking the cookies.** To decorate, sprinkle the unbaked cookies with granulated sugar. Bake the cookies in a preheated 350° F. [180° C.] oven until they are pale golden—12 to 15 minutes.

10 **Serving the cookies.** With a metal spatula, transfer the sugar cookies to a wire rack and allow them to cool before serving. Here, the cookies are stacked on a plate to display their fluted edges and the multicolored flecks of candied fruit.

Frameworks for Fillings

By combining a plain dough with a rich filling, you can create a galaxy of fancy cookies. A firm creamed dough *(pages 16-17)* makes an excellent base: It is strong enough to contain a bulky filling, and its mild flavor will counterpoint any of the sweet mixtures described on page 10. You may prepare the assembly before baking the cookies, either by concealing the filling in the dough *(right)* or partly revealing it in an open ring *(below)*. Alternatively, you can sandwich a filling between two already-baked cookies *(opposite, below)*.

If you prefer to conceal the filling, choose a dry nut or fruit mixture that will not spread during baking and thus leak through the dough. Moist lemon fillings or jam should be reserved for sandwiched or open-faced cookies—and can be used to lend a sharp note of contrasting color to the assemblies. Other decorative effects can be devised by sugaring the cookies or brushing their surfaces with icings or glazes *(pages 8-9)* after they are baked.

Hemispheres with Crunchy Cores

1 **Filling the dough.** Prepare a nut filling—here, chopped walnuts flavored with rose water *(page 10)*. Lightly butter baking sheets *(page 13)*. Break off a piece of dough the size of a walnut and roll it between your palms into a small ball *(above, left)*. Press your finger into the ball to make a pocket, and spoon a little filling into it *(center)*. Press the edges of the pocket over the filling to seal it *(right)*; place the cookie on a baking sheet. Shape and fill the rest of the dough in the same way.

Rings to Encircle Fruit Paste

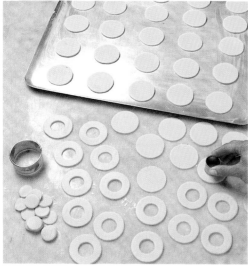

1 **Shaping the dough.** Roll creamed dough to a thickness of about ¼ inch [6 mm.] and stamp out cookies with a round cutter. Place half of the cookies on lightly buttered baking sheets. With a small round cutter, cut out the centers from the remaining cookies to form rings.

2 **Filling the cookies.** Prepare a dried-fruit filling *(pages 10-11)*—in this case, made with figs. Spoon some filling onto each of the cookies on the sheet, leaving a margin around the edge as wide as the rings of dough. Brush the margin with lightly beaten egg to serve as an adhesive. Firmly press a dough ring on each filled cookie.

3 **Baking the cookies.** Bake the cookies in a preheated 350° F. [180° C.] oven for 12 to 15 minutes—until they are a light golden brown. Before you serve them, transfer the cookies to a wire rack to cool.

2 **Baking the cookies.** Bake the cookies at 350° F. [180° C.] until lightly browned — 12 to 15 minutes. Roll them in confectioners' sugar while they are warm so that the sugar will cling to them *(above)*. Cool the cookies on a rack and roll them in sugar again before serving. At right, a cookie has been halved to display its filling.

Heart-shaped Sandwiches with Lemon Filling

1 **Spreading the filling.** Roll out creamed dough until it is about ¼ inch [6 mm.] thick. Stamp out decorative shapes with a cutter—a heart shape is shown. Bake the cookies in a preheated 350° F. [180° C.] oven for about 12 to 15 minutes. Transfer them to a rack to cool. Prepare filling—lemon filling is used here *(pages 10-11)*. With a spatula, spread the browned underside of half of the cookies with filling *(above, left)*; place the other cookies, underside down, on top of the filling *(right)*.

2 **Serving the cookies.** When all the cookies have been sandwiched together, return them to the wire rack and let them stand until the filling has set—about 30 minutes. Serve the cookies from a plate, stacking them to emphasize the bands of lemon filling.

The Artful Use of Line and Color

Flat surfaces of cookies stamped from creamed dough invite decoration. A simple sprinkling of sugar will suffice. So will a slathering of either of the icings shown on pages 8-9. But the most artistic approach is to pipe or paint designs onto the cookies as demonstrated here.

The best mediums for piping are soft and smooth, but not so runny that the design they form spreads after it is applied. Although melted and cooled chocolate is suitable, uncooked butter icing is more versatile because it may be dyed any color of the rainbow with a few drops of liquid food coloring. Sold in supermarkets in kits containing vials of red, yellow, blue and green, the colorings may be mixed to produce other hues.

The only equipment necessary for applying piping is a conical parchment-paper bag that is folded at the top to enclose the icing and cut open at the tip to extrude it. The bag will hold about ¼ cup [50 ml.] of icing. Inexpensive and easy to produce (Step 3, right), the bags can be made up for each color of icing—and disposed of after the piping is applied.

To create a slick background for the piped design, the porous surface of each cookie is sealed with a base coat of confectioners' sugar glaze or royal icing. The glaze will dry as a pearly, shiny base; the icing as an opaque surface. Both may be left white or tinted with food coloring.

The design can include both lines and dots. Their size will be determined by how deeply the bag tip is cut and how much pressure is applied; their arrangement and shape depend on the effect desired. Here the piping outlines the petals of a daisy-shaped cookie and creates dots to resemble the stamens in its center.

Painting gives even freer rein to the cook's imagination. The medium is raw egg white, mixed on a painter's brush with liquid food colorings and swabbed directly onto the cookie. For rich hues, the coloring is left at full strength, but for pastels it can be diluted with a drop or two of water. Either way, the colored egg white is easily painted onto a cookie, and it dries quickly to a bright sheen.

Drawing with a Piping Bag

1 **Forming the base coat.** Prepare confectioners' sugar glaze (recipe, page 164). Place one cookie at a time upside down on a table fork and dip the cookie into the glaze to coat its top surface. Allow the excess glaze to drip off, then turn the cookie upright onto your hand and set it on a wire rack to dry—approximately 15 minutes.

4 **Piping lines of the icing.** Snip off the tip of a piping cone. Holding the cut edge close to the surface of a cookie, squeeze the top of the piping bag gently to press the icing out in a thin strand (above, left). Moving the bag—not the cookie—form the desired outline on each of the cookies. To stop the flow at the end of each line, release the pressure on the bag. After decorating all of the cookies with one icing color, repeat the process with each subsequent color (right)—snipping off the tip of the bag just before you start to work.

5 **Piping dots of icing.** Snip the tip from the piping bag and hold the bag above the cookie at the point where you want to form a dot. Quickly squeeze the bag to push out a dab of icing, then immediately release the pressure. Lift the bag and repeat the process for each dot. Leave the cookies on a rack for a few minutes to allow the icing to set.

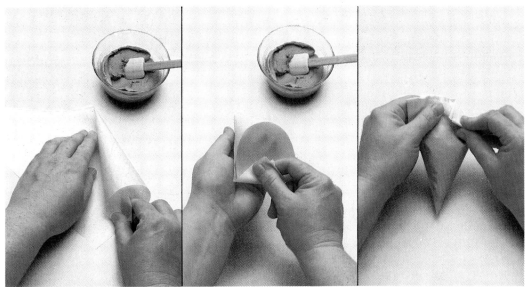

2 **Coloring the icing.** Prepare uncooked butter icing *(recipe, page 164)* and divide the batch among two or more small bowls. Stir liquid food coloring into each bowl of icing, adding a drop or two at a time until the desired color is achieved. Here the icing is mixed with blue and red colorings to produce lavender and purple.

3 **Making a piping bag.** Cut a 10-inch [25-cm.] square of parchment paper diagonally in half to make two triangles. Holding the right-angled point of one triangle, curl one short side until the underside of its oblique-angled point meets the right angle, forming a cone *(above, left)*. Hold the points together and curl the other half of the paper around the cone until all three points meet. Fold the points into the open end of the cone *(center)*. Using a rubber spatula, half-fill the cone with icing. Fold the top of the cone several times to enclose the icing tightly *(right)*.

Painting with a Brush

1 **Applying the base coat.** Prepare a royal icing *(recipe, page 164)*. With a narrow metal spatula, spread the icing smoothly over the top surface of each cookie. Let the cookies dry on a wire rack until the icing is firm to the touch—20 to 30 minutes.

2 **Painting the cookies.** Assemble separate bowls of egg white, water and liquid coloring—full strength or diluted. Moisten an artist's brush with egg white, dip it into the coloring and then paint the mixture onto a cookie. To change colors, clean the brush in the water and dry it on paper towels.

3 **Finishing the painting.** Paint all of the cookies with first one color, then another, until the design is complete. Leave the cookies on the rack for about five minutes until the paint is dry.

A Trio of Tools for Shaping

If a firm creamed dough is enriched with extra butter and moistened with an additional egg yolk *(recipe, page 166)*, it becomes soft enough to be forced through a wire strainer, pastry bag or cookie press as shown here. The resulting pressed, or spritzed, cookies are decorative even if left plain. For extra variety the dough can be colored with cocoa powder and the cookies topped with nuts or sugar.

A strainer *(right)* forms the dough into strands as thin as vermicelli. The strands cling together when scraped off the mesh and blend when baked, but their moss-like pattern remains distinct on the surface. By contrast, a canvas pastry bag equipped with a piping tube allows you to create a spectrum of designs from the rings, paired lines and S shapes shown below to figure 8s, coils and crescents.

A cookie press *(opposite, below)* is essentially a mechanical pastry bag—a metal tube with a plunger at one end and a disk at the other. When dough is forced through the holes in the disk, it forms a cookie with a pattern in its surface.

Using a Strainer for a Mossy Effect

1 **Shaping the dough.** Pull off a piece of the dough about the size of a walnut and shape it into a rough ball with your hands. Place the ball in a strainer and use the back of a spoon to force it through the mesh in thin strands. With a knife, scrape the ends of the strands from the underside of the strainer.

2 **Lifting the dough.** Lift the strands on the knife carefully and drop them onto a buttered baking sheet *(page 13)*; if necessary, use another knife to free the strands. Form the remaining dough into moss cookies in the same way.

Ridged Forms from a Star Tube

1 **Filling the pastry bag.** Fold down a collar at the top of the bag. Push a decorating tube—here, a large No. 7 star tube—into the opening at the tip. Spoon in dough until the bag is two thirds full. Unfold the collar and twist the top of the bag to enclose the dough. To eliminate air pockets, shake the bag—over a bowl to catch drips.

2 **Piping the dough.** Butter baking sheets. Pressing the bag from the top, pipe shapes—in this case, rings, paired lines and S shapes—onto the sheets. After each piping, stop the dough with a knife and twist the top of the bag to keep the dough tightly enclosed.

3 **Dusting with sugar.** Bake the cookies in a preheated 375° F. [190° C.] oven until lightly browned—12 to 15 minutes. Transfer the cookies to a rack to cool. If you wish, dust them with confectioners' sugar, tapping it through a sieve over the warm cookies.

3 **Baking the cookies.** If you like, sprinkle the cookies with finely chopped peeled nuts, such as hazelnuts, almonds or the pistachios shown above. Bake them in a preheated 375° F. [190° C.] oven for 12 to 15 minutes, or until they are lightly golden. Transfer the cookies to a wire rack to cool before you serve them *(right)*.

Neat Rosettes from a Cookie Press

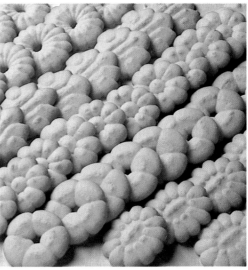

1 **Filling a cookie press.** Spoon rich creamed dough into the tubular body of a cookie press, filling it almost full. Select a decorative disk and place it in position to enclose the dough. Tightly screw on the ring that holds the disk at the end of the press.

2 **Shaping the dough.** Butter baking sheets. Place the bottom of the cookie press flat against a baking sheet. Then press down the handle and release it, at the same time carefully lifting the press straight up. Place the press alongside the first cookie to shape another. In this demonstration, the disk is changed after every row.

3 **Baking the cookies.** Bake the cookies in a preheated 375° F. [190° C.] oven for 12 to 15 minutes, or until they are a light golden brown. Using a metal spatula, transfer the cookies to a rack to cool. To serve the cookies, arrange them on a platter in rows to display the patterns made by the different disks.

Refrigerator Dough: A Medium for Molding

Shaped into a cylinder and chilled, a rich creamed dough becomes firm enough to slice neatly into cookies. Because chilling is essential, the baked slices are often called refrigerator, or icebox, cookies. They are always buttery and crumbly—the dough requires proportionally less flour than does a firm creamed dough (recipe, page 166). To keep the dough moist, it should be wrapped in an airtight covering such as plastic wrap before it is chilled. Firming the dough will take about an hour in the refrigerator or half that time in the freezer.

After chilling, the dough can be rolled or molded into various patterns as shown at right and on page 26, where—for emphasis—half of the dough is colored with cocoa powder. Here, trimmed sheets of plain and colored dough are rolled up together to produce a spiral design. In the successive demonstrations, four thin cylinders of alternating colors are wrapped in a sheet of plain dough to make checkered cookies, and a large cylinder is encircled by a contrasting sheet to create a log. For any pattern, a brushing of beaten egg white helps cement the surfaces of the plain and colored doughs.

After the dough is shaped, it must be chilled again for about twice as long as the first time. To have cookies ready for baking whenever convenient, the shaped dough can be kept refrigerated for 5 days or frozen for up to 3 months. Let the refrigerated dough soften slightly at room temperature for about 30 minutes before molding it; thaw the frozen dough in the refrigerator for two hours.

Refrigerator cookies could, of course, also be made from plain or colored dough used on its own. To define a spiral, checkerboard or log, the sheet can be sprinkled with chopped nuts or dried fruit before it is rolled up. Or, even more simply, the dough can be molded into a cylinder and rolled in chopped nuts or fruit to give the finished cookies rough-textured rims.

Spirals from Layered Sheets

1 **Coloring the dough.** Make two batches of rich creamed dough in separate bowls. Leave one batch plain, but use cocoa powder in the second batch to produce chocolate-colored—and flavored—dough.

2 **Finishing the dough.** Gather up the plain dough and place it on a floured work surface. Shape the dough into a ball, rolling it as you shape it to coat the surface lightly with flour. Shape the colored dough in the same way. Wrap the balls of dough in plastic wrap and chill them until firm—two hours in the refrigerator, 45 minutes in the freezer.

6 **Forming a cylinder.** Starting at one long edge, roll up the stack to form a cylinder; the egg white will make the layers stick together as you roll. Wrap the cylinder in plastic wrap and chill it for about two hours in the refrigerator or for 45 minutes in the freezer.

7 **Slicing the dough.** When the dough feels hard if prodded with a finger, unwrap it. Place the cylinder seam side down on the work surface. With a sharp knife, slice the cylinder into thin rounds—here, about ¼ inch [6 mm.] thick. Use a light sawing action to achieve a smooth, clean cut.

3 **Rolling the dough.** Roll the plain dough forward and crosswise, without turning it, into a rectangle ⅛ inch [3 mm.] thick and about twice as long as it is wide. In this case, the sheet of dough is 15 inches [38 cm.] long and 8 inches [20 cm.] wide. Then roll the colored dough into a rectangle of the same size.

4 **Stacking the dough.** In a small bowl, lightly beat an egg white with a fork until it begins to foam. Brush the surface of the plain dough with egg white. Carefully lay the colored dough on top of the plain dough. To ensure that the two sheets are firmly fixed together, lightly roll the surface with the rolling pin.

5 **Trimming the dough.** With a sharp knife, trim away the ragged edges of the dough to form a neat rectangle. Brush the surface of the stacked dough with the lightly beaten egg white.

8 **Baking the slices.** Lightly butter baking sheets *(page 13)*. Transfer the cookies to the sheets and bake in a preheated 375° F. [190° C.] oven until the cookies are firm to the touch— about 10 minutes. With a metal spatula, lift the cookies onto a wire rack to cool *(above)*. Serve them arranged on a plate to display their spiral pattern *(right)*.

Constructing a Checkerboard

1 **Shaping.** Make two batches of rich creamed dough—one with cocoa. Chill. Cut each batch into thirds; reserve a piece of colored dough for other use. Shape two colored and two plain pieces into 1-inch [2½-cm.] ropes. Brush them with egg white and stack them in pairs. Roll the remaining plain dough into a sheet as long as the stack and four times as wide; trim it.

2 **Wrapping the stack.** Brush the sheet of plain dough with egg white. Lift the stack and place it lengthwise on the center of the sheet. Fold the sheet around the stack to form a wrapper. Refrigerate the dough for two hours or freeze it for 45 minutes.

3 **Baking the cookies.** When the dough is firm, unwrap the cylinder and slice it into thin cookies. Lightly butter baking sheets (page 13), place the cookies on the sheets and bake them in a preheated 375° F. [190° C.] oven for about 10 minutes, until firm. Cool the cookies on a rack before serving.

Sheathing a Cylinder for Banded Cookies

1 **Rolling out the dough.** Make two batches of rich creamed dough, coloring one with cocoa. Form each batch into a ball and chill it. Mold the colored dough into a cylinder about 2 inches [5 cm.] in diameter. Cut off a third of the plain dough and roll it into a rectangle ¼ inch [6 mm.] thick. Reserve the remaining plain dough for another use.

2 **Wrapping the cylinder.** Trim the sheet of plain dough so that it is as long as the cylinder and wide enough to wrap around it. Brush the sheet of dough with beaten egg white. Place the cylinder close to one long edge of the rectangle. Roll the wrapper around the cylinder. Refrigerate the log for two hours or freeze it for 45 minutes.

3 **Baking the cookies.** Cut the firm log into slices about ¼ inch [6 mm.] thick. Place the cookies on a buttered baking sheet and bake in a preheated 375° F. [190° C.] oven for about 10 minutes. Transfer the cookies to a rack and let them cool before serving.

Chocolate Pretzels Fashioned by Hand

Fancy openwork cookies can be shaped by rolling a small portion of rich creamed dough *(recipe, page 166)* into a thin rope, and then twisting the rope into a pattern. Here, the dough is blended with cocoa powder and twisted into a loose knot to create a chocolate pretzel. Among the many other shapes possible are figure 8s, bows, corkscrew twists, numbers or alphabet letters. For color contrast, one length each of plain and colored dough can be twisted together in a single cookie.

The cookies require only a simple glaze of beaten egg or egg white to give them a shiny surface. They can be garnished with chopped nuts before baking or, as in this demonstration, sprinkled with coarse decorating sugar, which can be found in baking-supply stores, to simulate the salt crystals that garnish bread pretzels. Alternatively the cookies can be dusted with confectioners' sugar when they are removed from the oven.

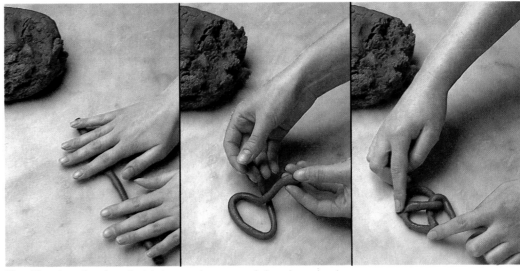

1 **Shaping the dough.** Make a rich creamed dough and color it with cocoa. Refrigerate the dough for one hour or freeze it for 30 minutes. Sprinkle a work surface with flour. Pull off a walnut-sized piece of dough and roll it into a thin rope *(above, left)* about 10 inches [25 cm.] long. Lay the rope in a curved shape with the ends toward you. Lift one end over the other and twist them *(center).* Turn the ends back and press them down onto the center of the curve *(right).* Shape the rest of the dough similarly.

2 **Baking the cookies.** As you shape each cookie, set it on a buttered baking sheet. Brush the cookies with lightly beaten egg white *(below)* and then sprinkle them with coarse decorating sugar. Bake the cookies in a preheated 375° F. [190° C.] oven for about 12 minutes. Cool them on a rack before serving them *(right).*

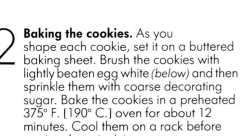

Drop Cookies: Quick and Easy Favorites

Adding more moistener or less flour to creamed dough makes it soft enough to be dropped from a spoon onto baking sheets—the quickest way of all to form individual cookies. Because it is so easy to handle, drop-cookie dough is the foundation for many of America's most popular confections, including the chocolate chip, oatmeal and peanut butter cookies shown on these pages.

Like all creamed doughs, the drop-cookie version requires a vigorous beating of the butter-and-sugar base to incorporate as much air as possible. However, because drop-cookie dough often includes heavy ingredients such as nuts, chocolate pieces, oatmeal or raisins, or acid ingredients such as brown sugar or honey, it usually needs the help of a chemical leavening—baking soda, baking powder or both—to rise fully during baking.

Baking soda, or sodium bicarbonate, will begin to produce carbon dioxide the instant it is moistened, so dough leavened with soda must be baked at once.

Otherwise the dough might release so much carbon dioxide into the air that too little would be left to lighten the cookies.

Baking powder, on the other hand, is double-acting and produces some gases when moistened, others when heated. Thus dough leavened with baking powder can be left to stand—even refrigerated overnight—before it is baked.

Drop-cookie dough is endlessly variable. Chocolate chip, or Toll House, cookies owe their fame to the bits of chocolate that are blended into the dough to melt in baking. They can be made with commercial chips or, as shown here, from hand-chopped chocolate.

Oatmeal cookies get their chewy quality from rolled or coarsely ground grain. The rolled oats shown here might be replaced by ground oat kernels, buckwheat grits or cracked wheat. Peanut butter cookies, of course, take their flavor and name from the peanut butter used as part of the basic fat. Cashew or almond nut butters would be delicious alternatives.

Studding with Chocolate

1 **Adding eggs.** In a large, heavy bowl set on a damp cloth to prevent slipping, cream butter, granulated sugar and brown sugar with a wooden spoon until the mixture is pale and fluffy. Quickly stir in lightly beaten eggs.

Incorporating Rolled Oats and Raisins

1 **Incorporating rolled oats.** Cream butter and sugar until fluffy, then stir in eggs. Sift flour with baking soda, cinnamon and salt. Gradually blend about half of the flour into the creamed mixture. Add rolled oats and, when the ingredients are well combined, blend in the remaining flour.

2 **Adding raisins.** Coarsely chop raisins and stir them into the dough. Using two spoons (Step 3, top), drop the dough onto buttered baking sheets, spacing the cookies well apart.

3 **Baking and cooling.** Bake the cookies in a preheated 400° F. [200° C.] oven until they are an even, light brown color—about 10 minutes. Use a metal spatula to transfer the cookies to wire racks to cool.

2 **Adding chocolate.** Gradually stir in flour that has been sifted with baking soda and salt. Coarsely chop chocolate—here, semisweet chocolate —and shake it in a sieve to eliminate dusty particles that might darken the batter. Chop nuts—here, walnuts. Working quickly, stir the chocolate, then the nuts into the dough.

3 **Shaping the cookies.** Butter baking sheets (page 13). Scoop up a walnut-sized piece of dough in one spoon and use another spoon to mold the dough into an oval and push it onto a baking sheet. Shape the remaining dough, placing the ovals 1 inch [2½ cm.] from the edges of the sheet and 2 inches [5 cm.] apart.

4 **Baking the cookies.** Bake the cookies in a preheated 375° F. [190° C.] oven until a dark brown ring forms around the edge of each one—10 to 12 minutes. With a metal spatula, remove the cookies immediately from the baking sheet and set them on a wire rack to cool before serving them.

Beating in Peanut Butter

1 **Creaming the peanut butter.** In a large, heavy bowl, cream softened butter until it is pale in color. Add peanut butter and beat the mixture vigorously against the sides of the bowl until it is fluffy. Beat in granulated and brown sugar, egg and vanilla extract. Slowly incorporate flour that has been sifted with baking soda and salt.

2 **Decorating the cookies.** Using two spoons (Step 3, top), drop the cookie dough onto buttered baking sheets at well-spaced intervals. To flatten the cookies and ornament them with a crosshatch pattern, dip the tines of a table fork in flour, tap off the excess flour and lightly press the tines into the top of each cookie.

3 **Baking and serving.** Bake the cookies in a preheated 350° F. [180° C.] oven for 10 minutes, or until the tops feel firm if prodded lightly with a finger. Cool the cookies on racks. To serve, arrange them on a platter in one layer to display their decorated tops.

Double Baking for Crispness

The kind of rich creamed dough generally used to make drop cookies can also be shaped into freestanding loaves. After baking, the loaves have a cakelike texture and a soft crust. But if they are sliced and baked a second time, their texture will become crunchy and their crust brittle. The result is the lightly toasted cookies, called rusks, that are demonstrated here *(recipe, page 129)*.

For the preliminary baking, the dough is spooned out onto a baking sheet lined with parchment paper, then shaped into loaves with a spatula. While they are hot from the oven, the loaves are fragile and they must be left on the paper to cool and firm. Then they can be removed from the paper and sliced for the second baking.

The classic flavoring for such loaves is almond. Here both almond extract and whole peeled almonds are mixed into the dough, along with vanilla extract and grated nutmeg. Other suitable spices are ground mace, allspice, cloves and cinnamon, used separately or blended. Hazelnuts, pecans, Brazil nuts or walnuts—chopped or whole—can replace almonds.

1 Forming loaves. Make a rich creamed dough. Cover a baking sheet with parchment paper *(page 13)*. Scooping up dough in a spoon and using a spatula to push it off the spoon onto the paper, form a strip of dough about 3½ by 10 inches [9 by 25 cm.] at one end of the baking sheet. Form a second strip with the rest of the dough.

2 Smoothing the loaves. Dip the spatula into cold water to moisten its blade and thus prevent its sticking to the dough. Smooth the tops and even the sides of the loaves with the spatula. Wet the spatula between strokes.

3 Cooling the loaves. Bake the loaves in a preheated 375° F. [190° C.] oven for 15 to 20 minutes, until they are pale golden. Remove the sheet from the oven and, holding it over a rack, carefully pull the paper and the loaves onto the rack.

4 Slicing the loaves. Let the loaves cool until they feel firm, then remove them from the paper. Using a sharp serrated knife, cut the loaves into ¾-inch [2-cm.] slices. Place the slices on a baking sheet and dry them out in a 300° F. [150° C.] oven for 15 minutes on each side, or until lightly browned.

5 Serving the cookies. Place the toasted slices on the rack: They will be ready to serve as soon as they are cool. If stored in an airtight tin, the cookies will keep for about a month.

A Soft Batter for Delicate Disks

With each additional egg that is blended into creamed dough, the mixture becomes increasingly fluid and the cookies it produces become crisper. In this demonstration, ladies' wafers (recipe, page 145) are made with approximately the same amounts of butter, sugar and flour used for a rich creamed cookie dough (pages 16-17). However, the number of eggs is increased from one to six, turning the dough into a batter that has to be shaped with a pastry bag.

Like tiny cakes, the finished cookies profit from icing. Here they are brushed with a glaze, made by sieving apricot jam, to seal their porous surface and make it smooth. Then they are brushed with a rum-flavored confectioners' sugar icing (page 8) that sets to a glittery coating when the cookies are returned briefly to the oven. The apricot glaze could be replaced by one based on any other fruit jam—strawberry, raspberry or cherry, for example. Melted chocolate would be as appropriate as confectioners' sugar icing and would harden without being dried in the oven.

1 **Filling a pastry bag.** Cream butter and sugar. Mix in eggs one at a time; blend in flour. Fold back the top of a pastry bag, insert a plain tube—in this case, a large No. 6 tube—into the bag and spoon in batter. When the bag is about two thirds full, twist the top to enclose the batter.

2 **Piping the batter.** Lightly butter baking sheets (page 13). Pipe the batter onto the baking sheets in small mounds, using a knife to stop the flow. Leave about 2 inches [5 cm.] of space between the mounds to allow for spreading during baking. If you wish, decorate the cookies by pressing dried currants or raisins onto them.

3 **Glazing the cookies.** Bake the cookies in a preheated 350° F. [180° C.] oven for about 10 minutes, or until lightly browned. Remove them from the oven. To color the cookies, brush on a little sieved apricot jam; it will set in seconds. Prepare a confectioners' sugar icing—here, flavored with rum—and brush it over the apricot glaze.

4 **Serving the cookies.** Return the baking sheets to the oven for about four minutes to set the confectioners' sugar icing. With a metal spatula, transfer the cookies to a rack. Serve the cookies when the icing has cooled and is firm to the touch.

Exploiting Egg Whites for Fine Texture

A creamed batter moistened with only the whites of eggs is the foundation for a range of fine-textured cookies that melt in the mouth. These cookies, exemplified by the cats' tongues in this demonstration *(recipe, page 147)*, owe their exceptional texture to the low proportion of fat in the batter. To make the batter, a relatively small amount of butter is creamed with sugar, and the mixture is moistened and bound with a large number of egg whites—the fatty yolks are reserved for other uses. Just enough flour is added to make the mixture hold its shape lightly. The resulting soft batter spreads during baking to yield a thin and crisp but still light cookie.

Granulated or superfine sugar can be used, but confectioners' sugar will give the cookies a finer texture. Typically the cookies are flavored with vanilla extract or a few spoonfuls of vanilla sugar. For a stronger taste, the grated peel of an orange or lemon, or a splash of orange-flavored liqueur or rum can be blended into the batter.

When all of the whites have been added to the creamed ingredients, the mixture will appear to be curdled, but there is no cause for alarm: The batter will bind together as soon as the flour is added. Because there is so little tenderizing fat in the mixture, it is especially important to blend in the flour gently. Vigorous beating would strengthen the gluten in the flour and toughen the cookies.

Creamed egg-white batters are so soft that they are usually shaped by being piped into rounds or—as shown here —into strips to make elongated cats' tongue shapes. Or the batter may be spooned into lightly buttered ladyfinger molds, which can be found where fine kitchen supplies are sold.

After baking and cooling, the cookies may be served plain. Alternatively, the ends of the cookies may be dipped into melted semisweet or sweet chocolate, or pairs of cookies may be sandwiched with jam or a creamy filling *(pages 10-12)*.

1 **Creaming the butter.** In a bowl set on a damp cloth to prevent slipping, cream softened butter and sugar— sifted confectioners' sugar is used here. Flavor the mixture with vanilla. Separate eggs and reserve the yolks for another use. With a fork, break up the whites until they foam. Add a little of the whites to the creamed ingredients.

2 **Incorporating egg whites.** Stir in the whites with the spoon. Continue to stir, mashing the creamed mixture against the sides of the bowl, until the ingredients are evenly blended.

5 **Folding in the flour.** With a spoon or spatula, blend the flour into the mixture, using a gentle cutting action and folding the batter over on itself. The flour will combine with the other ingredients to form a smooth, soft batter.

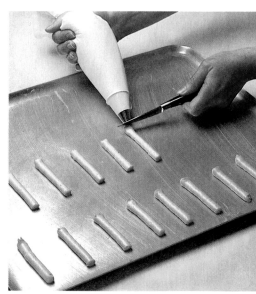

6 **Piping the batter.** Fold back the top of a pastry bag, insert a plain tube— here, a large No. 4 tube—and fill the bag two thirds full with batter. Twist the top. Pipe the batter onto lightly buttered baking sheets, forming strips about ⅜ inch [9 mm.] wide and 2¾ inches [7 cm.] long, spacing them well apart. Use a knife to stop the batter's flow and give the strips a neat end.

3 **Adding remaining whites.** Pour in the rest of the whites, a little at a time, stirring gently but thoroughly after each addition. As the whites are added, the mixture will begin to look curdled.

4 **Adding the flour.** When all of the whites have been added, sift flour into another bowl. Pour the sifted flour all at once into the egg-white mixture.

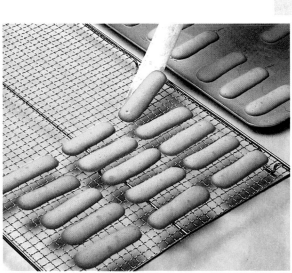 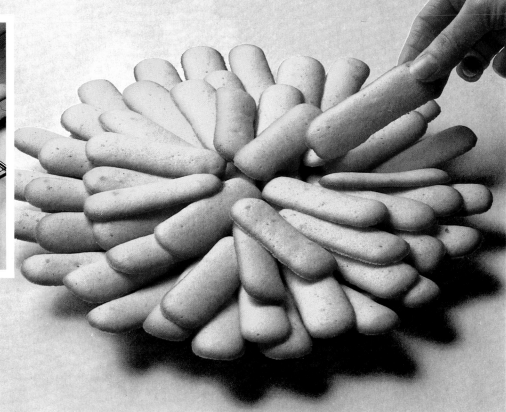

7 **Baking and serving.** Bake the cookies in a preheated 425° F. [220° C.] oven until their edges are browned— about seven or eight minutes. With a metal spatula, transfer the cookies to a wire rack to cool (above). Arrange them on a plate for serving (right).

The Molding of Just-baked Cookies

Reducing the quantities of flour in a creamed egg-white batter *(pages 32-33)* produces wafers that—while still warm from the oven—are flexible enough to be bent into curved shapes *(recipe, page 133)*. The cookies harden as they cool, becoming crisp and brittle.

The key to successful shaping lies in baking only a few wafers at a time and shaping them as soon as you remove them from the oven. Each wafer needs to be pressed against a mold for only a few seconds to take on its shape; it can then be placed on a rack to cool while you swiftly shape the next. If the wafers harden before you can shape them, return them to the oven and warm them until they are pliable again.

Various implements can be used for shaping. A wooden spoon with a rounded handle will produce the tubular cookies known as cigarettes *(top demonstration)*. A rolling pin will form curved disks that resemble roof tiles *(bottom demonstration)*. The wafers can also be pressed around a metal cream-horn mold to create cones, or into a tiny tart pan or a chocolate mold to form cups.

Cigarettes, cones and cups make attractive containers for soft fillings such as praline butter *(page 12)*, sieved jam or whipped cream, added just before serving to prevent the cookies from becoming soggy. For a more elaborate presentation, the filling may be garnished with chopped nuts or grated chocolate. Tiles will not hold filling, but they can be enriched with chopped or sliced nuts—pecans, hazelnuts, cashews or the almonds shown on these pages.

All of these cookies depend for their crispness on being kept perfectly dry. Store them in an airtight container and, if they soften despite this precaution, dry them in a 200° F. [100° C.] oven for a few minutes before serving them.

Rolling Warm Wafers around a Spoon Handle

1 **Piping the batter.** Make a creamed egg-white batter. Butter baking sheets *(page 13)*. Fit a pastry bag with a plain tube—here, a large No. 4 tube—and fill the bag two thirds full with batter. Pipe small mounds of batter onto a baking sheet, leaving plenty of space between mounds.

2 **Baking the cookies.** Place the sheet in a preheated 450° F. [230° C.] oven and bake the cookies until they are lightly browned at the edges—about four to five minutes; during baking, the batter will spread, forming thin wafers. Remove the sheet from the oven. Using a metal spatula, loosen all of the wafers from the baking sheet.

Sculpting Curves on a Rolling Pin

1 **Spooning out batter.** Make a creamed egg-white batter. Add sliced peeled almonds, mixing them into the batter with a spoon. Place small mounds of the mixture well apart on a lightly buttered baking sheet, pushing the batter off the spoon with your finger.

2 **Spreading the almonds.** Dip the tines of a fork in water, then smooth the mounds of batter with the back of the tines to distribute the almonds evenly. Wet the fork again if the batter sticks to it. Bake the cookies in a preheated 450° F. [230° C.] oven until their edges are brown—four to five minutes.

3 **Shaping the wafers.** Working quickly, take a wafer from the baking sheet and wrap it around the handle of a wooden spoon. Press down on the final edge to close the tube. Ease the cigarette off the spoon handle, place it on a rack to cool, and immediately shape the next wafer. Continue until all the wafers are shaped.

4 **Serving the cigarettes.** Let the cigarettes cool: They will become crisp and brittle. Serve them plain or, if you wish, pipe a little filling into both ends of each cigarette—praline butter is used here, but any soft, creamy filling is suitable.

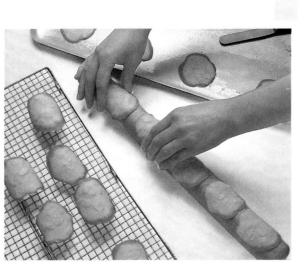

3 **Shaping the wafers.** Remove the wafers from the oven and loosen them from the baking sheet with a spatula. Place as many wafers as will fit over a rolling pin *(above)* and press them gently against the pin for a few seconds. Slide the molded wafers off the pin and place them on a rack to cool completely before serving *(right)*.

2
Pastry Doughs
A Repertoire of Simple Techniques

Rubbing or cutting fat into flour
Sweet toppings for bar cookies
The secrets of rough puff pastry
Crisp cookies from the deep fryer

The kinds of dough that provide cases and lids for tarts and pies also serve as the foundations for a wealth of cookies and crackers. Many of these start with short-crust and rough puff dough, others with slightly modified versions of these familiar pastry formulas. All are easy to make if you understand your ingredients and handle them lightly.

The base of any pastry dough combines flour, which provides bulk, and fat—usually butter—which provides tenderness. Sugar sweetens the dough for cookies and, more often than not, liquid binds it together. The overriding rules in all pastry making are to keep the ingredients cool and to manipulate them as little as possible. If the mixture gets warm, the fat will melt and become oily—resulting in greasy cookies or crackers. If the mixture is worked too much, the gluten in the flour will develop into a strong network that will toughen the dough.

The texture of the cookies or crackers depends on the ratio of fat to flour, the kind of liquid, and how the ingredients are blended. For example, rubbing a high proportion of butter into the dry ingredients produces moist crumbs that characterize shortbread dough—a mixture so soft it must be patted into shape *(pages 38-39)*. Reducing the butter and binding the rubbed ingredients with eggs yields a dough elastic enough for rolled cookies, but still tender and fine-textured *(pages 40-41)*.

Cutting, rather than rubbing, the butter into the dry ingredients and using water as a moistener produces an easily rolled short-crust dough —and crisp cookies *(pages 44-45)*. When the dough is repeatedly rolled, folded and chilled, short crust is transformed into rough puff that bakes to delicate flakiness in cookies *(opposite)* or crackers *(page 92)*. Whether produced by rubbing or cutting, a dough with a high percentage of flour and an acidic moistener such as buttermilk or yogurt is sturdy enough to deep fry into the crunchiest sort of pastry cookies *(pages 52-53)*.

All pastry doughs lend themselves to improvisation. Their mild flavor makes them excellent foils for many spices, ground nuts and extracts. Unbaked cookies can be given sheen with a glaze *(pages 8-9)* or texture with a topping of chopped nuts or dried fruit. More ambitiously, shortbread can be spread with a candy-like coating for doubly rich bar cookies *(page 39)*, and firm rubbed or cut dough can encircle a cylinder of nut paste to form a cookie log with a tender heart *(pages 42-43)*.

An alluring assortment of cookies, in a variety of shapes, has been created from rough puff dough *(pages 46-51)*. The twisted sticks are embellished with almonds, the tiny cases are filled with jam, and extra sugar provides the heart-shaped *palmiers* and pastry butterflies with a gleaming caramelized surface.

Rich Results from a Rubbed Dough

Forming a Disk of Crumbly Shortbread

A simple rubbed dough containing flour, sugar and a generous amount of butter—usually about one part of butter to two parts of flour—will produce rich, tender shortbread. The butter must be cut into cubes that can be incorporated quickly into the dry ingredients and it must be softened until it is malleable: firm but not hard. Rubbing the butter into the flour and sugar will then create moist crumbs that can cohere in a firm mass.

The flavor and texture of shortbread can be varied in many ways. All-purpose flour can be used alone or, as shown here, up to a third can be replaced by rice flour for a lighter texture (recipe, page 134). Using fine semolina instead of the rice flour will make the shortbread crunchy; ground almonds will give it a nutty taste.

A few drops of almond or vanilla extract are often added. Or, for a more pronounced effect, a few spoonfuls of the plain sugar can be replaced by vanilla sugar, made by storing sugar and a vanilla bean in a closed jar for a week or so.

After the ingredients are rubbed together by hand—or whirled together in a food processor—the dough is too mealy to roll, but is easily pressed into shape. The traditional form is a thick disk embossed with a thistle-patterned Scottish shortbread board (obtainable where fine kitchen supplies are sold). Alternatively, the edges can be decorated with a fork. In either case, the round should be pricked with a fork to let steam escape during baking and prevent buckling.

However, the shortbread dough can also be pressed into a baking pan to form the base for bar cookies (opposite, bottom). The base is baked long enough to set it, then coated with a sweet topping and the assembly returned to the oven until it is cooked through. The topping could start with chopped nuts, chopped figs or dates, or pieces of dried apricots—used alone or in combination. These are then sweetened with sugar, honey or jam and bound with flour and eggs.

The disk needs to be scored into portions before baking because afterward it quickly cools to a crumbly cookie that is difficult to cut. By contrast, the topping on bar cookies keeps the shortbread base integral so that it can be sliced neatly when the assembly is cool.

1 **Rubbing the butter into sugar and flour.** Sift sugar, a pinch of salt, and flour—here, a mixture of all-purpose and rice flours—into a large mixing bowl. Add softened butter cubes to the bowl. With the tips of your fingers and thumbs, pick up small amounts of the butter and the dry ingredients and rub them together into large flakes; let the flakes fall back into the bowl (above, left). Continue rubbing for two to three minutes, until the entire mixture is even and crumbly (right).

4 **Baking and serving.** Bake the shortbread at 350° F. [180° C.] for 20 minutes, or until golden. Loosen it from the baking sheet with a spatula, cut it into wedges, and leave it on the sheet until firm—about 15 minutes. Cool the wedges on a rack, then serve.

2 **Gathering the dough.** Using your finger tips and thumbs to press the mixture lightly, gather it gradually together. When you have formed a cohesive mass, shape it into a ball.

3 **Shaping the dough.** Place the dough on a lightly buttered baking sheet. Use the heel of your hand to flatten the ball into a rough round. Then, with the outstretched fingers of one hand, pat the dough into an evenly shaped disk about ½ to ¾ inch [1 to 2 cm.] thick—smoothing the edge with your free hand as you work (above, left). Indent the edge with the tines of a fork to decorate the disk and hold it flat. Then prick the middle repeatedly. Score the surface into wedge-shaped portions (right).

A Buttery Base for Bars

1 **Forming the base.** Prepare a shortbread dough (recipe, page 134), doubling the quantities of ingredients as here if you wish. Lightly butter a baking pan. Press the dough into a layer about ½ inch [1 cm.] thick to cover the bottom of the pan evenly. Bake the dough in a preheated 350° F. [180° C.] oven for 10 minutes.

2 **Adding the topping.** Prepare the topping—in this instance, a mixture of chopped pecans, brown sugar, sifted flour and eggs. Remove the partly cooked dough from the oven and increase the temperature to 375° F. [190° C.]. Spread the topping over the dough and bake the assembly until firm—about 25 minutes.

3 **Serving the cookies.** Remove the pan from the oven and set it on a rack to cool. Cut the assembly into individual bars—in this case, about 1 inch [2½ cm.] wide and 4 inches [10 cm.] long. Lift the bars out of the pan with a spatula and arrange them on a plate for serving.

39

Kneading to Develop Pliability

Not all rubbed doughs are as soft and buttery as those used for shortbread (pages 38-39): A rubbed dough based on one part of butter to four parts of flour is firm enough to be rolled. However, this formulation requires a moistener to hold the ingredients together. Water or milk will suffice, but eggs produce a more flavorful dough—and golden cookies as shown here (recipe, page 114).

To ensure a fine texture, the butter is cubed and softened just until it is malleable, then rubbed into flour and sugar to form sandlike particles. At this stage, the dough can be flavored to taste with spices, extract or grated citrus peel.

Adding eggs makes the dough sticky, and it has to be kneaded gently to become smooth and pliable. The dough then must be chilled to firm it for rolling and to relax the gluten in the flour so that the cookies will be tender. Once rolled, the dough can be stamped out with cutters, and the unbaked cookies decorated with a sprinkling of sugar or given a shiny coating of glaze as in this demonstration.

1 **Assembling the ingredients.** Sift flour, sugar and a pinch of salt into a large bowl; here, confectioners' sugar is used to give the dough a delicate texture. Add small cubes of firm—not hard—butter and, if you like, grate the peel of a lemon into the bowl.

2 **Rubbing in the butter.** Using your fingers and thumbs, pick up small amounts of the mixture and rub them together, letting them fall back into the bowl in large flakes. Continue rubbing until the flakes become fine crumbs and the mixture resembles damp sand.

5 **Kneading the dough.** Transfer the dough to a lightly floured work surface and knead it gently: Press the heel of your hand into the center of the dough and gently push it forward (above, left); fold the extended section of dough backward onto the mass (right). Give the dough a quarter turn and knead it once again. Shape the dough into a ball and wrap it in plastic wrap. To make it easier to roll, refrigerate the dough for about 30 minutes.

6 **Rolling the dough.** Place the chilled dough on a lightly floured work surface. Flatten the ball of dough slightly with a rolling pin. Using firm, light strokes, roll the dough forward; then give the dough a quarter turn and roll it forward again. Continue to roll and turn the dough until it forms an even round about ⅛ inch [3 mm.] thick.

3 **Adding eggs.** Make a well in the center of the mixture and add one whole egg. Over a small bowl, crack another egg; separate the egg and yolk by passing the yolk from one half shell to the other, letting the white drip into the small bowl. Add the egg yolk to the mixing bowl; you may reserve the egg white for another use.

4 **Blending the dough.** With a fork or, as here, the blade of a knife, cut the eggs into the rubbed mixture. Start by drawing in the flour around the well in the center *(above, left)* and gradually work outward until all the flour is incorporated; the mixture will become moist and crumbly *(right)*. Gather it into a ball with your hands.

7 **Cutting the cookies.** With a cookie cutter, stamp out as many shapes as possible from the sheet of dough. Pull away the trimmings and stack them. With a spatula, transfer the cookies to a lightly buttered baking sheet. Press the trimmings together, chill them, and then roll them to cut out more cookies.

8 **Glazing the cookies.** Prepare a caramel-colored egg glaze *(page 9)*; if you like, flavor the glaze with strong black coffee. Using a pastry brush, evenly coat the top of the cookies with the glaze. Let the glaze dry, then apply a second coat. Decorate the cookies by drawing a fork across the glaze.

9 **Baking and serving.** Bake the cookies in a preheated 375° F. [190° C.] oven for about 12 minutes, or until the undersides are golden: The tops will in any event be brown from the glaze. Put the cookies immediately on a wire rack and let them cool before serving.

A Spiced Wrapper for a Nut Log

Enclosing a filling in a long strip of firm dough creates a roll that, after baking, can be sliced into chunky filled cookies. Firm rubbed dough *(pages 40-41)* makes an excellent wrapping, since it is strong enough to support a bulky filling. In this demonstration, the dough, which is lightly leavened with baking powder and flavored with ground spices, encircles a cylinder of almond paste *(page 11)*. The rich, aromatic blend of spices—known in the Netherlands as *Speculaas* spice—complements the sweetness of the filling, and the assembly is decorated with almonds *(recipe, page 108)*.

If you prefer, the dough can be left plain, or it can be flavored with just a single spice, such as cinnamon. Fillings that contain figs, dates or mixed dried fruits *(pages 10-11)* can be used instead. These soft fillings are spooned onto the rolled dough, then enclosed by pressing the long sides of the dough together. Whatever the filling, the rolls are then glazed, baked and sliced as shown here.

1 Starting the dough. In a small bowl, beat eggs lightly with a fork. Sift flour, baking powder and salt into a large bowl, add cubes of butter and rub the mixture until it forms crumbs. Add sugar, grated lemon peel and spices—in this demonstration, cinnamon, nutmeg, cloves, ginger, cardamom and white pepper. Mix well.

2 Blending the dough. Make a well in the center of the dry ingredients and pour in the eggs. With a fork or knife, blend in the eggs. Gather the dough with your hand and press it into a ball. Wrap the dough in plastic wrap and refrigerate it for at least one hour to make it easier to roll.

6 Forming the rolls. To make the dough adhere to the filling, brush the surface of the dough with beaten egg—a whole egg and an extra yolk are used here. Lay a cylinder of nut paste in the center of a strip of dough. Roll the dough tightly around the nut paste. Trim the ends of the roll with a knife. Make the other rolls in the same way.

7 Glazing and garnishing. Place the rolls on a lightly buttered baking sheet with their seams downward. Brush the surface of the rolls with beaten egg. Press halved, peeled almonds into the top of each roll, placing the nuts close together and at a diagonal.

8 Finishing and baking. For extra gloss, coat the rolls again with beaten egg. Bake them in a preheated 350° F. [180° C.] oven for about 25 minutes. Remove the baking sheet from the oven and slide a metal spatula underneath the rolls to loosen them from the sheet. The rolls are fragile, so leave them on the baking sheet to cool.

3 **Shaping the nut paste.** Prepare an almond paste. Place the paste and the ball of dough on a lightly floured surface. Cut the paste into pieces—here, it is divided in four. Roll each piece of nut paste into a cylinder about 1 inch [2½ cm.] in diameter and as long as your baking sheet; in this instance, 14 inches [35 cm.] long.

4 **Rolling the dough.** Set the nut-paste cylinders aside. With quick, firm strokes, roll the dough about ⅛ inch [3 mm.] thick, turning it as you work to form a rectangle that is slightly longer than your baking sheet.

5 **Trimming the dough.** With a long, sharp knife, trim the edges of the dough to make an even rectangle— here, 14 by 16 inches [35 by 40 cm.]. Cut the rectangle into strips, each about 4 inches [10 cm.] wide and as long as the cylinders of nut paste. Gather up the trimmings to use for individual cookies.

9 **Slicing and serving.** Transfer the cooled rolls to a board and slice them diagonally between the almonds (above). Each slice forms a chunky cookie decorated with a nut; arrange the cookies to show off their filling (right).

Short-Crust Spirals with a Cinnamon Glaze

A short-crust dough made with about one part of butter for every three parts of flour will produce crisp, golden cookies—or crackers—with a flaky texture. Because the mixture contains less butter than shortbread dough *(pages 38-39)*, it must be moistened with a little water to produce a cohesive mass. The butter can be softened slightly and rubbed into the flour, but if instead you start with chilled cubes and cut the ingredients together as shown here, the butter will remain in larger pieces, and the cookies or crackers will be flakier.

To keep the butter pieces intact, it is important to handle the dough lightly so that the butter does not become oily. To firm the butter, the dough is chilled thoroughly before use. This resting period will also relax the gluten in the flour, making the dough easier to roll out.

For cookies, the short-crust dough can be made sugarless or sweetened with up to ¼ cup [50 ml.] of sugar to 1 cup [¼ liter] of flour, incorporated into the mixture by sifting it with the other dry ingre-

dients. Cracker dough should, of course, be sugarless, but might be enlivened with a pinch of savory spice such as black or cayenne pepper, dry mustard, even curry powder, sifted with the flour.

Whether plain or flavored, the rolled short-crust dough can be stamped into decorative shapes with cutters or cut into geometric forms with a knife. Cookies then can be sprinkled with sugar and sweet spices such as cinnamon or nutmeg, or topped with chopped nuts or dried fruits—patted into the surface to make them stick. Tangy seeds—caraway, dill, celery or poppy—make the best cracker toppings.

Alternatively, as demonstrated here, the rolled dough can be sprinkled with a flavoring, rolled and then sliced into spiral-patterned rounds. Again, sugar and spice, nuts and fruits are appropriate choices for short-crust cookies. Crackers might be filled with grated sharp cheese—Parmesan or Cheddar, for example—or finely chopped fresh herbs such as parsley, chives or tarragon.

1 **Cutting in the butter.** Sift flour and salt together into a large mixing bowl. Slice a block of chilled butter into ½-inch [1-cm.] cubes and drop the cubes into the flour. With two table knives, cut the butter into the flour by repeatedly crossing the blades and drawing them apart. Cut deeply so that the knife tips touch the bottom of the bowl.

5 **Adding flavorings.** Prepare a filling of your choice—a mixture of superfine sugar and ground cinnamon is used here for a sweet, spicy taste. Sprinkle the mixture evenly over the surface of the dough. Roll a pin lightly over the flavoring to ensure that it clings to the dough.

6 **Forming a roll.** Pick up a long edge of the rectangle and fold it over, to make a narrow hem that will form the center of the finished cookies. Then, applying light pressure and starting from the hem, roll the dough into a cylinder. To make the roll firm and easier to slice, chill it in the refrigerator for 30 minutes or in the freezer for 15 minutes.

7 **Slicing the roll.** Place the chilled roll on a work surface. Using a sharp knife with a narrow blade, slice the roll at intervals of ¼ inch [6 mm.] to produce thin cookies. Transfer the dough slices to a baking sheet.

2 **Stirring in the water.** When the butter is reduced to small pieces, pour a little cold water over the mixture. Stir the water in lightly with a fork or, as here, a knife. Add water a small amount at a time—stirring after each addition—until the mixture just clings together.

3 **Chilling the dough.** With your hand, gather up the dough. Firmly press the dough together and form it into a ball. Wrap the dough in plastic wrap to prevent it from drying out, and chill it in the refrigerator for at least one hour or in the freezer for half that time.

4 **Rolling.** Place the dough on a lightly floured work surface—here, a marble surface to help keep the dough cold. Flatten the ball by striking it firmly with a rolling pin. Then roll the dough into a rectangle about ⅛ inch [3 mm.] thick. With a knife, trim off the uneven edges. Reserve the trimmings; you can reroll them and cut individual cookies.

8 **Baking and serving.** Bake the cookies in a preheated 350° F. [180° C.] oven for about 10 minutes, or until they are firm to the touch and golden brown. With a spatula, transfer the cookies to a wire rack to cool *(above)*. Piled high on a napkin-lined plate *(right)*, the honey gold, buttery spirals make an attractive presentation.

Shaping a Many-layered Puff Dough

Rough puff dough, which rises into crisp, flaky layers in the oven's heat, yields a range of cookies and crackers *(page 92)* distinguished by their melting delicacy. As shown here, rough puff dough begins as a rich short crust *(pages 44-45),* but is transformed by repeated rolling, folding and chilling *(recipe, page 166).*

The lightness of rough puff depends upon the fact that the butter is not evenly incorporated into the flour. Instead, the butter remains in distinct pieces; these are reduced to thin films when the dough is rolled. Each folding sequence creates more layers of dough, and air is trapped between them. During baking, the moisture in the dough becomes steam, puffing the pastry, while the butter melts to keep the layers discrete.

The basic ingredients of the dough are flour, cold butter and liquid; a little sugar sweetens and tenderizes the mixture. The proportion of butter is extremely high—one part for every two parts of flour—and it is cut, not rubbed, into the dry ingredients so that it will remain in chunks large enough to be visible in streaks when the dough is rolled *(Step 5).*

The liquid can be water or—for more tender pastry—milk, cream or egg yolks thinned with a little water. Here, egg yolk, rum and cream bind the dough and give it an especially full flavor.

To keep the butter from becoming oily and making the cookies tough, chill the dough as soon as the liquid has been added, and again between each of the rolling and folding sequences—which are known as "turns"—that follow. Chilling will firm the butter, and during the resting periods the gluten in the flour will relax, making the dough easier to handle. The dough can be chilled in the refrigerator or freezer, but when placed in the freezer it must be removed at once if ice crystals develop on its surface.

For a golden finish, the dough can be rolled in sugar before it is fashioned into cookies such as the heart-shaped *palmiers* shown on pages 48-49. As the dough puffs during baking, some of the hearts will become distorted. But these minor imperfections will be compensated for by the sugar coating, which will caramelize in the oven to give the cookies an amber glaze.

1 Starting the dough. Sift flour, sugar and a pinch of salt into a large mixing bowl. With two knives, cut cold cubes of butter into the dry ingredients *(page 44, Step 1)* until the cubes are reduced to fairly small chunks. Put an egg yolk into a small bowl, add water or, as here, rum; pour in cream. Stir the liquids together with a fork.

2 Mixing the dough. Pour the liquid mixture all at once over the ingredients in the large bowl. With a fork, stir in the liquid lightly, distributing it evenly throughout the mixture to ensure that it does not form lumps.

5 Rolling and folding. With light, forward strokes, roll the dough into a rectangle about ½ inch [1 cm.] thick. If necessary, sprinkle on a little more flour to prevent sticking. At this stage, the edges of the dough will be uneven. Fold over the ends of the rectangle, so that they meet in the center *(above, left).* Then rest one hand in the center and fold over one end *(right)* to form a roughly square package. The original ends of the rectangle are now enclosed in a package four layers thick.

3 **Chilling the dough.** Gather the dough with your hands. Press it lightly into a ball, wrap it in plastic wrap, and chill it in the refrigerator for 45 minutes or in the freezer for half that time.

4 **Flattening the dough.** Lightly flour a cool work surface. Place the cold dough, which will be quite hard, on the surface. Sprinkle the dough lightly with flour. Press down on the ball of dough with the heel of your hand to flatten it slightly. To make the dough more malleable and to flatten it further for easier rolling, beat it with a rolling pin until the dough forms a roughly rectangular shape and is about ¾ inch [2 cm.] thick.

6 **Turning and rolling.** Turn the package 90 degrees so that the folds are at the side and an open end is directly in front of you. Rolling forward, roll the package into a rectangle three times as long as it is wide. Repeat Step 5 to fold the dough into a square shape again. Wrap the dough in plastic wrap and refrigerate it for at least 30 minutes.

7 **Completing the turns.** Unwrap the dough onto the work surface. With an open end in front of you and the folded edges at the sides, roll out a rectangle (Step 6). Then fold the dough into a square (Step 5) and chill it again. Repeat this rolling, folding and chilling sequence one or two more times.

8 **Cutting the dough.** After the final turning and chilling, cut off as much of the dough as you need— in this instance, a little more than half of the dough is removed to make *palmiers* as demonstrated on pages 48-49. Rewrap the rest of the dough and refrigerate it until you are ready to use it. ▶

9 **Rolling the dough in sugar.** Place the dough on a work surface sprinkled with superfine sugar and dribble more sugar over it *(above, left)*. Roll the dough forward into a long, narrow rectangle—here 12 inches [30 cm.] long *(center)*. Fold the ends of the rectangle to the center *(right)*, then fold the dough in half to make a square package. For an even sweeter dough, give the dough a quarter turn, roll it in sugar once more and fold it into a square again. Wrap it in plastic wrap, and refrigerate it for at least 30 minutes or freeze it for about 15 minutes.

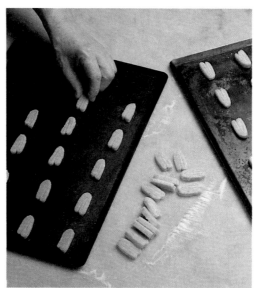

12 **Slicing the strip.** Chill the dough until it is firm—about 20 minutes in the refrigerator or half that time in the freezer—to make it easier to slice. Using a sharp, narrow-bladed knife, slice across the strips at ¼-inch [6-mm.] intervals.

13 **Baking the cookies.** Place the slices on baking sheets, leaving 2 to 3 inches [5 to 8 cm.] between the rows to allow the slices to expand during baking. Put the baking sheets in the refrigerator for 20 minutes or the freezer for 10 minutes. Then bake the cookies in a preheated 400° F. [200° C.] oven until the edges brown lightly—six to seven minutes.

14 **Turning the cookies.** Remove the baking sheets from the oven. With a metal spatula, turn the cookies over—working quickly, lest the caramelized surface harden as it cools and the cookies stick to the sheets. To color both sides evenly, return the cookies to the oven for two to three minutes. The second side needs less time than the first.

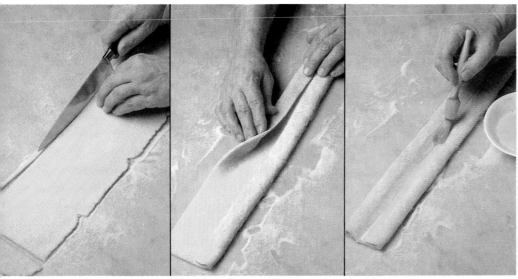

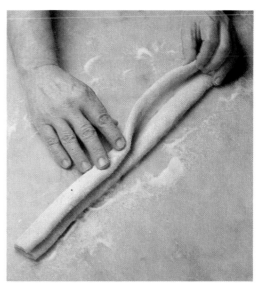

10 **Trimming and shaping the dough.** Dust the work surface with superfine sugar. Roll the dough into a long, narrow rectangle no more than ¼ inch [6 mm.] thick. With a sharp knife, trim the uneven edges *(above, left)*. Here, the trimmed rectangle measures about 5 by 20 inches [13 by 50 cm.]. Fold in the two long sides of the rectangle almost to the middle, but do not let them meet *(center)*. Press the rolling pin lengthwise down the middle to seal the edges and create an indented channel. Mix an egg yolk with water and brush this glaze along the channel *(right)*.

11 **Folding the strip.** Fold the dough in half lengthwise so that the folded edges meet. To make certain that the four layers will stick together, gently roll the shaped strip with the rolling pin.

15 **Cooling and serving.** Remove the cookies from the oven. Use the spatula to transfer the cookies to a wire rack *(above)*; they are very fragile while warm. Cool them to room temperature, then serve on a napkin-lined plate *(right)*.

A Medley of Puff-Dough Variations

The direction in which rough puff dough rises depends upon how the pieces are placed on a baking sheet: When laid flat, the layers expand upward, but if they are stood on end the layers expand sideways. Thus, varying the placement of the pieces as well as their size and shape produces dramatically different cookies as demonstrated here. Upended and crossed strands will fan out to form butterfly wings *(right);* twisted bands will spread in both directions *(below, left)* and the sides of tiny shells will climb so high they can encase jam *(opposite, bottom).*

Before it is cut and shaped, the dough can be enlivened by sprinkling the top with a flavoring such as chopped nuts, grated citrus peel or ground spices—cinnamon or nutmeg, for example. Here the dough for the twists is coated on both sides with a combination of equal amounts of chopped almonds and granulated sugar. To make it cling to the dough as it is shaped, any of these toppings must, of course, be pressed firmly into the surface with a rolling pin.

Strands That Spread into Butterfly Wings

1 **Cutting bands of dough.** Roll 1 pound [½ kg.] of rough puff dough *(pages 46-47)* into an 8-by-12-inch [20-by-30-cm.] rectangle ¼ inch [6 mm.] thick. Trim the edges with a sharp knife and cut the rectangle into four 3-by-8-inch [8-by-20-cm.] bands. Beat egg yolk with water and brush a strip of egg mixture down the center of three bands.

2 **Stacking the bands.** Stack the three brushed bands of dough, carefully aligning the edges, and lay the unbrushed band on top. To join the layers together, lay a rolling pin along the middle of the stack and press the pin down firmly. Keep the pin steady: The edges must remain well separated. Cut the stack into ½-inch [1-cm.] slices.

Nut-encrusted Twists

1 **Incorporating nuts.** Roll 1 pound [½ kg.] of rough puff dough into an 8-by-12-inch [20-by-30-cm.] rectangle ¼ inch [6 mm.] thick. Trim the edges. Brush on egg yolk beaten with water. Sprinkle with nuts and sugar; roll them in. Carefully turn the dough over. Brush the uncoated side with egg yolk, sprinkle on nuts and sugar, and roll them in.

2 **Cutting and twisting.** Cut the rectangle in half lengthwise, then cut each half crosswise into strips about ½ inch [1 cm.] wide. Hold a strip at each end and twist the ends in opposite directions. Lay the strip on a baking sheet and press the ends flat to prevent the strip from untwisting. Shape the remaining strips in the same way.

3 **Baking and serving.** Place the baking sheet in the refrigerator for 20 minutes or in the freezer for 10 minutes. Bake the twists in a preheated 400° F. [200° C.] oven until they are evenly golden—about 10 minutes. Cool the twists on a wire rack before serving them.

3 **Shaping the butterflies.** Hold a slice loosely at one end; with your free hand, twist the other end toward you; lower the slice onto a baking sheet, allowing the thin strips to fan out with their cut edges facing upward. Shape the remaining slices in the same way. Refrigerate the cookies for 20 minutes or freeze them for 10 minutes.

4 **Baking the cookies.** Bake the cookies at 400° F. [200° C.] for six to seven minutes, or until lightly browned. With a spatula, turn the cookies over. Bake them for three more minutes. Use the spatula to transfer the fragile cookies to a rack; cool before serving.

Fragile Shells to Fill with Jam

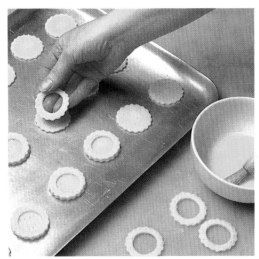

1 **Cutting the dough.** Roll about 1 pound [½ kg.] of rough puff dough ⅛ inch thick; to prevent the dough from rising too much, prick well with a fork, so steam can escape during baking. With a fluted cutter, stamp out rounds; place half on a baking sheet. With a smaller, plain cutter, cut out the centers of the remaining rounds *(above)*.

2 **Forming shells.** Beat an egg yolk with a little water. Brush the rim of each round base with the egg mixture, then place a ring of dough on top. Brush the surface of the ring with egg, taking care that no egg touches the cut sides and prevents the dough from rising. Refrigerate the shells for 20 minutes or freeze them for 10 minutes.

3 **Filling the shells.** Bake the shells in a preheated 450° F. [220° C.] oven for two minutes. Lower the heat to 350° F. [180° C.] and bake the shells for 10 to 12 minutes longer, until they are golden brown. Cool them on a rack. Dilute jam—in this case, raspberry—with a little water and melt it over low heat, then put a spoonful into each shell.

A Strong Dough for Deep Frying

The lightest and crunchiest of pastry-dough cookies are those that are deep fried in hot oil rather than baked in an oven. The dough must contain a high proportion of flour and, after butter has been rubbed or cut into it, should be moistened generously with an acidic liquid—wine, buttermilk or the sour-cream-and-rum mixture shown here (recipe, page 154). Kneading will then develop the flour's gluten into a strong, elastic meshwork that will hold the dough intact in the oil. The acidic liquid hastens development of the gluten while keeping it supple and—during frying—turns to steam, which creates air bubbles in the cookies.

For crispness, the dough must be rolled no more than ⅛ inch [3 mm.] thick so that it will cook through in the minute or so required to brown the cookies. The rolled dough can be shaped into bowknots (right), cut into strips and twisted into coils, or stamped into rounds and folded around a filling to create crescent turnovers (opposite, bottom). For turn-overs, the filling must be a firm one that will neither leak nor require cooking—the cookies are in the oil just long enough to warm the filling. Here the crescents contain a fig mixture; chopped nuts or another dried fruit would be as suitable a base for the filling (pages 10-11).

Any bland oil—peanut or corn oil, for example—is suitable for frying cookies. The layer of oil must be at least 1½ inches [4 cm.] deep to submerge them, but should not fill the pan by more than two thirds lest it bubble over the sides.

Temperature is critical. For perfect results, the oil must be preheated to 375° F. [190° C.] and kept at that temperature. If the oil is cooler, the cookies will become greasy; if the oil is hotter, the cookies will burn. The surest way to control the temperature is to use a deep-frying thermometer. Otherwise, test the oil from time to time by dropping a small piece of dough into it: The dough should sizzle and rise to the surface within a few seconds if the temperature is correct.

Tying Bowknots

1 Kneading the dough. Sift flour and sugar onto a cool work surface. Cut in cubes of butter, then add egg yolks, rum and sour cream. Mix well, gather the dough into a ball and knead it for about two minutes until smooth. Divide the dough into three parts, cover with plastic wrap, then refrigerate for an hour.

4 Frying the bowknots. Pour oil to a depth of 4 inches [10 cm.] into a heavy deep-frying pan and heat it until the oil registers 375° F. [190° C.] on a deep-frying thermometer. Using a skimmer or perforated spoon, lower several bowknots into the pan and fry them until golden brown—about 30 seconds on each side. Drain the bowknots on a rack covered with paper towels.

5 Sugaring the bowknots. While they are still hot, transfer the bowknots to a rack set over a shallow tray. Sift confectioners sugar over the bowknots to coat them evenly. Turn them over and sugar the other side. Serve the bowknots warm or at room temperature, sugaring them again before serving, if you like.

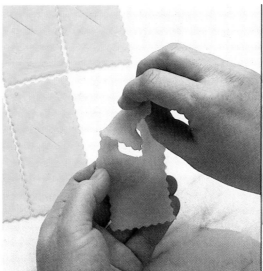

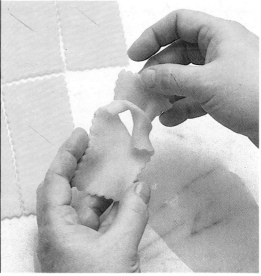

2 **Rolling the dough.** Flour the work surface lightly and roll one portion of the dough to a thickness of ⅛ inch [3 mm.]. With a pastry wheel and a straightedge, cut the dough into strips —in this case, 2 by 4 inches [5 by 10 cm.]. Save the scraps and chill them.

3 **Making a bowknot.** Cut a diagonal slit ¾ inch [2 cm.] long in the center of each strip. Carefully pick up one strip at a time. Fold the top narrow end forward to align one of its corners with the slit *(above, left)*. Work the corner through the slit and then gently pull the end through as far as it will go without tearing *(right)*. Set the bowknots aside while you roll out the other two portions of dough and all of the scraps, and shape as many bowknots as you can.

Shaping Fig-filled Crescents

1 **Applying an egg wash.** Roll the dough to a thickness of about ⅛ inch [3 mm.] and cut it into rounds 2½ inches [6 cm.] in diameter. Prepare a fig filling and dab about ½ teaspoon [2 ml.] of the filling onto each round. Brush the edges of the rounds with a mixture of egg yolk beaten with cream.

2 **Sealing the crescents.** Working quickly, fold one half of each dough round over the filling to form a crescent and press the edges together to seal them. Deep fry a few cookies at a time in oil preheated to 375° F. [190° C.] for about 30 seconds on each side. Drain the crescents on paper towels.

3 **Glazing the crescents.** Make a rum-flavored confectioners' sugar glaze *(page 8)*. While the crescents are warm, lift each one in turn on the tines of a large fork and lower it into the glaze, turning it over to coat both sides. Transfer the crescent to a rack, placed over a tray to catch drips, and let the glaze set.

3
Egg-White Confections
Textures from Dense to Airy

Pounding almonds in a mortar
Binding a blend of nuts and sugar
Tactics for beating egg whites
Sugar syrup for Italian meringue

The frosty beauty of plain meringues is reflected in a sparkling serving dish. To make the meringues, egg whites were whisked to soft peaks; sugar was blended in until the mixture became stiff and glossy. Spoon-dropped onto baking sheets and dried out in the gentlest of oven heats, the meringues slowly hardened and acquired a texture both crisp and meltingly light.

Macaroons and delicate meringues are only two of the kinds of cookies that can be produced from egg white without the addition of flour, fat or egg yolk. They owe their diversity to the different roles that egg whites play in cookie making.

Unbeaten egg white is a viscous liquid that, when lightly broken up with a fork, becomes a loose foam used to bind dry ingredients. Nuts are often the primary ingredient in such mixtures, replacing the flour that gives body to most cookie doughs. A blend of nuts and sugar, moistened with enough egg white to form a soft batter, will produce crunchy macaroons. These cookies will have a deliciously chewy texture if they are made with nuts pounded to a rough paste in a mortar *(pages 56-57)*. Smooth nut crescents *(pages 58-59)* contain the same ingredients, but in this case the nuts must be ground to a fine powder. Just enough egg white is added to the nut powder to make a stiff paste that can be molded by hand into various shapes, then decorated, baked and glazed.

When egg whites are beaten, the proteins they contain form thin films that trap air. Prolonged beating breaks these air cells into smaller and smaller bubbles until the whites increase dramatically in volume, becoming a dense, stable foam. Proper containers, scrupulously prepared, are essential to the creation of this foam: Egg whites interact with some metals and discolor—and even a trace of fat in a bowl will prevent whites from rising properly. For beating, you can use stainless-steel, ceramic or glass bowls that have been washed in hot soapy water, rinsed and dried. However, an unlined copper bowl is best: An interaction with the metal strengthens the proteins in the whites, creating a long-lasting foam. If you use a copper bowl, scrub it with a mixture of salt and vinegar or lemon juice—allow 2 teaspoons [10 ml.] of salt for each tablespoon [15 ml.] of acid—to remove potentially toxic oxides in the metal; then rinse and dry the bowl. Do not keep egg whites in a copper bowl for longer than 15 minutes, lest they discolor.

Properly prepared and sweetened, egg-white foam will produce the delicate meringues shown opposite; the addition of ground nuts makes a dense mixture that becomes firmer, crisper cookies *(pages 60-61)*. And a foam sweetened with hot sugar syrup—a so-called Italian meringue—will support such liquid flavorings as fresh fruit purées *(pages 62-63)*.

55

Macaroons: Chewy Cookies from a Granular Nut Paste

The simplest egg-white cookies are those in which the white—unbeaten—serves to bind a mixture of ground nuts and sugar. The type of nuts used determines the taste of these cookies. The way those nuts are prepared determines their texture, which may be smooth and homogeneous, as in the cookies demonstrated on pages 58-59, or appealingly rough, as in the macaroons shown here (recipe, page 150).

The word macaroon comes from *maccarone,* the Italian name for a cookie based on ground almonds, but macaroons can be made from any nuts—walnuts, hazelnuts and pecans, for instance, all make delectable macaroons. Any of these nuts may be blanched and peeled (page 6) if you prefer cookies with a subtle flavor; for a nuttier flavor—and darker color—leave the nuts in their skins. Almonds are mild-flavored in any case, so European cooks intensify the taste by including a few bitter almonds. Cousins of the commonly available sweet variety, bitter almonds contain small amounts of poison-ous prussic acid and are not sold in the United States; a few drops of almond extract will serve the same purpose.

Nuts for macaroons should be ground to a paste that is granular and moist, but not oily: Oiliness will keep the dough from cohering. Grinding the nuts with a mortar and pestle, as demonstrated at right, is tedious but gives you total control over their consistency. To ensure a perfect texture, add a little egg white to the nuts: The white will coat them, preventing the release of too much oil. If you use a food processor, operate it in short bursts and inspect the nuts often.

To transform nut paste into cookie batter, stir in sugar and egg whites gradually—alternating ingredients to control the consistency of the batter: It should be soft but not sticky. The batter may be dropped from a spoon onto a paper-lined baking sheet to create irregular rounds. Or, for more perfect circles, the batter may be piped from a pastry bag fitted with a large plain tube (page 31).

1 **Pounding almonds.** In a heavy mortar, combine blanched and peeled almonds (page 6) with a little egg white—and, if you like, almond extract. Pound the nuts for 30 minutes—or until they form a coarse paste.

3 **Completing the batter.** Add more sugar, stirring it into the mixture with the pestle. Gradually stir in more egg white—taking care not to add too much at a time—until the mixture is just soft enough to drop from a spoon.

4 **Forming the macaroons.** Line baking sheets with parchment paper (page 13). Drop the macaroon mixture onto the paper by spoonfuls, leaving about 2 inches [5 cm.] between mounds to allow for spreading during baking.

5 **Cooking the macaroons.** Bake the macaroons in a preheated 425° F. [220° C.] oven for 10 minutes—or until their edges are golden. Remove them from the oven. Press a blanched almond or, as shown here, a few pine nuts into the top of each macaroon, and then sift a fine coating of confectioners' sugar over them.

2 **Adding sugar and egg white.** In a small bowl, mix egg whites with a fork or whisk until they begin to foam. Add sugar to the almond paste in the mortar *(above, left)*. Mix the almonds and sugar together with the pestle *(center)*. Pour in half of the egg white *(right)* and stir it into the almonds and sugar.

6 **Finishing the macaroons.** Return the cookies to the oven for a minute to set the confectioners' sugar; then let them cool on the baking sheets. Do not try to lift the macaroons from the paper while they are still warm. Although they feel firm, they are soft inside and, if handled, will break. When the macaroons are cool, peel them from the paper and serve them.

Almond Crescents with a Crunchy Coating

Egg whites, ground nuts and sugar— the same ingredients used for macaroons *(pages 56-57)*—can yield a stiff dough that will produce decoratively shaped cookies, crisp outside and chewy inside. In this case the nuts must be reduced to powder: Use a food processor, food grinder or nut grinder to grind them fine.

Here the nut powder is made from blanched, peeled almonds *(page 6),* but walnuts, pecans or a mixture of nuts— peeled or not—are just as suitable. The ground nuts are combined with sugar; confectioners' sugar is used here because it produces a finer texture than granulated sugar. Jam is added for flavor and moisture, then the mixture is bound with egg white. This dough can be molded into individual shapes, as here, or into a large cylinder for slicing. It can also be rolled flat and shaped with cutters.

For a pleasingly textured exterior, the cookies can be coated with egg white and chopped nuts before baking. A coating of sweetened milk applied after baking gives the cookies a shiny glaze.

1 **Combining the ingredients.** In a food processor, grind blanched almonds to powder. Mix them with confectioners' sugar. Beat egg whites with a fork until they foam. Make a well in the center of the nut mixture and add a spoonful of jam—in this case, apricot jam—and a few drops of vanilla extract. Then pour about one third of the egg whites into the well *(above, left)*. Using a knife, stir the egg white and jam into the dry ingredients *(right)*. Stir in about half of the remaining egg white, a little at a time, until the mixture is moist enough to cohere.

4 **Coating the cylinders.** Chop nuts fine; almonds are used here. Place the chopped nuts on a plate. Using a pastry brush, coat a cylinder of dough on all sides with lightly beaten egg white *(above, left)*, then roll it in the chopped almonds *(right)* so that the cylinder is completely covered with nuts.

5 **Shaping the crescents.** Bend the nut-coated cylinder into a crescent shape, and place it on a buttered baking sheet. Coat and shape the other cylinders in the same way. Bake the crescents in a preheated 375° F. [190° C.] oven for 10 to 12 minutes—or until they are a pale golden color.

2 **Gathering the dough.** As the mixture begins to form a cohesive mass, gather it into a ball with your hand. Moisten any dry bits in the bottom of the bowl with a few drops of egg white and add them to the ball of dough. The finished dough should be moist enough to hold together, yet firm enough to be shaped by hand.

3 **Shaping the paste.** Transfer the ball of dough to a lightly floured work surface. Pull off pieces of dough—about the size of walnuts—and roll each of them under your hand to form thin cylinders about 3 inches [8 cm.] long.

6 **Glazing the crescents.** Remove the cookies from the oven. In a small bowl, stir a little confectioners' sugar into cold milk. While the cookies are still warm, brush them with a little of the sweetened milk *(inset)*. When they feel firm, transfer the cookies to a wire rack to finish cooling. Serve the crescents on a napkin-lined plate *(right)*.

Meringues: A Range of Effects

Egg whites whisked to a stiff, airy foam become the basis for a range of cookies known as meringues. Sugar provides the sweetening; vanilla, almond or peppermint extracts, ground cinnamon or grated nutmeg add flavor. And ground nuts can be included in different amounts, depending on whether you prefer the light meringues shown at right *(recipe, page 166)* or the denser cookies in the box at bottom *(recipe, page 149)*.

In any case, the first and most important step in preparation is the beating of the egg whites. The whites should be brought to room temperature before they are beaten: They will be more elastic and will absorb air more readily than when chilled. And the whites must be carefully separated from the yolks to ensure that not even a speck of the yolks' fat contaminates them.

To hold the whites, an unlined copper bowl, prepared as described on page 60, is ideal. The best implement for beating the whites is a wire whisk, which can be lifted during beating *(Step 1, right)* to incorporate the maximum amount of air into the whites.

To sweeten the beaten egg whites, use granulated sugar or, if you prefer, superfine or confectioners' sugar, which dissolve faster than the plain granulated variety. Sugar should be added gradually as you beat the whites so that they can absorb it evenly. Spices and extracts are added toward the end of beating.

Any nut—ground to powder in a food processor or nut grinder—may be folded into the whites for flavor and body. You may flavor an entire meringue mixture or—for the two-tiered cookies shown on these pages—only part of one, saving some of the meringue for a topping. For light, nut-flavored meringues, use up to ¾ cup [175 ml.] of ground nuts for each egg white; for mixtures firm enough to roll, double the volume of nuts.

Baking time and temperature for meringues vary according to the density of the mixture. Light meringues are simply dried out for several hours in a slow oven so that they will firm without browning. Dense meringues require higher temperatures and shorter baking periods.

1 **Beating egg whites.** Separate an egg over a small bowl, let the white fall into the bowl and reserve the yolk for another use. Transfer the white to a large bowl set on a damp cloth to prevent it from slipping. Repeat this procedure with each egg in turn, so that any mishap will affect only one egg. Using a wire whisk, beat the whites with a slow, lifting motion. When the whites start to foam *(above, left)*, beat them with a rapid figure-8 motion until they form soft peaks *(right)*.

Dense Dough from a Foamy Base

1 **Forming.** Fold ground almonds into half of a cinnamon-flavored meringue to make a stiff dough. Coat a work surface and rolling pin with flour or confectioners' sugar and roll the dough ¼ inch [6 mm.] thick. Stamp out cookies and place them on lined baking sheets. Brush the remaining plain meringue on top of each cookie.

2 **Baking and serving.** Bake the cookies in a preheated 325° F. [160° C.] oven for about 15 minutes—or until they are stiff and dry. Let the cookies cool on the lined baking sheets; then remove them from the paper and arrange them on a platter for serving.

2 **Incorporating sugar.** Sprinkle a small amount of superfine sugar over the whites and whisk it in *(above, left)*. Repeat the process until about one third of the sugar has been added and the mixture is fairly dense. Incorporate the remaining sugar in larger batches than before, whisking vigorously, until the mixture forms stiff, glossy peaks *(right)*.

3 **Flavoring the meringue.** Transfer two thirds of the mixture to a separate bowl and add to it finely ground nuts—in this case, hazelnuts. With a spatula, fold the nuts into the meringue, until they are evenly distributed.

4 **Layering the meringue.** Line a baking sheet with parchment paper *(page 13)*. Spoon small, even-sized mounds of nut-flavored meringue onto the paper. Top each mound with a dollop of the plain meringue.

5 **Baking.** Bake the cookies on a low shelf in a 200° F. [100° C.] oven for three hours—or until they are dry and firm. If they start to brown, set the oven door ajar. Cool the cookies completely before moving them from the paper. If you like, serve the cookies in individual paper cases, as shown here.

A Hot Syrup to Stabilize Foam

Blending beaten egg whites with hot, concentrated sugar syrup—rather than with plain sugar—produces Italian meringue, which is finer in texture than a basic meringue *(pages 60-61)* and yields crisper cookies. More important, the syrup method broadens the choice of liquid flavorings for meringue. Strong-tasting extracts can, of course, be used, but so can milder liquids—such as black coffee, liqueur, puréed raspberries or the strawberry purée shown in this demonstration *(recipe, page 149)*.

A mild liquid flavoring, added in a quantity large enough to be effective, would break down the egg-white foam of a basic meringue. However, for Italian meringue, the flavoring can be incorporated into the hot syrup before it is beaten into the egg whites. The syrup's heat sets the egg whites by partially cooking them, thereby stabilizing the foam so that it can hold extra liquid.

The syrup is a solution of sugar and water that is boiled to concentrate it—and it requires careful cooking. If undissolved sugar crystals remain in the solution when it boils, they will produce a grainy syrup. To prevent this, stir the syrup as it heats and brush any crystals from the pan sides *(Step 2, right)*. Do not stir the syrup after it boils.

As the syrup boils, its concentration is measured by its temperature and simple water tests. If you are using coffee or liqueur as flavoring, boil the syrup until its temperature reaches 250° F. [120° C.] on a candy thermometer and it reaches the hard-ball stage—that is, a spoonful of syrup dropped in ice water solidifies at once. Then stir in the coffee or liqueur—about 2 tablespoons [30 ml.] for a four-egg-white meringue.

Fruit purées must be used in more generous amounts—¼ cup [50 ml.] or so for a four-egg-white meringue—and require a denser solution: Boil the syrup to 300° F. [150° C.]; this is known as the hard-crack stage because, when a spoonful is dropped in ice water, the syrup forms a rigid mass that can be snapped in two. The purée will quickly cool the syrup to the proper temperature—250° F.—for forming the meringue.

1 **Puréeing berries.** Swirl strawberries briefly in water to cleanse them and immediately drain them in a colander. Hull the berries, dropping them into a fine-meshed strainer set over a bowl. Using a pestle or the back of a wooden spoon, press the berries through the strainer to make a smooth purée.

4 **Adding the syrup to the beaten whites.** Beating continuously, pour the hot syrup into the beaten egg whites in a thin, steady stream. Ask a helper to pour in the syrup while you use a whisk, as here *(above, left)*, or beat the whites with an electric beater while you add the syrup yourself. Increase the flow slightly as you proceed *(center)*; the mixture may soften, but it will regain its stiffness when all of the syrup has been added as it is beaten *(right)*.

2 **Making the sugar syrup.** Put sugar and water in a heavy saucepan set over medium heat. Stir the mixture lightly with a wooden spoon until the sugar completely dissolves. To remove any remaining crystals, brush down the sides of the pan with a pastry brush dipped in water.

3 **Finishing the syrup.** When the sugar has dissolved, place a candy thermometer—warmed in hot water to keep it from cracking—in the pan. Bring the syrup to a boil *(above, left)*. Beat egg whites in a large bowl until they form stiff peaks. When the syrup reaches 300° F. [150° C.], turn off the heat. Carefully pour the fruit purée into the syrup *(right)*; the syrup will bubble and the temperature will fall. When the temperature reaches 250° F. [120° C.], lift the hot thermometer out with a hot pad or cloth towel and stir the mixture once.

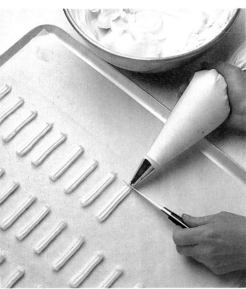

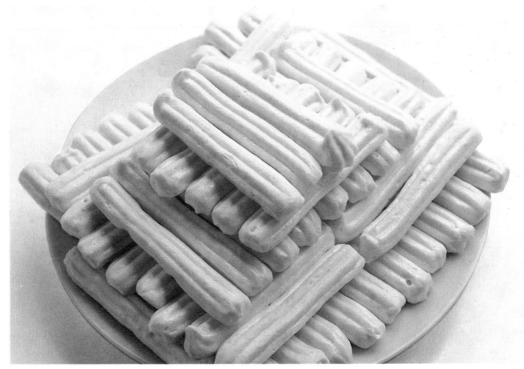

5 **Piping the meringue.** Line baking sheets with parchment paper *(page 13)*. Fit a pastry bag with a tube—here, a large No. 4 star tube—and fill the bag two thirds full with meringue. Holding the bag almost horizontal, pipe strips about ⅜ inch [9 mm.] wide and 3 inches [8 cm.] long onto the baking sheets; use a knife to stop the flow and give the strips neat ends.

6 **Baking and serving.** Bake the meringues in a 200° F. [100° C.] oven for three hours—or until the cookies are dry; do not let them color. Let the meringues cool on the baking sheets. Here, the meringues are stacked on a plate to form a pale pink lattice.

4
Sponge Foundations
Capturing Lightness in Beaten Eggs

Patterns from a carved rolling pin
How to soften cookies in a container
Preparing molds for baking batters
Separating eggs for maximum aeration

The last cookie is added to a plate of shell-shaped madeleines that have been arranged in tiers for serving. Made with a butter-enriched sponge batter, the madeleines were baked in molds (pages 68-69). After unmolding, they were given a dusting of sugar to highlight their attractive ridged surfaces.

Among the pleasures of cookie making is discovering how the same basic ingredients and techniques can be subtly modified to produce dramatically different textural results. This is particularly true when the cookies have a foundation of beaten eggs and sugar. The changes that can be rung on this so-called sponge base yield cookies as diverse as dense-textured springerle, cakelike madeleines and airily light ladyfingers.

All sponge-based cookies are made by first beating eggs and sugar together until their volume trebles. In the process, air bubbles are trapped by the egg proteins; as the mixture expands, the sugar dissolves and stabilizes the foam. The trapped air is the major leavening agent for the cookies: The bubbles increase in size in the oven's heat, raising the other ingredients. Additionally, the eggs supply water, which helps to leaven the cookies further when it becomes steam during baking.

Flour is a fundamental determinant of texture. If a sponge that contains but a few eggs is used to bind a substantial quantity of flour, the result will be a dough firm enough to knead and roll out. Because such handling presses out much of the air, cookies made from the dough rise hardly at all. Nonetheless, the dough retains some of its sponginess—and it can be rolled with a carved pin or pressed with a wood mold to create an embossed design that will spring up slightly when the appropriately named springerle are baked. If the same amount of flour is added to a sponge made with twice as many eggs, the result will be a soft batter that can be piped or spooned in mounds onto a baking sheet. These will rise noticeably in baking to create tender domes with crisp tops. Leaving either type of cookie to dry before baking will help ensure that it develops a pale, brittle crust (pages 66-67).

Another textural effect is achieved by adding melted butter to a sponge after the flour has been folded in. This tactic will create a madeleine batter, which is so fluid that it must be baked in molds (opposite). The butter also tenderizes the mixture, ensuring a light and delicate texture as well as a rich flavor.

But the lightest of all sponge batters depends on separating the eggs and whisking the whites to a stiff foam before incorporating them into the beaten yolks and sugar. The volume of air suspended in the egg whites is responsible for the crisp texture of ladyfingers (pages 70-71).

Embossed Shapes with a Sugary Crust

The simplest sponge-based cookies start with whole eggs that are beaten together with sugar, then blended with flavorings and flour. The consistency of the finished mixture—and texture of the cookies—depends on the ratio of flour to eggs. A high proportion of flour produces the dry and crunchy German springerle demonstrated at right *(recipe, page 117)*. A low proportion of flour yields soft and fragile cookies such as the anise caps shown in the box below *(recipe, page 101)*.

Because trapped air serves as the only form of leavening for the cookies, the eggs and sugar should be beaten until they form a sponge firm enough to fall from the beater in ribbons—a process that takes up to 20 minutes with a whisk or rotary beater, about 10 minutes with an electric mixer. Although granulated sugar may be used, superfine or confectioners' sugar will dissolve more readily in the eggs.

Traditionally, springerle are flavored with lemon and anise. Here, an anise liqueur is added to the sponge; you could substitute ground anise or fennel—or give the cookies an unexpected taste by using ground cinnamon or cardamom.

For springerle the sponge is thickened with so much flour that the resulting firm dough must be kneaded lightly to smooth it for rolling. The rolled dough is then embossed with a carved rolling pin or board, obtainable where fine kitchen supplies are sold, and cut into square cookies. For softer cookies, flour is folded into the sponge—a little at a time to avoid driving out air—to form a light batter that is either piped or spooned onto baking sheets.

Before baking, springerle are set aside overnight to allow their surfaces to dry and their designs to set. In the oven the embossed pattern rises, forming a decorative crust. Softer cookies are set aside for a shorter time because the moist batter more quickly forms a sugary crust. During baking, the air incorporated into the eggs expands, creating the domed surface that is a feature of these cookies.

The anise caps can be served as soon as they cool. By contrast, the springerle are so hard they are first ripened in a loosely covered container for one to three weeks until moisture from the air softens them.

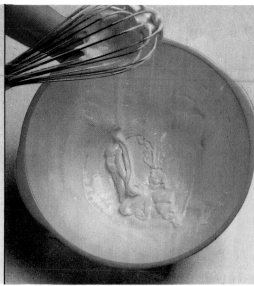

1 **Forming the sponge.** In a large mixing bowl, set on a damp cloth to keep it steady, beat whole eggs to blend the whites and yolks together. Sift sugar—in this case, confectioners' sugar—into the bowl and whisk it together with the eggs *(above, left)*. Continue whisking until the mixture trebles in bulk and becomes pale and thick. It will fall smoothly from the whisk in wide ribbons that hold their shape and remain visible on the surface *(right)*.

Snowy Domes Scattered with Anise Seeds

1 **Spooning the batter.** Beat whole eggs and superfine sugar in a bowl until the mixture reaches the ribbon stage *(Step 1, above)*. Gradually fold in sifted flour. Drop spoonfuls of the batter onto buttered baking sheets, pushing the batter off the spoon with your finger. Leave enough space between the cookies for the batter to expand.

2 **Baking and serving.** Garnish the surface of the cookies with a sprinkling of anise seeds. Set the cookies aside in a cool, dry place for two hours. Then bake them in a preheated 350° F. [180° C.] oven for about 10 minutes, or until they are slightly colored. Cool the cookies on a wire rack before serving them.

2 **Adding flour.** With the whisk, stir in flavorings—grated lemon peel and a small amount of anise-flavored liqueur are used here. Gradually add sifted flour, whisking it lightly into the egg-and-sugar mixture.

3 **Mixing the dough.** When the dough becomes too stiff to whisk, use your hands to mix in the rest of the flour. Gather the dough into a ball.

4 **Kneading the dough.** Transfer the ball of dough to a lightly floured work surface. Knead the dough only until it is smooth, dusting it with a little flour if it feels sticky. Do not overwork the dough, lest it become tough. With a lightly floured pin, roll the dough about ¼ inch [6 mm.] thick.

5 **Making patterns.** Before imprinting the dough with a carved rolling pin, as shown here, cut the dough into strips slightly wider than the pin. Lightly flour the pin, and roll it firmly over each strip of dough. If using a carved board instead, repeatedly press its surface into the dough.

6 **Drying the cookies.** Using a sharp knife, cut between the raised designs on the dough to make individual squares. For extra flavor, sprinkle buttered baking sheets with anise seeds before setting the squares on the sheets. Cover the cookies with parchment or wax paper and set them aside in a cool, dry place overnight.

7 **Baking and serving.** Bake the cookies in a preheated 300° F. [150° C.] oven for 15 to 20 minutes—the springerle are ready when their tops rise up to form a brittle, white crust and their bottom surfaces are lightly colored. Cool the springerle on a wire rack; then store them, covered, for at least a week before serving them.

Madeleines: Molded Cookies with a Cakelike Texture

Like spongecakes, madeleines start from a buttery sponge batter, but they are baked in molds to become cookie-sized shells *(recipe, page 131)*. Because the butter is melted and cooled before it is added, it blends in evenly without curdling the egg sponge and gives the batter a pourable consistency. The result is so rich that madeleines are only subtly flavored with a little lemon or orange peel, a splash of vanilla extract or—to add flecks of color as well as contribute taste —with scrapings from a vanilla bean.

The pans for madeleines—obtainable where fine kitchen supplies are sold— can have two to 48 molds that range in size from the miniatures only 1½ inches [4 cm.] long, shown here, to larger, deeper types 3 inches [8 cm.] long. Before the batter is spooned in, the molds are coated with butter and flour to keep the madeleines from sticking to the ridges. After each batch is baked, the molds should be wiped clean with paper towels—washing would remove any residue of fat— and given a fresh film of butter and flour.

1 Sifting in flour. In a large bowl set on a damp cloth to prevent it from slipping, whisk whole eggs and superfine sugar until the mixture is pale and thick *(page 66, top demonstration, Step 1)*. Add flavorings—in this case, finely grated lemon peel is used. Sift flour into the mixture.

2 Folding in flour. Gently fold the flour into the eggs and sugar with a rubber spatula or, as here, a wooden spoon. Cut downward through the batter with the spoon, then lift the batter on the spoon and fold it over on itself until all the flour is incorporated and the batter is smooth.

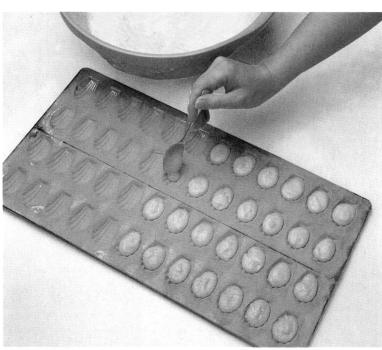

5 Filling the molds. Spoon the batter into the prepared madeleine pan. To allow for the expansion of the batter during baking, spoon in just enough batter so that each of the molded indentations will be approximately two thirds full.

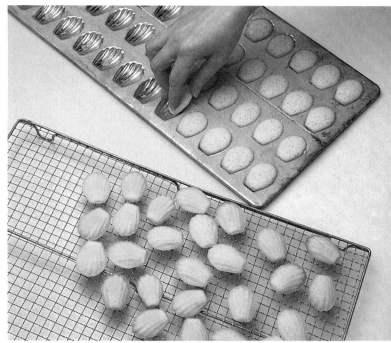

6 Baking. Bake the madeleines in a preheated 375° F. [190° C.] oven until they are firm and have shrunk from the sides of the molds. Miniature madeleines, as here, will be done in about 10 minutes; larger ones will take one or two minutes longer. Press down on the narrow ends of the madeleines to free them from the mold, and put them on a rack with their patterned sides upward.

3 **Adding butter.** A little at a time, pour in butter that has been melted and cooled. Fold each addition into the batter before adding more.

4 **Preparing the molds.** Dip a pastry brush in softened butter—or, as here, melted butter—and lightly coat each molded indentation of a madeleine pan. Sift a dusting of flour over the buttered surfaces. To remove any excess flour, invert the pan and sharply tap its underside.

7 **Coating with sugar.** If you like, finish the madeleines by sprinkling them with a little sugar. Here, superfine sugar is sifted over the surface of the madeleines while they are still warm; the sugar will cling to the warm cookies, emphasizing their decorative ridges. Leave the madeleines on the rack to cool before serving them.

Ladyfingers with a Beaded Surface

The delicate cookies called ladyfingers owe their lightness to the fact that egg whites whisked alone will trap much more air than when they are beaten with yolks. The fluffy mass of beaten whites, folded into the yolks, sugar and flour, produces a particularly soft batter (recipe, page 145). The heat of the oven then makes the air bubbles in the batter expand, puffing up the ladyfingers and giving them their characteristic crisp but not dry texture.

Ladyfingers can be piped into special pans with molded depressions in order to form cookies that are rounded on the bottoms as well as the tops. However, most cooks simply pipe the batter into finger-length strips on baking sheets, as demonstrated here. Either way, the piped batter can be dusted with sugar and sprinkled with water. During baking the coating will crystallize, frosting the ladyfingers with little sugar pearls.

1 Forming the sponge. Separate eggs. Drop the yolks into a heavy mixing bowl, the whites into a prepared copper bowl (page 55). Whisk the yolks until smooth, then add sugar and continue whisking until the sponge reaches the ribbon stage (page 66, top demonstration, Step 1). This may take 20 minutes by hand, 10 minutes with an electric mixer.

2 Folding in flour. Beat the whites until they form stiff peaks (page 60, Step 1). Working quickly, stir a few drops of orange-flower water into the egg-yolk sponge, then add sifted flour. Fold in the flour by cutting through the batter with the edge of a spatula or large spoon, then folding the batter over on itself.

5 Piping the batter. Spoon batter into a pastry bag fitted with a large No. 4 plain tube; twist the bag closed. Holding the bag almost horizontal to ensure straight lines, pipe strips of batter about 4 inches [10 cm.] long and ⅜ inch [9 mm.] wide onto buttered baking sheets. Space the strips well apart, and use a knife to stop the flow of batter at the end of each one.

6 Sprinkling on sugar. Through a sieve, sprinkle a light dusting of confectioners' sugar over the strips of batter. Flick a few drops of water over the batter strips and the sheet.

7 Baking the ladyfingers. To keep the batter from deflating, place the baking sheet at once in a preheated 325° F. [160° C.] oven. Bake the ladyfingers for about 20 minutes, or until they are very lightly colored and feel firm. Using a metal spatula, transfer the ladyfingers to a wire rack to cool.

3 **Lightening the batter.** To prevent lumps from forming when the bulk of the egg whites are incorporated, add one or two large spoonfuls of the beaten egg whites to the batter. With the spoon, cut and fold the whites into the mixture.

4 **Completing the batter.** Transfer the rest of the beaten egg whites to the bowl of batter all at once, using a spatula to scrape the bowl *(above, left)*. With the spoon, cut the mixture and fold it over on itself, gradually incorporating the whites into the rest of the ingredients *(right)*. Although the batter should be smooth, do not overwork it lest the egg whites lose their aeration and liquefy.

8 **Serving.** When the ladyfingers have cooled, arrange them on a platter for serving—perhaps as an accompaniment for ice cream. For a more elegant presentation, first coat the tips of the ladyfingers with chocolate by dipping them into sweet dark chocolate that has been melted in a bowl set over boiling water.

5
Syrup-flavored Mixtures
Melting In Sweetness

Experimenting with blends of spices
Robust gingerbread men
Constructing a gingerbread house
Nuts and fruit in candied wafers
Applying a chocolate coating

Syrup cookies are confections classified together because all contain ingredients that are melted to a syrupy consistency before the batter or dough is formed. In some cases the cookies are flavored with honey, molasses or chocolate, all of which require melting to reduce them to the right consistency for even blending; in other cases ingredients such as sugar and butter are melted in order to endow cookies with unique textures or tastes.

Among cookies flavored by melted honey or molasses are those relics of the Middle Ages, German lebkuchen and their various descendants. Lebkuchen are unsophisticated cookies, first made when honey—rather than rarer sugar—was Europe's primary sweetening agent. Spices from Asia, especially ginger, were used with abandon then. And doughs, not far removed from primitive bread doughs, were stiff and heavy. The thick medieval doughs were just malleable enough to be forced into elaborate wooden molds, then baked to form sturdy cookie knights, ladies and even Biblical scenes, as they still are in Central Europe today. The basic dough that forms lebkuchen can be refined and lightened by altering the proportions of flour, fat and liquid to produce tender cookie doughs that are still firm enough to turn into festive shapes—the gingerbread men pictured opposite, for instance, or the richly garnished gingerbread house demonstrated on pages 78-79.

The melting of ingredients is used to quite different effect for elegant cookies such as the florentines *(pages 80-81),* named for their supposed origin in the Italian city of Florence. To make cookies of this type, sugar is heated in cream and butter so that the ingredients dissolve together into a rich syrup, a sweetener much smoother than unmelted sugar because dissolving reduces the sugar granules to minuscule crystals. The addition of a small amount of flour turns the syrup into a thin batter that bakes to delicate, candy-like wafers. These may be left plain, or can be studded with fruit or coated with icing, as the cook chooses.

Melted sugar lends smoothness to some types of American brownies, too, and can add distinctive flavors. As shown on page 83, brown sugar, melted with butter, caramelizes slightly, acquiring the rich flavor and deep color that distinguish butterscotch—a pleasant variation of the more traditional chocolate brownies, also shown on those pages.

Clustered in a napkin-lined basket, a contingent of gingerbread men stand ready to be presented. The cookies are made from a syrup dough spiced with ginger, cinnamon and cloves. Pliable enough to roll out thin, the dough bakes to a crisp consistency.

A Generous Use of Syrup for Spicy Lebkuchen

The traditional syrup cookies called leb-kuchen owe their dense, hard texture to the proportions of the ingredients in the dough. To promote the gluten development that results in firmness, the dough contains high amounts of liquid and flour and low amounts of tenderizing fat.

A major part of the liquid for dough of this type is provided by the syrup sweetener, which may be honey or molasses and must be heated to reduce its viscosity so that it will combine smoothly with dry ingredients. Granular sugar augments the sweetness of the syrup and, for even blending, both the sugar and the fat— brown sugar and butter, in this case— are melted in the syrup *(recipe, page 167)*. The melted ingredients should be allowed to cool before flour is added: Heat from the syrup might otherwise partially cook the flour, causing it to congeal.

To give the cookies a fine, even texture, dry ingredients should be sifted together before they are combined with the syrup. Besides flour, dry ingredients for cookies of this type commonly include spices that complement the sweetness of the dough. Some appropriate spices are nutmeg, cinnamon, cloves, fennel and anise; for optimum flavor, buy the spices whole and store them in airtight, lightproof containers. Grate or grind small quantities as needed, using a nutmeg grater for the nutmeg and a mortar and pestle, electric coffee grinder or rotary pepper grinder for other spices.

Another dry ingredient for basic syrup doughs is baking soda, which reacts with the acid in honey or molasses to produce carbon-dioxide bubbles that lighten the cookies slightly without depriving them of their characteristic density.

The cookie dough can be augmented in many ways, before and after it is shaped and baked. For an interesting texture, stir chopped nuts and candied fruit or fruit peel into the dough, as here. Or roll the dough, cut out shapes—rectangles are traditional—and use nuts and fruits for a topping. After baking, the cookies can be topped with royal icing or confectioners' sugar glaze *(pages 8-9)*.

The baked cookies are very hard. But if stored with a slice of apple in an airtight container, they will absorb the fruit's moisture and soften in a week or so.

1 Adding the syrup. Put sugar—in this case, dark brown sugar—butter, and water into a heavy pan. Before measuring syrup sweetener—honey is shown here—lightly oil the inside of the cup to prevent sticking, then pour in the sweetener. Add the measured sweetener to the pan.

2 Melting the syrup. Over low heat, stir the mixture with a wooden spoon until the sugar dissolves and the ingredients are thoroughly blended. Increase the heat and, without stirring, bring the mixture to a boil. Remove the pan from the heat at once and let the mixture cool to room temperature.

6 Rolling out the dough. With your hands or a rolling pin, flatten the ball of dough. Roll the dough out lengthwise and then crosswise, into a long narrow rectangle about ⅓ inch [8 mm.] thick.

7 Cutting and baking. Trim off the uneven edges of dough with a knife. Cut the rectangle lengthwise into strips, then crosswise into bars—here, about 1 by 3 inches [2½ by 8 cm.]. Transfer the bars to buttered baking sheets and bake them in a preheated 325° F. [160° C.] oven for 25 to 30 minutes, or until they are dry and firm to the touch.

3 **Blending in flour.** Parboil candied fruit peel *(page 7)* and chop it fine; blanch and peel almonds and slice them into slivers. Set aside the peel and nuts. Sift flour, baking soda and spices into a bowl. Gradually add these dry ingredients to the syrup, stirring well after each addition.

4 **Stirring in nuts and peel.** Tip the chopped peel and nuts into the pan, stirring vigorously to combine the ingredients. The dough will be quite dry and crumbly at this stage.

5 **Kneading the dough.** To prevent sticking, lightly flour a work surface— and your hands as well. Spoon the dough onto the work surface. Gather the dough into a ball with your fingers; then knead the dough lightly until it forms a smooth, compact mass.

8 **Glazing and serving.** Transfer the bars to a wire rack and allow them to cool. Prepare a confectioners' sugar glaze, flavored—if you like—with a little fresh lemon juice. Brush the top of the cookies with the sugar glaze *(inset)*. Let the glaze set before serving the cookies *(right)* or storing them in a covered container to soften them.

Scope for Inventive Shaping

Decreasing the proportion of liquid in a syrup dough while increasing the fat limits the development of the flour's gluten and produces cookies that are much more tender and light than those demonstrated on pages 74-75. The result is a soft and sticky dough that can be easily molded into balls and that will spread during baking to form thick, domed cookies *(box, below; recipe, page 142)*. The addition of egg to the dough will strengthen it, making it sufficiently pliable to roll out thin, yet cohesive enough to maintain its shape in the oven *(recipe, page 119)*. Because it spreads very little during baking, this egg-enriched dough is ideal for cutting into decorative shapes, as shown at right.

The syrup sweetener for both doughs demonstrated here is molasses, which contributes a deep color and strong flavor; for a milder taste, substitute honey, dark corn syrup or English golden syrup, a refined form of molasses sold at specialty markets. As with most syrup cookies, spices add flavor and color, and these also can be varied, from a blend of several ground spices, such as the one described on pages 74-75, to one distinctive flavoring, such as ground ginger.

A dough firm enough for rolling requires leavening if it is to be appropriately light when baked. The leavening is provided by two ingredients. Beating the egg before adding it will incorporate some air, which will expand during baking to raise the cookies. And baking powder—its action is more pronounced than that of the baking soda used for basic syrup cookies—will produce carbon dioxide during baking for additional leavening.

Any cutters can be used to shape the rolled dough; figures are used here to make classic gingerbread men. If you wish to decorate the men after they are cooked, use raisins for eyes, pressing them into place while the cookies are still soft. Once the cookies have cooled, you can pipe royal icing *(page 9)* onto them to form noses, mouths and buttons.

1 Melting the syrup. Place sugar, syrup sweetener—here, molasses—butter, and ground cinnamon, ginger and cloves in a small, heavy saucepan. Set the pan over low heat and stir the mixture with a wooden spoon until the sugar dissolves and the butter melts.

2 Adding beaten egg. As soon as the syrup comes to a boil, remove the pan from the heat. Let the syrup cool to room temperature, then stir in baking powder. Sift flour into a large bowl. Add a pinch of salt. Make a well in the center and pour in the cooled syrup *(above)*. Beat an egg lightly and add it to the ingredients in the bowl.

Golden Brown Nuggets from a Sticky Dough

1 Shaping dough. Melt molasses, butter and brown sugar. After the mixture cools, stir in spices, flour and baking soda. Roll nut-sized pieces of dough into balls between your palms, oiling your hands to keep the dough from sticking. Place the balls on buttered baking sheets, leaving enough room between them for expansion during baking.

2 Baking and serving. Bake the cookies in a preheated 325° F. [160° C.] oven for 15 to 20 minutes. Using a metal spatula, move them to a wire rack to cool completely. If they are stored in an airtight tin, the cookies will keep for up to two months.

3 **Mixing the dough.** Using the wooden spoon, stir the ingredients until they are evenly blended. Flour your hands and gather the dough into a ball; place it on a lightly floured work surface. Knead the dough into a smooth ball, flouring your hands as necessary to prevent sticking. Refrigerate the dough for half an hour to firm it.

4 **Rolling the dough.** With a rolling pin, flatten the chilled dough on a floured work surface. Roll the dough into an even disk about ⅛ inch [3 mm.] thick.

5 **Cutting the cookies.** Stamp out shapes—in this case, little men—with a cookie cutter. Turn the cutter around while you work in order to produce as many cookies as possible.

6 **Baking the cookies.** Lift the scraps from around the shapes *(inset)* and press them into a ball. Chill it, roll and cut as before. Transfer the cookies to lightly buttered baking sheets. Bake them in a preheated 325° F. [160° C.] oven for 10 minutes, until their edges darken. Cool them on a rack *(right)*.

A Blueprint for a Gingerbread House

The dough that is the stuff of gingerbread men *(pages 76-77)* also provides the construction material for a festive gingerbread house *(recipe, page 119)*. Baked in broad slabs, gingerbread can be cut into house elements that will fit together readily if shaped with the aid of the cardboard templates described below. Their scale can be varied according to the size you want for the house: The plan will provide you with the correct proportions.

The slabs must be cut while they are warm and soft; they harden when they cool. The house then should be built on a board you can turn as you work. Thick royal icing *(page 9)*, which dries quickly, will cement the pieces together. The same icing can be spread over the roof to simulate snow, and piped onto the walls to outline windows.

Half the pleasure of creating a gingerbread house is decorating it. Nuts—including grated coconut—candied fruits and small candies such as gumdrops are among the traditional ornaments. Royal icing will hold these, too, in their places.

1 Cutting the gingerbread. Make templates *(box, below)*. Roll gingerbread dough ½ inch [1 cm.] thick. Bake it in slabs—here, 15 by 18 inches [38 by 46 cm.]—in a 350° F. [180° C.] oven for 25 minutes. Lay the templates on the warm gingerbread and cut around them with a knife; the rectangle cut from the front wall will be the door.

2 Beginning the house. Prepare a thick royal icing. Set the base of the house on a board or tray. Lay one end wall on the work surface. With a metal spatula, spread a wall support with icing. Lay the support face down parallel to one side of the wall and ½ inch [1 cm.] from the edge. Affix a second support to the other side.

Cutting Cardboard Templates

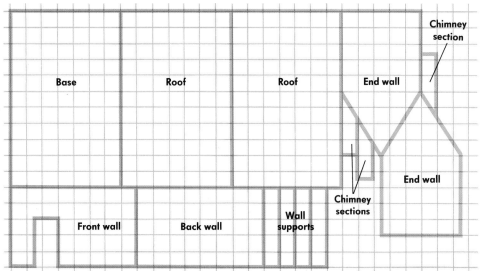

Base | Roof | Roof | End wall
Chimney section
Chimney sections
End wall
Front wall | Back wall | Wall supports

Making templates. Using a pencil and ruler, draw the shapes shown above on stiff cardboard. Work to scale—for this demonstration, each square of the grid represents 1 inch [2½ cm.]. With a sharp knife and the ruler, cut out templates for the base, two roof pieces, front wall, back wall, two end walls, four wall supports and three chimney sections.

6 Icing the roof. Apply icing to a small section of the roof at a time, swirling the icing with the tip of the spatula to create a rough finish. Then ice the chimney, leaving the inner side of the chimney plain, if you like.

3 **Joining the walls.** Ice two adjoining edges of both the back wall and the prepared end wall. Join the two walls to form a corner, pressing the side edge of the back wall to the wall support. Set the joined walls in place on the base. Prepare the second end wall in the same fashion as the first, cement it to the front wall and set the two on the base.

4 **Adding the door and roof.** Ice one long edge of the door. Working from the inside, secure the door—opening inward and slightly ajar—at the opening in the front wall. Spread the top edges of the walls with icing. Gently press one roof piece into position, holding it until it does not slip. Affix the second roof piece. Ice the ridge.

5 **Erecting the chimney.** Join the three chimney sections together with icing, making sure that their tops and bottoms are parallel. Ice the slanting bottom of the assembled chimney and press it into place on the roof on the front of the house so that it rests in a perpendicular position.

7 **Decorating.** Make decorations— here, whole blanched almonds, strips of angelica and candied fruits cut into various shapes. Before the icing hardens, stick almonds onto the roof ridge (inset). Pipe icing onto the walls to make windows. Use dabs of icing to stick the other decorations onto the walls (right).

A Molten Binding for Fruit and Nuts

A syrup-cookie mixture containing minimal amounts of flour and large amounts of syrup and butter becomes a thin batter that spreads, when baked, to form delicate, candy-like cookies. The syrup for these cookies must be a thin one if they are to have the proper lacy texture; if you use a syrup such as honey, you must not only heat it to reduce its viscosity, but also dilute it with water or cream. Or you can make your own rich syrup by dissolving granulated sugar with butter and cream, as for the florentines demonstrated here *(recipe, page 95)*.

A syrup batter of this type may be left plain, or—for a richer flavor and a more varied texture—the batter can be used as a binder for generous amounts of slivered, diced or chopped nuts and candied fruit and peel. After baking, while they are still soft and warm, the cookies can be shaped around a spoon handle or rolling pin to form containers for filling *(pages 10-11)*. Or the wafers can be left flat to harden, then coated with chocolate, as shown, or with royal icing *(page 9)*.

1 **Forming the syrup.** Put butter and sugar in a heavy pan. Pour in cream. Warm the mixture over medium heat, stirring continuously with a wooden spoon until the butter melts and the sugar dissolves.

2 **Bringing to a boil.** When the sugar has dissolved, let the syrup come to a boil, stirring gently to keep it from burning on the bottom of the pan. Remove the pan from the heat and let the syrup cool to room temperature.

5 **Spreading the batter.** Lightly butter and flour a baking sheet. Spoon the batter into mounds on the baking sheet, leaving 3 inches [8 cm.] between mounds to allow for the spreading of the batter. Dip a fork in a bowl of water to prevent sticking, and use the fork to spread the mounds into rounds, distributing the nuts and fruit evenly. Bake the florentines in a preheated 350° F. [180° C.] oven for 12 to 15 minutes, until their edges are browned. Using a metal spatula, transfer the cookies to a wire rack to cool.

6 **Spreading the chocolate.** Bring a pan of water to a boil, then reduce the heat until the water barely simmers. Place pieces of semisweet chocolate in a small, heatproof bowl. Set the bowl over (but not touching) the water, stirring the chocolate until it melts. Remove the pan from the heat. With a spatula, spread the underside of each cookie with melted chocolate. Place the cookies on a tray, chocolate side up.

3 **Adding the dry ingredients.** Blanch and peel almonds, then chop some of the nuts and cut the rest into slivers. Cut candied fruit and peel into fine dice. Sift flour. Tip the slivered almonds into the melted ingredients in the pan, then add the chopped almonds, the diced fruit and peel, and the sifted flour.

4 **Blending the batter.** Using a wooden spoon, stir the mixture until the nuts, fruit and flour are thoroughly incorporated. Make sure that all of the flavorings are coated with batter.

7 **Decorating the cookies.** Holding a fork at a slight angle *(inset)*, score parallel sets of wavy lines into the chocolate. Score the cookies in the same order in which you coated them, to prevent the chocolate coatings from becoming too firm to decorate. Let the chocolate set before arranging the cookies on a serving plate *(right)*.

Brownies: Traditional Favorites

Among the most popular of syrup cookies are brownies—included in the group because the ingredients that give these bar cookies their distinctive flavors are melted before the batters are formed *(recipes, pages 103-104)*. For instance, the solid chocolate that flavors traditional brownies *(right)* must be melted to a syrup that will blend evenly with the other batter ingredients.

The flavoring for butterscotch brownies *(box, opposite)* is brown sugar, which also is melted before it is mixed into the batter, not only for even blending, but also to cook the brown sugar slightly, endowing it with the nutty taste characteristic of butterscotch. As for any syrup mixture, the melted ingredients must be cooled before they are mixed with dry ingredients, in order to prevent lumping.

High in sugar and butter and relatively low in flour, brownies may be either cakelike or chewy—but they are always tender. The density of the bars is controlled by the number of eggs included in

the batter and by the treatment accorded those eggs. Light-textured brownies contain a large number of eggs, which are beaten to the ribbon stage *(page 66, Step 1)* to lighten the batter. For a firmer result, a brownie batter is made with a lower proportion of eggs—beaten just enough to break them up for easy mixing. Batters for light-textured brownies also generally include more leavening—in the form of baking powder or soda—than do denser brownie batters.

Besides the basic ingredients—a syrup, butter, sugar, eggs and flour—most brownie batters contain elements added for extra taste and variety of texture. Chopped nuts, dried fruit such as raisins, and candied fruit all may be included.

Brownies, like other bar cookies, are baked in single sheets, then divided into bars. It is important that the baked sheets be cooled completely before they are cut up: Premature cutting releases moisture in the form of steam, resulting in brownies that dry out quickly.

The Chocolate Classic

1 **Melting chocolate.** In a small pan, bring a 1-inch [2½-cm.] layer of water just to a simmer. Place pieces of unsweetened chocolate in a heatproof bowl and set the bowl over the water. Stir the chocolate until it melts, then add butter and stir until it melts. Let the mixture cool to room temperature.

4 **Baking.** Butter a baking pan—one 9-by-13-inch [23-by-33-cm.] pan is used here—and pour in the batter. Level the top with a spatula. Set the pan in a preheated 350° F. [180° C.] oven.

5 **Testing for doneness.** After 20 to 25 minutes, the batter will begin to pull away from the sides of the pan. Insert a cake tester in the center *(above)*. If the tester comes out clean, the brownie sheet is done. Let the sheet cool completely, then cut it into 2-inch [5-cm.] squares and lift them from the pan with a metal spatula *(inset)* for serving.

2 **Mixing the ingredients.** Beat eggs and salt until the eggs are foamy and pale yellow. Gradually beat in sugar and vanilla extract. Continue to beat for about 10 minutes, or until this sponge doubles in volume and falls from the beater in a thick ribbon. Stir in the cooled chocolate mixture.

3 **Adding flour.** When the chocolate and egg mixtures are partly combined, fold in sifted flour *(above, left)*. When the mixture is streaky, fold in coarsely chopped nuts—in this case, pecans *(right)*. Continue folding until the ingredients are evenly combined.

Butterscotch for a Special Flavor

1 **Making butterscotch.** In a small, heavy pan set over low heat, melt butter. Stir in brown sugar. When the sugar dissolves and the mixture bubbles, set it aside to cool. Mix into this syrup a beaten egg, vanilla extract, and sifted flour, salt and baking powder. Stir in chopped nuts—here, walnuts.

2 **Baking.** Butter a baking pan—in this instance, 8 inches [20 cm.] square. Pour in the batter and spread it evenly with a spatula. Bake in a preheated 350° F. [180° C.] oven for 20 minutes, or until a cake tester inserted into the center comes out clean. Set the pan on a wire rack to cool.

3 **Serving the brownies.** Let the pan and its contents cool completely before you cut the layer into bars 2 inches [5 cm.] square. Arrange the bars attractively on a plate for serving.

6
Crackers
Crisp and Tasty Treats

The uses of specialty flours
Kneading a supple dough
Working with yeast
Ways to incorporate seasoning

The morsels we know as crackers got their name from Josiah Bent, an enterprising sea captain who went into the baking business in Massachusetts shortly after 1800. He developed a thinner, lighter and thus more palatable version of hardtack—the heavy unleavened biscuit that was then the sailor's staple for long sea voyages—and dubbed his creation after the cracking noise it made when broken or eaten.

Captain Bent's cracker was a simple flatbread, a type as popular now as then and as easy to produce (pages 86-87). Indeed, compared to cookies, most crackers make minimal demands on the cook: They call for few ingredients and usually are assembled with little fuss. Flatbreads require just flour and water, kneaded together. Other crackers, based on pastry doughs—short crust (opposite) or rough puff (page 92)—include tenderizing fats; some need acidic liquids to moisten them and leavening to make them rise (page 89). So-called soda crackers are the most complex, beginning with a yeast mixture that is left to rise like bread dough before it is transformed into flaky snacks (pages 90-91).

Ordinarily, crackers are based on all-purpose flour, which has a high percentage of the gluten needed to bind the dough. But as Captain Bent proved, there is ample room for experimentation. In any cracker dough, up to 10 per cent of the all-purpose flour may be replaced with flour chosen for its flavor rather than its gluten content. In flatbread, all-purpose flour may be omitted, providing at least a third of the flour content is whole wheat—a flour with ample gluten, but also with bran to lend a crunchy texture and earthy taste. Other options are malty-tasting barley flour and the somewhat musty buckwheat flour. Oat flour is sweet; millet flour is nutty. And rye flour has a bittersweet flavor that may be faint or strong, depending on whether it is medium or dark rye.

Improvisation can also extend to seasonings and spices. A favorite addition is cheese, of a variety hard enough to be grated into tiny fragments that will disperse through the dough and strong-flavored enough to retain its character. Cheddar, Gruyère, Parmesan and Romano are all good choices. Zesty herbs such as sage or spices such as cayenne can be mixed with the flour, whereas seeds—celery, sesame, poppy or caraway seeds among them—can either be incorporated into the dough or sprinkled over the crackers before they are baked.

Classic water biscuits owe their crispness to the fact that they contain only a small quantity of fat—usually lard, which gives the crackers a mild, faintly sweet flavor. The fat is cut into pieces and rubbed into flour by the same method used for other short-crust doughs (page 88). Water serves as the moistener to bind the two ingredients.

Cooking a Flatbread on a Griddle

The most elemental of crackers is crisp, thin flatbread, made of nothing more than flour, water and salt *(recipe, page 156)*. Any kind of flour, or combination of flours, can be used. The only constant is that at least one third of it must be all-purpose or whole-wheat flour, either one of which will supply enough gluten to make the dough cohere.

Whatever flour is selected, the dough must be kneaded thoroughly. When a piece is shaped into a cylinder it should bend double without cracking. If time allows, cover the kneaded dough with plastic wrap or a damp cloth, and let it rest for at least half an hour—or as long as two hours. Resting will relax the gluten, thus tenderizing the dough and making it easier to roll.

Before it is rolled, the dough is divided into pieces of the size desired. Traditionally, flatbread is rolled into large thin disks as demonstrated here. However, the dough also can be rolled and cut into small crackers of any shape. And, if you like, you can sprinkle the rolled dough with seasonings—coarse salt or caraway, poppy or sesame seeds—and press them lightly into the surface of the dough with the rolling pin.

Prick each flatbread with a fork so that during the cooking steam can escape, rather than bubbling within the dough and causing it to buckle. The flatbreads can then be baked on sheets in a hot—425° F. [220° C.]—oven or on a griddle on top of the stove as shown at right. In either case, turn the rounds over halfway through the cooking process. Turning will ensure that they dry out completely and attain maximum crispness.

1 **Mixing the dough.** Sift flour—in this case, a mixture of barley and whole-wheat flours—and salt into a large mixing bowl. Stirring the mixture with a knife, gradually pour in just enough water to moisten the flour evenly *(above, left)*. When the dough forms a cohesive mass and comes away cleanly from the sides of the bowl, gather it up into a ball with your hands *(right)*.

5 **Cooking the flatbread.** Set the griddle over low heat for two or three minutes. Using both hands, carefully transfer a disk of dough from the tray to the hot griddle.

6 **Turning the flatbread.** Cook the flatbread for about 15 minutes, pushing its edges down with a metal spatula if they curl. When the underside has browned, turn the flatbread over, steadying it on the spatula with one hand.

2 **Kneading the dough.** Place the ball of dough on a lightly floured work surface. Press down on the dough with the heel of your hand and push it away from you; fold the dough back over on itself, give it a quarter turn, and repeat. Continue kneading for at least five minutes, or until the dough is completely smooth.

3 **Rolling out the dough.** With a knife, divide the dough into equal-sized pieces—here, it is cut into quarters. With a floured rolling pin, roll one piece as thin as possible. To make an even disk, roll forward only, from one edge to the other, and give the dough a quarter turn after every few strokes.

4 **Pricking the dough.** Lightly flour the surface of a heavy griddle. Prick the disk of dough all over with a fork; transfer the pricked round to a tray. Roll out and prick the other pieces of dough in the same way.

7 **Serving the flatbread.** Cook the flatbread for a further 10 to 15 minutes, until it is brown and crisp. Transfer it to a rack to cool. Cook the remaining rounds of dough in the same way, flouring the griddle for each one. Serve the flatbreads whole—they are so crisp that they can be broken cleanly into smaller pieces.

Puffy Biscuits from a Rubbed Dough

Crackers gain flakiness and tenderness when the flour is sifted with baking powder, then rubbed together with chilled fat—either butter or the lard used in the water biscuits shown here *(recipe, page 157)*. The fat coats some, but not all, of the flour particles, forming a barrier to water. Thus, gluten in the coated particles does not develop, and the dough is more tender than it would be if all the flour were well moistened.

The baking powder leavens the dough and makes it rise slightly in the oven. At the same time, the tiny bits of fat liquefy to keep the flour particles discrete and impart a flaky quality to the crackers.

Whatever the fat, it should be kept chilled throughout the mixing process. If it melts, too many flour particles will get coated with fat and the dough will not cohere properly. Use cold water to bind the dough, and roll it on a cool surface.

The rolled dough may be cut into any geometric shape. For variety, sprinkle the crackers before baking with coarse salt or caraway or poppy seeds.

1 Rubbing fat into flour. Sift flour, baking powder and salt into a large bowl and add small cubes of chilled fat—in this case, lard. Pick up small amounts of fat and flour, and rub them together with your finger tips to form flakes. Continue the process until all the fat has been rubbed into the flour and the mixture resembles coarse crumbs.

2 Adding water. Make a small well in the center of the mixture and pour in cold water a little at a time, stirring constantly with a knife or fork until the dough forms a cohesive mass.

3 Rolling the dough. Gather up the dough and press it lightly against the sides of the bowl to form a smooth ball. Sprinkle a little flour over the dough and place it on a lightly floured work surface. Roll the dough forward, give it a quarter turn and roll again. Repeat until the dough is ⅛ inch [3 mm.] thick.

4 Cutting out the crackers. Prick the sheet of dough all over with a fork to let steam escape during baking. Then, using a cookie cutter—here, 3½ inches [9 cm.] in diameter—cut rounds from the dough; with a metal spatula, place them on a lightly buttered baking sheet. Gather the scraps of dough into a ball, roll it and cut more rounds.

5 Baking. Bake the crackers in a preheated 350° F. [180° C.] oven for 10 to 15 minutes, or until they turn a pale golden color. Transfer the crackers to a rack to cool before serving them.

Firm Deep-fried Wafers

Adding melted fat and a generous proportion of warm acidic liquid to flour produces firm, chewy crackers such as the savory Indian wafers called *matthi* that are shown here *(recipe, page 159)*. Because it is melted, the fat lubricates the flour during the kneading process and helps the strands of gluten proteins become strong and elastic. The warm liquid—in this case, yogurt dissolved in tepid water—ensures maximum gluten development; a bit of baking soda counteracts the acid taste of the yogurt.

For extra flavor, crushed lovage seeds, which taste like celery, are added to the dough. Among other possible seasonings are slightly bitter coriander seeds, or licorice-like fennel or anise seeds.

The cut-out rounds of dough are crispest if deep fried, but they also can be baked if the fat content is doubled to offset the drying effect of the oven. In either case, slash the rounds in several places to let steam escape, thus preventing the crackers from puffing up too much.

1 **Rubbing in the fat.** Put flour into a bowl and pour in cooled melted fat—butter, lard or, as here, vegetable shortening. Pick up some flour and fat in one hand and rub the other hand over it until the ingredients are mixed evenly. Keep rubbing the fat and flour until no lumps remain. Add baking soda, salt and crushed lovage seeds.

2 **Adding yogurt and water.** Stir warm water into unflavored yogurt and pour the mixture over the flour. Mix the liquid and rubbed ingredients with your hands until they cohere enough to form a rough mass. Turn the dough out onto a lightly floured work surface.

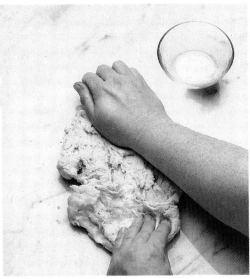

3 **Kneading the dough.** Spread a little fat on your hands to keep the dough from sticking to them. Knead the dough for 10 minutes, or until it becomes silky and elastic. Put it in a greased bowl, cover with plastic wrap and leave it at room temperature for 30 minutes. Then knead the dough for one minute and divide it into eight equal balls.

4 **Cutting the dough.** Place one dough ball at a time on a lightly floured surface and cover the others with plastic wrap. Roll each ball about ⅛ inch [3 mm.] thick. Stamp out 2-inch [5-cm.] rounds with a cutter. With a small, sharp knife make four ¼-inch [6-mm.] slashes in the center of each cracker.

5 **Frying the crackers.** In a deep, heavy pan, heat oil to 325° F. [160° C.] on a deep-frying thermometer. Drop in a few crackers at a time and, turning them frequently with a metal skimmer, fry them for about three minutes, or until they become a pale golden color. Transfer the fried crackers to a rack covered with paper towels to drain.

Old-fashioned Soda Crackers Made at Home

Despite their name, soda crackers are based on a yeast dough that is repeatedly rolled and folded to form a multiplicity of flaky paper-thin layers. The chief role of baking soda is to neutralize the acidity of the dough and thus ensure that the crackers have a mildly sweet taste.

In its first stage, soda-cracker dough is a simple mixture of flour, yeast and water. To minimize the yeast's flavor, very little of it is used, and the dough requires 18 to 30 hours to rise to double its volume. However, because the rising time is so long the dough ferments slightly; once risen it needs to be mixed with alkaline soda to counteract its acids.

At the same time, sour milk or buttermilk is added to make the dough supple, and lard is worked in to give it tenderness. The dough is then kneaded and allowed to rest for four hours to relax the flour's gluten and prevent toughness. Finally, the dough is rolled out and folded several times in rapid succession: Speed is necessary to prevent the dough from drying out and becoming too stiff to manipulate. A judicious dusting of flour after each rolling helps to keep the layers separate and ensure flaky crackers.

During baking, the crackers will rise to approximately three times their original height. To produce the thin crackers shown in this demonstration, the dough is rolled $\frac{1}{16}$ inch [$1\frac{1}{2}$ mm.] thick and cut into small squares. For more substantial cracker-barrel crackers, the dough can be rolled $\frac{1}{3}$ inch [1 cm.] thick and cut into 3-inch [8-cm.] rounds.

Because gluten is so essential in giving them their finished texture, soda crackers are lightest if made with all-purpose flour. However, up to 10 per cent of the all-purpose flour can be replaced, if you like, with rye, whole-wheat, buckwheat or oat flour. For further flavor variation, the unbaked crackers can be topped with seeds or coarse salt—or cayenne pepper, paprika or crumbled dried sage can be incorporated into the dough while it is being kneaded.

1 **Making the basic dough.** Pour tepid water into a large mixing bowl and add yeast, stirring to dissolve it. After the yeast foams—about 10 minutes—add sifted flour. When the mixture becomes too stiff to stir with a spoon, finish mixing it with your hand. Cover the bowl with plastic wrap and set the dough in a warm, draft-free place.

4 **Rolling the dough.** Place the dough on a floured work surface and pound it with a rolling pin to flatten it. Roll the dough into a rectangle $\frac{1}{4}$ inch [6 mm.] thick and about 18 by 24 inches [23 by 61 cm.]. Use only enough flour on the rolling pin and work surface to keep the dough from sticking— excess flour will toughen the dough.

5 **Folding the dough.** Brush the dough very lightly with flour; then fold its long sides into the center to make three layers. Roll the package into a rectangle $\frac{1}{4}$ inch [6 mm.] thick, pushing the pin both crosswise and lengthwise. Repeat this folding and rolling process twice more, then fold the dough into thirds as before and cut it crosswise into four pieces.

6 **Rolling out the pieces.** Cover three of the pieces and place the fourth on the floured work surface. Roll the dough into a rectangle $\frac{1}{16}$ inch [$1\frac{1}{2}$ mm.] thick; it will be so thin that you can see through it. If there is any excess flour on the underside, lift the dough up and brush it off.

2 **Adding the baking soda.** When the dough has doubled in volume—about 20 hours—punch it down with your fist to deflate it. Then add baking soda, salt, water and chunks of lard. Pour in sour milk or buttermilk. Using your hands, work the ingredients together until the dough is fairly smooth, but sticky.

3 **Kneading the dough.** Turn the dough onto a floured work surface. Holding the dough with one hand, push it forward with the heel of your other hand *(above, left)*. Work in a little sifted flour, then fold the dough back over on itself. Repeat until all of the flour is incorporated, then knead the dough for about 10 minutes, or until it is silky and smooth *(right)*. Put the dough in a large clean bowl, cover it tightly and let the dough rest at room temperature for four hours; it may again double in volume.

7 **Cutting the dough.** Using a straightedge and a sharp knife, trim the uneven edges from the rectangle. Prick the dough with a fork and cut it into 2-inch [5-cm.] squares. Lift each square with a knife or spatula to make sure it is not stuck to the work surface.

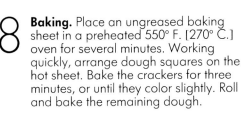

8 **Baking.** Place an ungreased baking sheet in a preheated 550° F. [270° C.] oven for several minutes. Working quickly, arrange dough squares on the hot sheet. Bake the crackers for three minutes, or until they color slightly. Roll and bake the remaining dough.

A Cheese Coating for Crunchy Straws

When it is blended with tart flavorings, rough puff dough *(pages 46-47)* yields a buttery pastry that has the crumbly texture of a cookie and the savory taste of a cracker. For the cheese straws shown here, the dough is moistened with water; if you want to underscore the dough's richness, substitute milk or cream, or egg yolk thinned with a little water.

To ensure crisp pastry, the flavorings must be dry ones—grated cheese such as Gruyère, Cheddar or the Parmesan used in this demonstration; chopped pecans, walnuts or hazelnuts; or whole seeds such as caraway, sesame or lovage. The flavorings are added in two operations: First the dough and work surface are dusted with the flavoring element, which is incorporated by rolling and folding the dough. Then, when the dough is rolled for cutting, it is given a final, flavorful coat.

The rolled rough puff dough will lend itself to any of the shaping techniques demonstrated on pages 48-51. Or it can be stamped into rounds, cut into rectangles or diamonds, or sliced into strips and twisted into straws.

1 Rolling in cheese. Make a sugarless rough puff dough and give it three turns *(pages 46-47, Steps 1 to 10).* Sprinkle grated cheese—in this case, Parmesan—over the work surface and the dough. Roll the dough into a rectangle ¼ inch [6 mm.] thick and three times as long as it is wide. Fold the ends to the center *(above, left),* then fold the parcel in half *(center)* to make four layers. With the open end of the parcel toward you, roll the dough into a rectangle *(right)* and fold it into four again. Chill the dough for 30 minutes in the refrigerator or 15 minutes in the freezer.

2 Cutting strips. Sprinkle grated cheese over the work surface and again roll the dough into a rectangle. Sprinkle more cheese and a little cayenne pepper over the rectangle. Roll the flavorings lightly into the surface. Turn the rectangle over and flavor the other side. Cut the dough crosswise into strips about ½ inch [1 cm.] wide.

3 Twisting straws. Hold the ends of one strip of dough between your fingers and twist the ends in opposite directions. Lay the strip on a buttered baking sheet, pressing the ends down flat to prevent untwisting. Shape the remaining strips in the same way. Chill the straws in the refrigerator for 30 minutes or the freezer for 15 minutes.

4 Baking and serving. Bake the straws in a preheated 450° F. [230° C.] oven until they are evenly colored—about seven minutes. Transfer them carefully to a rack to cool; they are very fragile when hot. Serve the straws while slightly warm or cooled to room temperature, arranging them—if you wish—on a napkin-lined plate.

Anthology of Recipes

Drawing upon the cooking literature of more than 25 countries, the editors and consultants for this volume have selected 222 published recipes for the Anthology that follows. The selections range from the familiar to the exotic—from four variations of brownies to cookies formed by baking a coat of fruit-flavored almond paste on diamond-shaped pieces of edible rice paper.

Many of the recipes were written by world-renowned exponents of the culinary art, but the Anthology also includes selections from rare and out-of-print books and from works that have never been published in English. Whatever the sources, the emphasis in these recipes is always on fresh, natural ingredients that blend harmoniously and on techniques that are practical for the home cook.

Since many early recipe writers did not specify amounts of ingredients, sizes of pans or even cooking times and temperatures, the missing information has been judiciously added. In some cases, clarifying introductory notes have also been supplied; they are printed in italics. Modern recipe terms have been substituted for archaic language and some instructions have been expanded; but to preserve the character of the original recipes and to create a true anthology, the authors' texts have been changed as little as possible.

The cookie recipes are categorized chiefly by the methods used to shape them—rolling, piping or molding, for example. The exceptions are meringues and macaroons, which are grouped together because both are based on egg whites, and the cookies that are fried rather than baked. Cracker recipes appear as one group, regardless of how they are shaped or cooked. Recipes for standard preparations—icings, fillings and basic cookie doughs among them—appear at the end of the Anthology. Unfamiliar cooking terms and uncommon ingredients are explained in the combined General Index and Glossary.

All ingredients are listed within each recipe in order of use, with the customary U.S. measurements and the metric measurements provided in separate columns. All quantities reflect the American practice of measuring such solid ingredients as flour by volume rather than by weight, as is done in Europe.

To make the quantities simpler to measure, many of the figures have been rounded off to correspond to the gradations on U.S. metric spoons and cups. (One cup, for example, equals 237 milliliters; however, wherever practicable in these recipes, the metric equivalent of 1 cup appears as a more readily measured 250 milliliters—¼ liter.) Similarly, the weight, temperature and linear metric equivalents have been rounded off slightly. Thus the American and metric figures do not exactly match, but using one set or the other will produce the same good results.

Drop Cookies	94
Bar Cookies	103
Rolled Cookies	112
Refrigerator Cookies	126
Molded and Hand-shaped Cookies	129
Pressed and Piped Cookies	144
Meringues and Macaroons	148
Fried Cookies	152
Crackers	155
Standard Preparations	164
Recipe Index	168

Drop Cookies

Mariette's Cookies

Biscuits de Mariette

To make about 50

1 cup	flour	¼ liter
½ cup	superfine sugar	125 ml.
½ cup	heavy cream	125 ml.
3	egg whites, stiffly beaten	3

Put the flour and sugar in a large bowl. Add the cream and mix together well. Gently fold in the egg whites. Butter two baking sheets. Using a teaspoon, place little heaps of the dough, spaced well apart, on the sheets. Bake the cookies in a preheated 450° F. [230° C.] oven until brown—less than five minutes. Watch them carefully; they cook very quickly.

ÉLIANE AND JACQUETTE DE RIVOYRE
LA CUISINE LANDAISE

Tea Crackers

Nuts, dried currants, raisins, candied orange or lemon peel, or pieces of dried fruit may be used for decoration.

To make about 25

4 tbsp.	butter, softened	60 ml.
¼ cup	sugar	50 ml.
½ tsp.	vanilla or almond extract, or fresh lemon juice	2 ml.
1	egg, beaten	1
¼ tsp.	salt	1 ml.
½ cup	flour	125 ml.

Cream the butter; add the sugar, then cream again. Add the flavoring, egg, salt and flour. Drop teaspoonfuls of the batter, well spaced, onto buttered baking sheets and bake in a preheated 350° F. [180° C.] oven for 13 to 15 minutes. Do not let the cookies get too brown.

LOIS LINTNER SUMPTION AND MARGUERITE LINTNER ASHBROOK
AROUND-THE-WORLD COOKY BOOK

Drop Cookies

To make about 100

8	eggs, beaten	8
2 cups	superfine sugar	½ liter
3 cups	flour	¾ liter
1 tbsp.	caraway seeds (optional)	15 ml.

Whisk the eggs and sugar until pale and fluffy—about 15 minutes—then gradually fold in the flour, beating well after each addition. Drop teaspoonfuls of the mixture onto floured baking sheets and bake in a preheated 350° F. [180° C.] oven for 20 minutes. When you see the cookies rising, watch them carefully and take them out of the oven as soon as they begin to color; if they are not sufficiently cooked through, return them to the oven briefly. Once the cookies have been baked, you may scatter on caraway seeds, if you please. Switch off the heat and return them to the oven until they are very dry.

E. SMITH
THE COMPLEAT HOUSEWIFE

Vanilla Wafers

Vanille Kager

To make about 100

¾ lb.	butter, softened	350 g.
2 cups	sugar	½ liter
2	eggs	2
1 tsp.	vanilla extract	5 ml.
1½ cups	sifted flour	375 ml.
1½ cups	cornstarch	375 ml.
½ tsp.	cream of tartar	2 ml.

Cream the butter and sugar smooth; beat in the eggs and vanilla extract. Sift together the flour, cornstarch and cream of tartar, and beat them gradually into the butter mixture. Drop the batter by spoonfuls spaced about 2 inches [5 cm.] apart onto buttered baking sheets. Bake in a preheated 400° F. [200° C.] oven for about eight minutes, until the cookies are golden brown at the edges. When removed from the baking sheets, the cookies will be soft; they will become crisp when they cool.

FLORENCE BROBECK AND MONIKA B. KJELLBERG
SMÖRGÅSBORD AND SCANDINAVIAN COOKERY

Light Cookies

Bizcotelas

To make about 50

8	eggs, the yolks separated from the whites, and the whites stiffly beaten	8
2 cups	superfine sugar	½ liter
1 cup	water	¼ liter
½ cup	flour	125 ml.

Beat the egg yolks very thoroughly with 1¾ cups [425 ml.] of the sugar and the water until the sugar has dissolved and the yolks are thick and pale—about 10 to 15 minutes. Fold in the flour carefully, and then the egg whites.

Place sheets of parchment paper or foil over baking sheets, and butter the paper or foil. Place small elongated teaspoonfuls of the batter on the lined baking sheets, and sprinkle them with the remaining sugar. Bake the cookies in a preheated 350° F. [180° C.] oven for six to eight minutes, or until they are puffed slightly and firm to the touch.

MARIA DEL CARMEN CASCANTE
150 RECETAS DE DULCES DE FÁCIL PREPARACIÓN

Applesauce Gems

To make about 60

½ lb.	butter, softened	¼ kg.
2 cups	firmly packed light brown sugar	½ liter
½ cup	cold black coffee	125 ml.
1 cup	applesauce	¼ liter
3½ cups	sifted flour	875 ml.
½ tsp.	baking soda	2 ml.
1 tsp.	baking powder	5 ml.
1 tsp.	salt	5 ml.
1 tsp.	grated nutmeg	5 ml.
1 tsp.	ground cinnamon	5 ml.
1 cup	seedless white raisins or diced candied fruit	¼ liter
1 cup	dried currants	¼ liter

Cream the butter and sugar well. Add the coffee and applesauce. Sift together the flour, soda, baking powder, salt and spices, and blend them in. Stir in the fruits. Drop spoonfuls of the batter onto lightly buttered baking sheets and bake in a preheated 375° F. [190° C.] oven for about 10 minutes, or until lightly browned. To keep these cookies soft, store them in airtight containers.

ANNETTE LASLETT ROSS AND JEAN ADAMS DISNEY
THE ART OF MAKING GOOD COOKIES PLAIN AND FANCY

Florentines

To make about 30

3 tbsp.	butter	45 ml.
½ cup	heavy cream	125 ml.
⅔ cup	sugar	150 ml.
¼ cup	candied cherries, soaked in hot water for 2 minutes, drained and quartered	50 ml.
6 oz.	almonds, blanched and peeled (about 1½ cups [375 ml.]), 1¼ cups [300 ml.] finely chopped, the rest cut into slivers	175 g.
¾ cup	finely chopped candied orange peel	175 ml.
⅓ cup	flour	75 ml.
Topping		
8 oz.	semisweet baking chocolate, chopped	¼ kg.

In a heavy pan, bring the butter, cream and sugar slowly to a boil. Remove the pan from the heat and stir in the cherries, almonds, orange peel and flour. Drop the batter by teaspoonfuls onto buttered and lightly floured baking sheets, leaving plenty of room between the mounds for spreading; flatten each mound with a wet fork.

Bake the cookies in a preheated 350° F. [180° C.] oven for five to six minutes. Take them from the oven and, with a round cutter 3 inches [8 cm.] in diameter, pull in the edges of each cookie. Return the cookies to the oven and bake them for five to six minutes longer, or until lightly browned at the edges. Cool the cookies briefly on the baking sheets; then lift them off with a sharp knife and transfer them to a rack to cool completely.

Melt the chocolate in a heatproof bowl set over a pan of hot water, stirring the chocolate with a wooden spoon until it is smooth. Spread the undersides of the cookies with chocolate and, if you like, when the chocolate is at the point of setting, mark it with wavy lines, using a cake decorating comb or a serrated knife.

FAYE LEVY
LA VARENNE TOUR BOOK

Fruited Cornmeal Cookies
Gialletti or Zaletti

The ammonium bicarbonate in this recipe is a leavening agent that was used before the days of commercial baking powder. It is the hartshorn salt of old recipes. It gives an especially crisp texture to a cookie. Ammonium bicarbonate can be bought in drugstores. It comes in small lumps and should be crushed with a rolling pin just before being used. An equal quantity of baking powder may be substituted for the ammonium bicarbonate.

To make about 40

1 cup plus 2 tbsp.	fine yellow cornmeal	280 ml.
1¼ cups	flour	300 ml.
1 tsp.	crushed ammonium bicarbonate	5 ml.
½ tsp.	salt	2 ml.
3	egg yolks	3
½ cup	superfine sugar	125 ml.
2 tsp.	grated lemon peel	10 ml.
6 tbsp.	butter, melted and cooled	90 ml.
1 cup	dried currants, soaked in warm water for 15 minutes, drained and dried	¼ liter
	confectioners' sugar	

Sift together the cornmeal, flour, ammonium bicarbonate and salt. Beat the egg yolks and gradually beat in the superfine sugar, beating well after each addition. Beat in the lemon peel and butter; mix thoroughly. Gradually beat in the cornmeal mixture, beating until smooth. Stir in the currants and mix them through the batter. The batter should be firm, but not too stiff. (Cornmeal varies in its ability to absorb liquid; if necessary, add 1 to 2 teaspoonfuls [5 to 10 ml.] of water to soften the dough slightly.)

Drop the dough by heaping tablespoons onto buttered and floured baking sheets, leaving spaces of 2 inches [5 cm.] between the cookies. Pat the cookies into diamond shapes. Bake them in a preheated 375° F. [190° C.] oven for about 15 minutes, or until crisp. Cool on the baking sheets for a few minutes, then transfer the cookies to a rack to cool completely. Sprinkle with confectioners' sugar before serving.

NIKA HAZELTON
THE REGIONAL ITALIAN KITCHEN

Jam Cookies
Biscottini di Confetture

Crystallized orange blossoms are obtainable at some specialty food stores. If not available, add 2 teaspoons of orange-flower water to the apricot jam and pound the candied citron with 3 tablespoons [45 ml.] of the superfine sugar.

To make about 35

1 cup	chopped candied citron	¼ liter
5	crystallized orange blossoms	5
2 tbsp.	apricot jam	30 ml.
½ cup	superfine sugar	125 ml.
4	eggs, the yolks separated from the whites, and the whites stiffly beaten	4

In a mortar pound the citron to a paste with the orange blossoms. Add the jam, ⅓ cup [75 ml.] of the sugar and the egg yolks. Mix and put through a food grinder. Then fold in the egg whites.

Drop the mixture by teaspoonfuls onto baking sheets lined with parchment paper—spacing the mounds well apart. Sprinkle the mounds with the remaining sugar to form a glaze, and bake in a preheated 275° F. [140° C.] oven for about 30 minutes, or until the cookies are firm.

IPPOLITO CAVALCANTI, DUCA DI BUONVICINO
CUCINA TEORICO-PRATICA

Orange Jumbles

To make about 35

½ cup	sugar	125 ml.
6 tbsp.	butter, softened	90 ml.
1 cup	almonds, blanched, peeled and slivered	¼ liter
½ cup	flour	125 ml.
4 tbsp.	grated orange peel	60 ml.
¾ cup	fresh orange juice	175 ml.
	red food coloring	

Beat together the sugar and butter, and add the almonds, flour, orange peel and juice, and a few drops of the coloring. Mix and put on lightly buttered baking sheets in quantities of about 1 teaspoon [5 ml.] to each jumble, allowing room to spread, and bake in a preheated 350° F. [180° C.] oven for about 15 minutes. The jumbles will be the size of teacup rims, and should curl their crisp edges, faintly pink as the underneath of a young mushroom.

LADY JEKYLL
KITCHEN ESSAYS

Orange Juice Cookies

To make about 70

2½ cups	sifted flour	625 ml.
½ tsp.	baking soda	2 ml.
¼ tsp.	salt	1 ml.
12 tbsp.	butter, softened	180 ml.
1 cup	sugar	¼ liter
2	eggs, lightly beaten	2
¾ cup	strained fresh orange juice	175 ml.
1 cup	shredded coconut, finely chopped	¼ liter

Sift the flour with the baking soda and salt; set it aside. Cream the butter and sugar together, add the eggs and continue creaming. Add the flour alternately with the orange juice, then add the coconut. Drop the batter by the teaspoonful onto lightly buttered baking sheets, spacing the mounds well apart. If desired, sprinkle the cookies with additional coconut. Bake in a preheated 400° F. [200° C.] oven for 10 to 12 minutes, or until a cookie springs back when pressed with a finger.

NEW JERSEY RECIPES, OLDE & NEW

Cherokee Date Rocks

These cookies keep well if wrapped, when cold, in wax paper and stored in an airtight container.

To make about 50

¾ lb.	butter, softened	350 g.
1½ cups	firmly packed light brown sugar	375 ml.
3	eggs, the yolks separated from the whites, and the whites stiffly beaten	3
1 tsp.	baking soda, dissolved in 2 tsp. [10 ml.] water	5 ml.
4 cups	flour, sifted with 1 tsp. [5 ml.] ground allspice and 1 tbsp. [15 ml.] ground cinnamon	1 liter
½ lb.	dates, pitted and chopped (about 1⅔ cups [400 ml.])	¼ kg.
½ lb.	pecans or walnuts, coarsely chopped (about 2 cups [½ liter])	¼ kg.
	superfine sugar	

Cream the butter and brown sugar, and add the egg yolks and baking soda. Combine the sifted flour mixture with the butter mixture. Fold the egg whites into the batter and, last of all, fold in the dates and nuts. Drop by teaspoonfuls onto well-buttered baking sheets, leaving about 3 inches [8 cm.] between the mounds. Bake in a preheated 375° F. [190° C.]

oven for 15 to 18 minutes, or until the cookies are done in the center. Do not cook them too long or they will be as hard as their name implies. Remove the cookies from the baking sheets with a spatula and dust them with superfine sugar.

MARION FLEXNER
OUT OF KENTUCKY KITCHENS

Raisin Cookies

"Galetes" aux Raisins

To make about 50

4 tbsp.	butter	60 ml.
¼ cup	superfine sugar	50 ml.
1	egg	1
⅔ cup	flour	150 ml.
⅓ cup	raisins	75 ml.
1 tsp.	rum	5 ml.

Place the butter in a bowl and work with a fork until soft. Stir in the sugar and beat the mixture for three to four minutes. Break in the egg and continue beating until the mixture is smooth. Add the flour, a spoonful at a time, and then mix in the raisins and the rum. Drop the dough by spoonfuls onto buttered baking sheets, spacing the mounds well apart. Bake the cookies in a preheated 425° F. [220° C.] oven for four to six minutes, or until they are firm and light brown.

ÉLIANE THIBAUT COMELADE
LA CUISINE CATALANE

Peanut Butter Cookies

To make 60

½ cup	peanut butter	125 ml.
8 tbsp.	butter, softened	120 ml.
½ cup	granulated sugar	125 ml.
½ cup	firmly packed light brown sugar	125 ml.
1	egg	1
½ tsp.	vanilla extract	2 ml.
½ tsp.	salt	2 ml.
½ tsp.	baking soda	2 ml.
1 cup	flour	¼ liter

Cream together the peanut butter and butter, beat in the two sugars and then stir in the remaining ingredients. Arrange by teaspoonfuls on baking sheets. Press flat with a floured spoon or a floured fork. Bake in a preheated 350° F. [180° C.] oven until firm—about 10 minutes.

WILMA LORD PERKINS (EDITOR)
THE FANNIE FARMER COOKBOOK

Best Peanut Butter and Chocolate Cookies

To make about 50

¾ cup	flour	175 ml.
½ tsp.	baking soda	2 ml.
8 tbsp.	butter, softened	120 ml.
½ cup	smooth or chunky peanut butter	125 ml.
½ cup	firmly packed light brown sugar	125 ml.
½ cup	granulated sugar	125 ml.
1	egg, lightly beaten	1
1 tsp.	vanilla extract	5 ml.
½ cup	salted Spanish peanuts, red skins left on	125 ml.
½ cup	semisweet chocolate bits	125 g.

On wax paper, thoroughly stir together the flour and soda. In a medium-sized mixing bowl, cream the butter and peanut butter; beat in—one ingredient at a time—the brown sugar, granulated sugar, egg and vanilla. Add the flour mixture; with a spoon, mix well. Stir in the peanuts and chocolate.

Drop the batter by heaping teaspoonfuls about 2 inches [5 cm.] apart onto ungreased baking sheets. Press down on each cookie with a floured fork to make a crisscross pattern; reflour the fork for each cookie. (This procedure will flatten the cookies, but the marking will not show after baking.)

Bake the cookies in a preheated 350° F. [180° C.] oven until lightly browned—about 10 minutes. Leave the cookies on the sheets for about one minute, then use a wide metal spatula to transfer them to wire racks to cool. Store in an airtight container.

CECILY BROWNSTONE
CECILY BROWNSTONE'S ASSOCIATED PRESS COOK BOOK

Chocolate Snaps

To make 36

1 cup	flour	¼ liter
1 tsp.	baking powder	5 ml.
8	egg whites	8
2 cups	confectioners' sugar	½ liter
2 oz.	unsweetened baking chocolate, grated	60 g.
2 tsp.	grated orange peel	10 ml.

Sift together the flour and baking powder. Beat the egg whites until firm, then gradually beat in the confectioners' sugar to make a stiff meringue. Fold in the grated chocolate, the sifted flour mixture and the grated orange peel.

Drop teaspoonfuls of the batter 2 inches [5 cm.] apart on buttered baking sheets. Bake in a preheated 350° F. [180° C.]

oven for eight to 10 minutes, or until the cookies are dry and firm to the touch.

JULIETTE ELKON
THE CHOCOLATE COOKBOOK

Crackled Chocolate Drops

To make about 30

8	egg yolks	8
½ cup	sugar	125 ml.
1 tsp.	vanilla extract	5 ml.
½ lb.	semisweet baking chocolate, melted and cooled	¼ kg.
1 cup	almonds, blanched, peeled and ground	¼ liter
⅞ cup	flour, sifted with a pinch of salt	205 ml.

Beat the egg yolks and sugar together until pale and fluffy. Add the vanilla extract. Stir in the melted chocolate, almonds and flour. Drop or pipe small rounds of batter onto a buttered and floured baking sheet, leaving 1 inch [2½ cm.] between the cookies. Bake in a preheated 350° F. [180° C.] oven for approximately 25 minutes, or until the cookies are crackled and dry.

PAULA PECK
THE ART OF FINE BAKING

Chocolate Chip Cookies

To make about 70

12 tbsp.	butter, softened	180 ml.
1 cup	firmly packed light brown sugar	¼ liter
½ cup	granulated sugar	125 ml.
2	eggs, lightly beaten	2
2¼ cups	sifted flour	550 ml.
½ tsp.	salt	2 ml.
1 tsp.	baking soda	5 ml.
1½ tsp.	vanilla extract	7 ml.
1 cup	chopped nuts	¼ liter
6 oz.	semisweet chocolate bits	175 g.

Cream the butter and sugars together. Add the eggs. Sift together the dry ingredients and add them to the mixture, then add the vanilla, nuts and chocolate bits. Drop the dough by spoonfuls onto baking sheets. Bake in a preheated 375° F. [190° C.] oven for 10 to 12 minutes, or until the cookies are firm and lightly colored.

ANNETTE LASLETT ROSS AND JEAN ADAMS DISNEY
THE ART OF MAKING GOOD COOKIES PLAIN AND FANCY

Chocolate Walnut Wheels

To make 24

6 tbsp.	butter, softened	90 ml.
1 cup	sugar	¼ liter
1	egg, lightly beaten	1
2 oz.	unsweetened baking chocolate, melted	60 g.
¼ tsp.	vanilla extract	1 ml.
⅔ cup	sifted cake flour	150 ml.
¼ tsp.	salt	1 ml.
½ lb.	walnuts (about 2 cups [½ liter]), 24 halves reserved, the rest finely chopped	¼ kg.

Cream the butter and add the sugar gradually. Add the egg, a little at a time, then the chocolate and vanilla extract. Add the flour, salt and chopped nuts, and beat the batter well. Drop the batter from the tip of a spoon into mounds spaced 1 inch [2½ cm.] apart on a buttered baking sheet. Garnish each mound with a walnut half. Bake in a preheated 350° F. [180° C.] oven for 10 minutes, or until the cookies are lightly browned.

JOSH GASPERO (EDITOR)
HERSHEY'S 1934 COOKBOOK

Toll House Chocolate Crunch Cookies

Toll House cookies—the original chocolate chip cookies—were created by the author in the 1930s, when she and her husband operated the Toll House Inn, an 18th Century stagecoach stop on the toll road between Boston and New Bedford.

Because baking soda begins to release some of its carbon dioxide as soon as it is moistened, you will obtain lighter cookies if you omit the water and sift the soda with the flour as demonstrated on pages 28-29.

To make 100

½ lb.	butter, softened	¼ kg.
¾ cup	firmly packed light brown sugar	175 ml.
¾ cup	granulated sugar	175 ml.
2	eggs, beaten	2
1 tsp.	vanilla extract	5 ml.
2¼ cups	flour	550 ml.
1 tsp.	salt	5 ml.
1 tsp.	baking soda	5 ml.
1 cup	chopped nuts	¼ liter
12 oz.	semisweet chocolate bits	350 g.

Cream the butter. Beat in the brown and granulated sugars, and then the eggs and vanilla. Sift the flour with the salt.

Dissolve the soda in 1 teaspoon [5 ml.] of hot water and add it to the butter mixture alternately with the flour. Stir in the nuts and chocolate.

Drop the dough by spoonfuls—spaced about 3 inches [8 cm.] apart—onto buttered baking sheets. Bake in a preheated 375° F. [190° C.] oven for 10 to 12 minutes, or until the cookies are uniformly browned and crisp.

Alternatively, chill the dough overnight. Break off teaspoonfuls of dough and roll them between the palms of your hands. Place the balls 2 inches [5 cm.] apart on buttered baking sheets. Then press the balls with your finger tips to form flat disks. This way the cookies do not spread as much in the baking and they stay uniformly round.

RUTH GRAVES WAKEFIELD
TOLL HOUSE TRIED AND TRUE RECIPES

Pecan Oatmeal Cookies

The batter may be chilled, rolled into cookie-sized balls and frozen on a baking sheet until firm. These may then be kept in small containers in the freezer to cook a few at a time.

To make about 50

½ lb.	butter, softened	¼ kg.
1 cup	firmly packed light brown sugar	¼ liter
1 cup	granulated sugar	¼ liter
2	eggs	2
1½ cups	sifted flour	375 ml.
1 tsp.	salt	5 ml.
1 tsp.	baking soda	5 ml.
1 tsp.	vanilla extract	5 ml.
1 cup	chopped pecans	¼ liter
3 cups	rolled oats	¾ liter

Cream the butter, brown sugar and granulated sugar together. Add the eggs and beat until the mixture is fluffy. Sift together the flour, salt and soda and slowly add to the mixture. Add the vanilla. Fold in the pecans and rolled oats. Drop the batter by spoonfuls onto buttered baking sheets. Bake in a preheated 350° F. [180° C.] oven for 10 to 15 minutes, or until lightly browned.

THE JUNIOR CHARITY LEAGUE OF MONROE, LOUISIANA
THE COTTON COUNTRY COLLECTION

Chocolate Oatmeal Cookies

To make about 50

8 tbsp.	unsalted butter, softened	120 ml.
⅓ cup	granulated sugar	75 ml.
⅓ cup	firmly packed light brown sugar	75 ml.
1	egg, beaten	1
½ tsp.	vanilla extract	2 ml.
¾ cup	flour	175 ml.
½ tsp.	salt	2 ml.
1 tsp.	baking powder	5 ml.
¼ cup	milk	50 ml.
½ cup	chopped nuts	125 ml.
1 ½ cups	rolled oats	375 ml.
1 cup	semisweet chocolate bits	¼ liter

Cream together the butter and sugars. Mix in the egg and vanilla extract. Sift together the flour, salt and baking powder, and add the dry ingredients to the butter mixture alternately with the milk. Stir in the nuts, oats and chocolate.

Drop teaspoonfuls of the mixture onto lightly buttered baking sheets. Bake in a preheated 375° F. [190° C.] oven for 10 to 12 minutes, or until lightly browned.

JULIETTE ELKON
THE CHOCOLATE COOKBOOK

Oatmeal Raisin Cookies

To make about 70

2 cups	flour	½ liter
1 tsp.	baking soda	5 ml.
1 tsp.	salt	5 ml.
1 tsp.	ground cinnamon	5 ml.
12 tbsp.	butter, softened	180 ml.
1 cup	sugar	¼ liter
2	eggs	2
2 cups	rolled oats	½ liter
1 cup	raisins, chopped	¼ liter

Sift together the flour, baking soda, salt and cinnamon. Cream the butter with the sugar. Beat in the eggs. Add half of the flour mixture and stir well. Add all of the rolled oats and stir well. Add the remainder of the flour mixture, stirring the batter just enough to blend in the flour. Add the raisins. Drop the batter by spoonfuls onto baking sheets and bake in a preheated 400° F. [200° C.] oven for 10 to 15 minutes, or until the cookies are firm and lightly browned.

JOSEPHINE PERRY
COOKIES FROM MANY LANDS

Cottage Cheese Cookies

To make 48

8 tbsp.	butter or lard, softened	120 ml.
1 ½ cups	sugar	375 ml.
2	eggs, lightly beaten	2
2 ½ tbsp.	fresh lemon juice	37 ml.
2 tsp.	grated lemon peel	10 ml.
1 cup	cottage cheese	¼ liter
2 cups	flour	½ liter
1 tsp.	baking powder	5 ml.
1 tsp.	salt	5 ml.

Cream the butter with the sugar until fluffy. Beat in the eggs, lemon juice and lemon peel. Press the cottage cheese through a sieve and add it to the batter, beating well. Sift the dry ingredients together, add them to the batter and mix thoroughly. Drop the batter by the teaspoonful onto buttered baking sheets—spacing the mounds well apart. Bake in a preheated 400° F. [200° C.] oven for about 15 minutes, or until the cookies are lightly browned.

BEATRICE VAUGHAN
YANKEE HILL-COUNTRY COOKING

Country Cookies

Galletas Campesinas

The oatmeal called for in this recipe is finely ground oat kernels—not the familiar rolled oats. Oatmeal is obtainable at health-food stores.

To make about 60

2¾ cups	fine oatmeal	675 ml.
1 cup	whole-wheat flour	¼ liter
¼ cup	sugar	50 ml.
2 tsp.	baking powder	10 ml.
	salt	
2	eggs, beaten	2
½ cup	honey, warmed	125 ml.

Put the oatmeal, whole-wheat flour, sugar, baking powder and a pinch of salt in a bowl. Mix well, then make a well in the center of the mixture. Pour into it the eggs and warm honey. Mix and knead thoroughly. Place teaspoonfuls of the batter on buttered and floured baking sheets, leaving a little space between the mounds. Bake in a preheated 350° F. [180° C.] oven for 20 minutes, or until lightly browned.

MARIA DEL CARMEN CASCANTE
MANUAL MODERNO DE PASTELERIA CASERA

Anise Caps
Aniskuchen

Instead of being mixed into the dough, the anise seeds can be sprinkled over the cookies after they are shaped.

Another way of preparing this dough is to mix 2½ cups [625 ml.] of sugar with six eggs and four yolks in a bowl set over a pan of simmering water. Whisk the mixture until it is warm and very thick and frothy—about 10 minutes. Remove the bowl from the heat and continue whisking the mixture until cold. Fold in 5 cups [1¼ liters] of flour and the anise seeds, and continue as below.

To make 100 to 120		
2 cups	superfine sugar	½ liter
7	eggs	7
4 cups	flour	1 liter
3½ tbsp.	anise seeds	52 ml.

Beat the sugar and eggs until thick, pale and frothy—about 15 minutes. Gradually fold in the flour and anise seeds. Let stand for two hours. With a spoon, drop the dough by heaping tablespoonfuls onto buttered baking sheets—spacing the mounds about 2 inches [5 cm.] apart. Let the cookies stand in a warm place for several hours, or until the surface of each cookie is smooth and slightly dried.

Bake the cookies in a preheated 350° F. [180° C.] oven for about 10 minutes, or until they are just beginning to change color. Remove them from the baking sheets while still warm.

SOPHIE WILHELMINE SCHEIBLER
ALLGEMEINES DEUTSCHES KOCHBUCH FÜR ALLE STÄNDE

Almond-Paste Cookies
Calissons d'Aix

Edible rice paper is made by pressing a rice-flour paste between hot irons to form a very thin sheet; it can be obtained from confectionery-supply stores.

To make about 50		
½ lb.	almonds, blanched and peeled (about 2 cups [½ liter])	¼ kg.
¼ cup	syrup from preserved fruits	50 ml.
1 cup	superfine sugar	¼ liter
	royal icing (recipe, page 164)	

In a mortar, grind the almonds fine with the fruit syrup; add the sugar and continue to grind the mixture into a paste. Take the paste out of the mortar, put it into a saucepan set over low heat and stir it for five to six minutes, or until the paste is so compact and dry that it will not adhere to your finger. Take the paste off the heat and spread it, as evenly as possible, onto rice paper in a layer about ½ inch [1 cm.] thick. Spread a thin layer of icing over the paste. Slicing through the paper, cut out diamond-shaped cookies with a sharp knife. Set the paper-backed cookies on baking sheets. Bake in a preheated 300° F. [150° C.] oven with the door ajar for 50 minutes, or until the cookies are dried and firm.

ÉMILE HÉRISSÉ
THE ART OF PASTRY MAKING

Pistachio Cookies
Biscottini di Pistacchi

The paper cups called for in this recipe are usually used to hold candies and are much smaller than those used for cupcakes. They are obtainable at bakery and confectionery supply stores. For these cookies, buy paper candy cups 1½ inches [4 cm.] in diameter and fill each of them about three quarters full with the batter.

To make about 35		
½ cup	pistachios, blanched and peeled	125 ml.
½ cup	finely chopped candied citron	125 ml.
7	egg whites, 1 lightly beaten, 6 stiffly beaten	7
⅔ cup	sugar	150 ml.
2	egg yolks	2
1 tsp.	flour	5 ml.

In a mortar, pound the pistachios and citron together to form a smooth paste. Add the lightly beaten egg white, little by little. Pour the mixture into a bowl and add ½ cup [125 ml.] of the sugar and the egg yolks. Stir until well combined. Beat the flour into the stiffly beaten egg whites and fold them into the nut mixture. Pour the batter into paper cups set side by side on one or two baking sheets, or place teaspoonfuls of the batter—at least an inch [2½ cm.] apart—on baking sheets covered with parchment paper. Sprinkle the batter with the remaining sugar and bake the cookies in a preheated 275° F. [140° C.] oven for about 30 minutes, or until firm and lightly browned.

IPPOLITO CAVALCANTI, DUCA DI BUONVICINO
CUCINA TEORICO-PRATICA

Eulalia Cookies

Bollos Eulalia

Wafers are very thin 1¼-inch [3-cm.] rounds made by press-
ing and drying potato-flour paste. They are obtainable where
bakery or confectionery supplies are sold. If they are not avail-
able, cut similar disks from sheets of edible rice paper.

To make 36

½ lb.	almonds, blanched, peeled and ground (about 2 cups [½ liter])	¼ kg.
1 cup	sugar	¼ liter
2 cups	flour	½ liter
½ lb.	butter, softened	¼ kg.
6	egg yolks	6
	salt	
½ tsp.	ground cinnamon	2 ml.
36	wafers	36

Mix the almonds with the sugar to make a paste. Sift the
flour onto a pastry board, add the butter, egg yolks, almond
paste and a small pinch of salt. Stir, add the cinnamon and
mix well. Spread this mixture on the wafers, put them on a
baking sheet and bake in a preheated 300° F. [150° C.] oven
for 20 minutes, or until the cookies are firm but not colored.

VICTORIA SERRA
TÍA VICTORIA'S SPANISH KITCHEN

Millennial Cookies

Tausendjahrkuchen

The original version of this recipe calls for bitter almonds.
Almond extract makes a suitable substitute.

To make 80 to 90

1 cup	almonds, blanched and peeled	¼ liter
1 tsp.	egg white	5 ml.
3¼ cups	superfine sugar	800 ml.
7	eggs	7
8 tbsp.	butter, melted	120 ml.
¼ tsp.	almond extract	1 ml.
1 tsp.	ground cinnamon	5 ml.
2	sugar tablets, rubbed over the rind of a lemon, then coarsely crushed (or 1 tsp. [5 ml.] granulated sugar)	2
¼ cup	finely chopped candied orange peel	50 ml.
4 cups	flour	1 liter

Combine the almonds and spoonful of egg white in a mortar
and pound the nuts to a fine paste. In a bowl, mix the paste

with the superfine sugar and whole eggs, and whisk until
the mixture is thick and foamy. Stir in the butter, almond
extract, cinnamon, crushed lemon-flavored sugar, candied
peel and flour. Drop this batter by tablespoonfuls onto buttered baking sheets—spacing the mounds well apart. Bake
in a preheated 350° F. [180° C.] oven for 15 minutes, or until
the cookies are browned. Remove the cookies from the baking sheets as soon as they come out of the oven.

SOPHIE WILHELMINE SCHEIBLER
ALLGEMEINES DEUTSCHES KOCHBUCH FÜR ALLE STÄNDE

Pumpkin Cookies

To make about 40

¾ cup	firmly packed light brown sugar	175 ml.
2 tbsp.	honey	30 ml.
1 cup	puréed cooked pumpkin	¼ liter
½ cup	vegetable oil	125 ml.
1 tsp.	vanilla extract	5 ml.
2 cups	flour	½ liter
1 tsp.	baking powder	5 ml.
1 tsp.	baking soda	5 ml.
½ tsp.	salt	2 ml.
½ tsp.	ground cinnamon	2 ml.
½ tsp.	grated nutmeg	2 ml.
¼ tsp.	ground ginger	1 ml.
1 cup	pitted prunes or seedless raisins, chopped	¼ liter
½ cup	chopped walnuts	125 ml.

Place the brown sugar, honey, pumpkin, oil and vanilla extract in a mixing bowl. Beat until blended. In a separate
bowl, stir together the flour, baking powder, baking soda,
salt, cinnamon, nutmeg and ginger. Add the dry ingredients
to the pumpkin mixture. Mix well. Stir in the prunes or
raisins and the walnuts. Drop the batter by rounded teaspoonfuls onto buttered baking sheets, spacing the cookies
well apart. Bake in a 350° F. [180° C.] oven for 12 to 15
minutes, or until the cookies are golden brown. Cool them
on wire racks.

LOU SEIBERT PAPPAS
COOKIES

Carrot Cookies

To make about 40

½ cup	butter, softened	125 ml.
1 cup	firmly packed light brown sugar	¼ liter
½ cup	granulated sugar	125 ml.
1 tsp.	vanilla extract	2 ml.
1	egg	1
1 cup	boiled and puréed carrots, cooled	¼ liter
2 cups	flour, sifted	½ liter
½ tsp.	salt	2 ml.
1½ tsp.	baking powder	7 ml.
¾ cup	raisins, chopped	175 ml.

Cream the butter and sugars together until smooth and pale. Add the vanilla extract and the egg. Beat until fluffy. Add the carrots. Sift together the flour, salt and baking powder and add to the creamed mixture, beating until smooth. Add the chopped raisins and blend them into the batter. Drop the batter by teaspoonfuls onto buttered baking sheets, spacing the mounds 2 to 3 inches [5 to 8 cm.] apart. Bake in a preheated 375° F. [190° C.] oven for 10 to 12 minutes, or until the cookies are golden brown and firm.

MARY EMMA SHOWALTER
MENNONITE COMMUNITY COOKBOOK

Sweet-Potato Cookies

To make about 60

2 cups	sifted flour	½ liter
4 tsp.	baking powder	20 ml.
1 tsp.	grated nutmeg	5 ml.
8 tbsp.	butter, softened	120 ml.
1½ cups	firmly packed light brown sugar	375 ml.
2	eggs	2
2	medium-sized sweet potatoes, boiled, peeled and mashed (about 1¼ cups [300 ml.])	2
1 tsp.	vanilla extract	5 ml.
1 tsp.	grated lemon peel	5 ml.
1 cup	shredded coconut	¼ liter
¼ cup	chopped candied ginger	50 ml.
½ cup	chopped nuts	125 ml.

Sift together the flour, baking powder and nutmeg; set the mixture aside. Cream the butter and sugar, and beat in the

eggs, sweet potatoes, vanilla extract and lemon peel. Add the sifted ingredients and mix in the coconut, ginger and nuts. Lightly oil two baking sheets and drop tablespoonfuls of the mixture onto them 1½ inches [4 cm.] apart. Bake the cookies in a preheated 400° F. [200° C.] oven for 12 to 15 minutes, or until well browned.

NEW JERSEY RECIPES, OLDE & NEW

Bar Cookies

Brownies Cockaigne

Almost everyone wants to make this classic American confection. Brownies may vary greatly in richness and contain anywhere from ¾ pound [350 g.] of butter and 5 ounces [150 g.] of chocolate to 2 tablespoons [30 ml.] of butter and 2 ounces [60 g.] of chocolate for every cup [¼ liter] of flour. If you want them chewy and moist, use a 9-by-13-inch [23-by-32½-cm.] pan; if cakey, a 9-by-9-inch [23-by-23-cm.] pan.

To make 30

8 tbsp.	butter	120 ml.
4 oz.	unsweetened baking chocolate	125 g.
4	eggs, at room temperature	4
¼ tsp.	salt	1 ml.
2 cups	sugar	½ liter
1 tsp.	vanilla extract	5 ml.
1 cup	sifted flour	¼ liter
1 cup	pecans, chopped	¼ liter

Melt in a double boiler the butter and unsweetened chocolate. Cool this mixture. If you do not, your brownies will be heavy and dry. Beat the eggs and salt until light in color and foamy in texture. Add the sugar and vanilla gradually and continue beating until well creamed.

With a few swift strokes, combine the cooled chocolate mixture and the egg-and-sugar mixture. Even if you normally use an electric mixer, do this manually. Before the mixture becomes uniformly colored, fold in—again by hand—the flour. Before the flour becomes uniformly colored, gently stir in the pecans.

Pour the mixture into a buttered 9-by-13-inch [23-by-32½-cm.] pan and bake in a preheated 350° F. [180° C.] oven for about 25 minutes. Cut when cool: The interiors are still moist when fresh from the oven.

IRMA S. ROMBAUER AND MARION ROMBAUER BECKER
THE JOY OF COOKING

Peanut Butter Brownies

To make 36

2	eggs	2
1 cup	granulated sugar	¼ liter
½ cup	firmly packed light brown sugar	125 ml.
¼ cup	chunky peanut butter	50 ml.
1 tsp.	vanilla extract	5 ml.
2 tbsp.	butter, softened	30 ml.
1⅓ cups	flour	325 ml.
2 tsp.	baking powder	10 ml.
½ tsp.	salt	2 ml.
¼ cup	salted peanuts, chopped	50 ml.

Beat the eggs, sugars, peanut butter, vanilla extract and butter thoroughly with an electric mixer or rotary beater. Sift together the remaining dry ingredients and stir them into the batter. Spread the batter into a buttered 9-inch [23-cm.] square baking pan. Sprinkle the peanuts over the top and press them in lightly. Bake in a preheated 350° F. [180° C.] oven for about 30 minutes, or until a knife inserted into the center comes out clean. Cut into 1½-inch [4-cm.] squares while warm.

WILMA LORD PERKINS (EDITOR)
THE FANNIE FARMER COOKBOOK

Marbled Brownies

German's sweet chocolate is a unique chocolate product developed in 1851 by Samuel German.

To make 36

4 oz.	German's sweet chocolate	125 g.
5 tbsp.	butter, 2 tbsp. [30 ml.] softened	75 ml.
3 oz.	cream cheese, softened	90 g.
1 cup	sugar	¼ liter
3	eggs	3
½ cup plus 1 tbsp.	flour	140 ml.
1½ tsp.	vanilla extract	7 ml.
½ tsp.	baking powder	2 ml.
¼ tsp.	salt	1 ml.
½ cup	coarsely chopped nuts	125 ml.
¼ tsp.	almond extract	1 ml.

Stirring constantly, melt the chocolate and 3 tablespoons [45 ml.] of the butter in a small saucepan over very low heat. Let the mixture cool. Cream the softened butter with the cream cheese. Gradually add ¼ cup [50 ml.] of the sugar, creaming until light and fluffy. Blend in one egg, 1 tablespoon [15 ml.] of the flour and ¼ teaspoon [2 ml.] of the vanilla. Set aside. In a large bowl beat the remaining two eggs until thick and light in color—about 10 minutes. Gradually add the remaining sugar, beating until thickened. Add the baking powder, salt and remaining flour. Blend in the cooled chocolate mixture, the remaining vanilla, the nuts and almond extract. Spread about half of the chocolate batter in a buttered 9-inch [23-cm.] square baking pan. Then spread the cream-cheese batter evenly over the chocolate layer. Spoon the remaining chocolate batter gently over the cream-cheese layer. Zigzag a spatula through the batter once in each direction to create a marble effect. Bake in a preheated 350° F. [180° C.] oven for 30 minutes, or until the top springs back when pressed lightly in the center. Let the cake cool and cut it into 1½-inch [4-cm.] squares.

JUNIOR LEAGUE OF HOUSTON, INC.
HOUSTON JUNIOR LEAGUE COOKBOOK: FAVORITE RECIPES

Butterscotch Brownies

To make 15

4 tbsp.	butter, melted and cooled	60 ml.
1 cup	firmly packed light brown sugar	¼ liter
1	egg	1
½ tsp.	vanilla extract	2 ml.
1 cup	sifted flour	¼ liter
1 tsp.	baking powder	5 ml.
½ tsp.	salt	2 ml.
½ cup	chopped walnuts	125 ml.

Brown butter frosting

2 oz.	semisweet baking chocolate	60 g.
2 tbsp.	butter	30 ml.

Combine the melted butter and brown sugar; mix until thoroughly blended. Stir in the egg and vanilla. Sift together the flour, baking powder and salt; stir into the brown-sugar mixture. Add the walnuts. Spread the mixture in a buttered baking pan 8 inches [20 cm.] square. Bake in a preheated 350° F. [180° C.] oven for 20 minutes, or until a knife inserted in the center comes out clean. Cool in the pan on a rack.

To make the frosting, melt the chocolate and butter together over low heat, stirring constantly. Cool slightly. Pour the frosting over the brownies and tilt the pan back and forth to distribute the frosting evenly. When the frosting has set, cut the brownies into 1½-by-2½-inch [3-by-6-cm.] bars.

ELISE W. MANNING (EDITOR)
COUNTRY FAIR COOKBOOK

Maple Sugar Bars

To make 16

1 cup	crushed maple sugar (about ½ lb. [¼ kg.])	¼ liter
4 tbsp.	butter, softened	60 ml.
1	egg, lightly beaten	1
1 cup	flour	¼ liter
1 tsp.	baking powder	5 ml.
¼ tsp.	salt	1 ml.
1 cup	chopped nuts	¼ liter
½ tsp.	vanilla extract	2 ml.

Cream the maple sugar with the softened butter and beat in the egg. Sift the flour with the baking powder and salt, then add the nuts. Add the flour mixture to the egg mixture. Add the vanilla extract. Blend well and pour the batter into a buttered 8-inch [20-cm.] square baking pan. Bake in a preheated 350° F. [180° C.] oven for about 25 minutes, or until a knife inserted in the center comes out clean. When cool, cut the cake into 2-inch [5-cm.] squares.

BEATRICE VAUGHAN
YANKEE HILL-COUNTRY COOKING

Coffee Bars

To make about 25

4 tbsp.	butter, softened	60 ml.
1 cup	firmly packed light brown sugar	¼ liter
1	egg	1
½ cup	hot coffee	125 ml.
1½ cups	sifted flour	375 ml.
½ tsp.	baking soda	2 ml.
½ tsp.	baking powder	2 ml.
¼ tsp.	ground cloves	1 ml.
¼ tsp.	ground cinnamon	1 ml.
½ cup	raisins	125 ml.
½ cup	chopped nuts	125 ml.
1 cup	confectioners' sugar	¼ liter
2 tbsp.	warm coffee	30 ml.

Cream the butter, add the sugar and egg, and beat well. Add the hot coffee gradually, mixing well. Sift the flour, baking soda, baking powder and spices together and add them to the coffee mixture. Beat well, then add the raisins and the nuts. Pour the batter into a buttered 10-by-15-inch [25-by-38-cm.] baking pan. Bake in a preheated 350° F. [180° C.] oven for 15 to 20 minutes, or until a wooden pick inserted into the center comes out clean. Mix together the confectioners' sugar and warm coffee. Smooth this icing on top of the cake, cool, and cut it into 2-by-3-inch [5-by-8-cm.] bars.

THE JEKYLL ISLAND GARDEN CLUB
GOLDEN ISLES CUISINE

Citron Sponge Cookies

Biscottini Ordinari al Cedro

This recipe is from a 19th Century book written by the pastry chef to the King of Sardinia—and produces a regal supply of cookies. The amounts of ingredients called for can safely be halved or quartered. If you cannot obtain a citron to flavor the cookies, use a large lemon instead.

To make about 120

2	sugar tablets, rubbed over the peel of a citron, then crushed to a powder	2
24	eggs, the yolks separated from the whites, and the whites stiffly beaten	24
1¾ cups	superfine sugar	425 ml.
2½ cups	flour, sifted	625 ml.
	jam (optional)	
	confectioners' sugar glaze (recipe, page 164) or melted chocolate (optional)	

Beat the citron-flavored sugar, egg yolks and superfine sugar together until the mixture is quite firm, then add the flour. Gently fold in the egg whites. Pour the batter into buttered rectangular cake pans and bake them in a preheated 350° F. [180° C.] oven for 45 minutes, or until the tops are golden. Cool the sheets on a rack, then cut them into small squares. If the squares are thick, they may be split in half, spread with jam and covered with glaze or melted chocolate.

GIOVANNI VIALARDI
TRATTATO DI CUCINA, PASTICCERIA MODERNA

Cheesecake Cookies

To make 16

6 tbsp.	butter, softened	90 ml.
⅓ cup	firmly packed light brown sugar	75 ml.
1 cup	flour	¼ liter
½ cup	finely chopped walnuts	125 ml.

Cream cheese filling

¼ cup	granulated sugar	50 ml.
½ lb.	cream cheese, softened	¼ kg.
1	egg, lightly beaten	1
2 tbsp.	milk	30 ml.
2 tbsp.	fresh lemon juice	30 ml.
½ tsp.	vanilla extract	2 ml.

Cream the butter with the brown sugar in a small bowl. Add the flour and nuts, and stir until the mixture is crumbly. Reserve 1 cup [¼ liter] of this mixture for the topping. Press the remainder into the bottom of a buttered 8-inch [20-cm.] square baking pan. Bake in a preheated 350° F. [180° C.] oven for 12 to 15 minutes.

For the filling, first blend the sugar and cream cheese until smooth. Add the egg, milk, lemon juice and vanilla extract, and beat well. Spread the filling over the baked crust and sprinkle with the reserved topping. Bake at 350° F. for 25 minutes, or until a knife inserted into the filling comes out clean. Let the cake cool, then cut it into 2-inch [5-cm.] squares.

THE JUNIOR LEAGUE OF CHARLESTON, WEST VIRGINIA, INC.
MOUNTAIN MEASURES

Lemon Bars

To make about 30

8 tbsp.	butter, softened	120 ml.
¼ cup	confectioners' sugar, sifted	50 ml.
1 cup plus 2 tbsp.	flour	280 ml.
1 cup	granulated sugar	¼ liter
½ tsp.	baking powder	2 ml.
2	eggs	2
2 tbsp.	strained fresh lemon juice	30 ml.
2 tsp.	grated lemon peel	10 ml.
1 cup	confectioners' sugar glaze (recipe, page 164), made with lemon juice	¼ liter

In a deep bowl, cream the butter and confectioners' sugar together until the mixture is light and fluffy. Beat in 1 cup [¼ liter] of the flour, ½ cup [125 ml.] at a time. Place the mixture in a buttered baking pan 8 inches [20 cm.] square and, with your fingers, pat it smooth. Bake in the middle of a preheated 350° F. [180° C.] oven for 15 minutes, or until the cookie base is delicately colored and firm to the touch.

Meanwhile, combine the granulated sugar, the remaining 2 tablespoons [30 ml.] of flour and the baking powder, and sift them into a bowl. Add the eggs and beat vigorously with a spoon until the mixture is smooth. Stir in the lemon juice and lemon peel.

When the cookie base has baked its allotted time, pour the egg batter over it and smooth the top with the back of a spoon. Bake for about 25 minutes, or until the top is golden brown and firm. Let the cake cool to room temperature.

With a rubber spatula, spread the confectioners' sugar glaze evenly over the cooled cake. Let the glaze harden for about 15 minutes, then cut the cake into 1-by-2-inch [2½-by-5-cm.] bars. Drape foil or wax paper over the pan and let the lemon bars rest at room temperature for about a day before serving them. The three layers—cookie base, lemon topping and glaze—will blend with one another and give the lemon bars the chewy, somewhat sticky consistency of gumdrops.

FOODS OF THE WORLD
AMERICAN COOKING: THE GREAT WEST

Apricot Bars

To make about 15

8 tbsp.	butter, cut into pieces	120 ml.
¼ cup	granulated sugar	50 ml.
1 cup	flour	¼ liter
	confectioners' sugar	

Apricot topping

½ lb.	dried apricots	¼ kg.
2	eggs, beaten	2
1 cup	firmly packed light brown sugar	¼ liter
⅓ cup	flour	75 ml.
½ tsp.	baking powder	2 ml.
¼ tsp.	salt	1 ml.
½ tsp.	vanilla extract	2 ml.
½ cup	chopped nuts	125 ml.

Blend the butter, granulated sugar and flour until crumbly. Pack into a buttered 9-inch [23-cm.] square baking pan. Bake in a preheated 350° F. [180° C.] oven for 15 minutes.

Meanwhile, in a covered saucepan, simmer the dried apricots in water to cover for 15 minutes; drain the apricots and chop them. Combine the apricots with the remaining topping ingredients; beat until well mixed. Pour the filling over the baked crust and bake for 30 minutes at 350° F., or until the topping is firm to the touch and lightly browned. Cool the cake, dust it with confectioners' sugar and cut it into 2-inch [5-cm.] square bars.

THE JUNIOR LEAGUE OF PINE BLUFF, INC.
SOUTHERN ACCENT

Spicy Apple Bars

To make 48

½ cup	butter	125 ml.
1 cup	sugar	¼ liter
2	eggs	2
1 cup	sifted flour	¼ liter
1 tsp.	baking powder	5 ml.
½ tsp.	baking soda	2 ml.
½ tsp.	salt	2 ml.
1 tbsp.	cocoa powder	15 ml.
1 tsp.	ground cinnamon	5 ml.
½ tsp.	grated nutmeg	2 ml.
¼ tsp.	ground cloves	1 ml.
1 cup	rolled oats	¼ liter
1½ cups	diced peeled apples	375 ml.
½ cup	walnuts, coarsely chopped	125 ml.
	confectioners' sugar	

Cream the butter and sugar together until pale and fluffy; beat in the eggs, one at a time. Sift together the dry ingredients; add them to the creamed mixture. Stir in the oatmeal, apples and nuts. Spread the batter into a buttered 12-by-16-inch [30-by-40-cm.] baking pan. Bake in a preheated 375° F. [190° C.] oven for about 25 minutes, or until a knife inserted in the center comes out clean. Cool the cake slightly; cut it into 2-inch [5-cm.] squares. Sprinkle the bars with confectioners' sugar.

NELL B. NICHOLS (EDITOR)
FARM JOURNAL'S COUNTRY COOKBOOK

Chick-pea Flour Squares

Bereshtook Nokhochi

Chick-pea flour is obtainable at health-food stores and stores specializing in Middle Eastern foods.

To make about 30

1 lb.	butter or shortening	½ kg.
4 cups	chick-pea flour	1 liter
2 cups	confectioners' sugar	½ liter
1 tbsp.	ground cardamom	15 ml.
2 to 3 tbsp.	ground or slivered pistachios or almonds (optional)	30 to 45 ml.

Melt the butter in a skillet. Turn the heat very low and sift the chick-pea flour in gradually, stirring it constantly with a wire whisk. Remove the skillet from the heat and let the flour cool slightly. Stir in the confectioners' sugar and cardamom. With a spatula, spread the dough onto an oiled baking sheet, forming a smooth layer about ¼ inch [6 mm.] thick. Sprinkle on the pistachios or almonds, if using. Bake the dough in a preheated 300° F. [150° C.] oven for about one hour. When cool, cut it into tiny squares.

NESTA RAMAZANI
PERSIAN COOKING

Genoese Cookies

Dolcetti di Genova

To make 49

5 tbsp.	butter, melted and cooled	75 ml.
⅔ cup	granulated sugar	150 ml.
3	eggs	3
⅓ cup	flour	75 ml.
1 cup	almonds, blanched, peeled and finely chopped	¼ liter
¼ cup	kirsch	50 ml.
	superfine or vanilla sugar	

Put the butter in a bowl with the granulated sugar and beat until the mixture is light and fluffy. Stirring constantly, add the eggs, then the flour and the almonds. Finally, add the kirsch. Butter and flour a 7-inch [18-cm.] square baking pan and pour in the mixture. Bake in a preheated 350° F. [180° C.] oven for 20 to 25 minutes, or until the top is firm to the touch and delicately browned. Let the cookie cool before cutting it into 1-inch [2½-cm.] squares. Arrange these on a serving plate and sprinkle with superfine or vanilla sugar.

ERINA GAVOTTI (EDITOR)
MILLERICETTE

Spicy Speculaas

Gevulde Speculaas

Speculaas spice is a flavoring mixture sold packaged in the Netherlands. It can be made by combining ground spices in the following proportions: 3½ tablespoons [52 ml.] of cinnamon, 1 tablespoon [15 ml.] each of nutmeg and cloves, 2 teaspoons [10 ml.] of ginger and 1 teaspoon [5 ml.] each of cardamom and white pepper.

Instead of being used to sandwich an almond-paste filling, the dough can be rolled around the paste, as shown on pages 42-43. Or the dough can be used alone—rolled ½ inch [1 cm.] thick and stamped into individual cookies with wooden Speculaas molds, available where fine kitchen supplies are sold.

	To make about 80	
9 cups	flour	2¼ liters
1 tbsp.	baking powder	15 ml.
1½ tsp.	salt	7 ml.
1¼ lb.	butter, cut into pieces	600 g.
2 cups	superfine sugar	½ liter
2 tsp.	grated lemon peel	10 ml.
1 tbsp.	*Speculaas* spice	15 ml.
3	eggs, beaten	3
2 lb.	nut paste *(recipe, page 165)*, made with almonds	1 kg.
1	egg yolk, beaten with 1 tbsp. [15 ml.] water	1
	almonds, blanched, peeled and halved	

Sift the flour, baking powder and salt into a bowl, then rub in the butter until the mixture resembles bread crumbs. Mix in the sugar, lemon peel and *Speculaas* spice. Add the beaten eggs and mix with a fork or knife until the dough is smooth and elastic. Let it rest in a cool place for at least one hour.

Divide the dough in half and roll one half about ⅛ inch [3 mm.] thick. Cut it into rectangles to cover three 12-by-15-inch [30-by-38-cm.] buttered baking sheets. Roll out the nut paste into similar-sized rectangles 1/16 inch [1½ mm.] thick, then place it on top of the rolled dough. Roll out the other half of the dough and use it to cover the nut paste. Brush the top of each sandwich with egg yolk, cover it well with the halved almonds and brush with the rest of the egg yolk. Bake in a preheated 350° F. [180° C.] oven for about 25 minutes, or until light golden brown. When cool, cut the cookies into 1½-by-3-inch [4-by-8-cm.] slices.

WILFRED J. FANCE (EDITOR)
THE NEW INTERNATIONAL CONFECTIONER

Almond Sponge Slices

Spongata

	To make about 20	
⅔ cup	honey	150 ml.
⅔ cup	sugar	150 ml.
¾ cup	white wine	175 ml.
1 cup	almonds, finely chopped	¼ liter
½ lb.	walnuts, finely chopped (about 2 cups [½ liter])	¼ kg.
½ cup	fresh bread crumbs	125 ml.
½ cup	crumbled almond macaroons	125 ml.
¼ cup	pine nuts	50 ml.
½ cup	white raisins	125 ml.
2 tbsp.	grated orange peel	30 ml.
¼ tsp.	ground cloves	1 ml.
¼ tsp.	grated nutmeg	1 ml.
1 tsp.	ground cinnamon	5 ml.
	Wine dough	
about 5 cups	flour	about 1¼ liters
⅔ cup	sugar	150 ml.
1 tbsp.	oil	15 ml.
10 tbsp.	butter, softened	150 ml.
⅔ cup	milk	150 ml.
⅔ cup	white wine	150 ml.

In a large, heavy pan, melt the honey over low heat. Add the sugar and wine and, stirring continuously, the almonds, walnuts, bread crumbs and macaroons. Add the pine nuts, raisins, orange peel and spices, and mix well. Remove the pan from the heat and cover it to keep this filling warm.

For the dough, mix together the flour and sugar, work in the oil and butter, and moisten with the milk and wine. The dough should be firm but malleable; if necessary, add more flour. On a floured board, roll the dough ¼ inch [6 mm.] thick. Use two thirds of the dough to line the bottom and sides of a buttered 12-by-18-inch [30-by-45-cm.] jelly-roll pan. Pour in the filling and spread it out evenly. Cover with the remaining dough and press the edges together. Bake in a preheated 350° F. [180° C.] oven for 30 minutes, or until a wooden pick inserted into the filling emerges moist, but not sticky. Cut the cake into 2-by-2½-inch [5-by-6-cm.] slices and cool them in the pan.

CARMEN ARTOCCHINI
400 RICETTE DELLA CUCINA PIACENTINA

Almond and Cinnamon Cookies

Zimt-Pitte

Zimt-pitte are cinnamon-flavored shortbread cookies. This recipe is from Chur, in Graubünden, a Romansh-speaking district where many terms are borrowed from the Italian, as for instance *"pitte"* from the Italian *"pizza,"* meaning pie.

To make about 70

⅓ cup	ground cinnamon	75 ml.
¼ cup	granulated sugar	50 ml.
14 oz.	almonds, ground (about 3½ cups [875 ml.])	400 g.
18 tbsp.	butter	270 ml.
2½ cups	flour	625 ml.
3	egg yolks, lightly beaten	3
1	egg, lightly beaten	1
Almond topping		
1¼ cups	almonds, blanched, peeled and cut into slivers	300 ml.
3	egg whites, stiffly beaten	3
⅔ cup	superfine sugar	150 ml.

Knead the cinnamon, granulated sugar, ground almonds, butter, flour, egg yolks and whole egg to a smooth paste. Roll the paste about ¼ inch [6 mm.] thick, and place it on buttered and floured baking sheets. Mix the topping ingredients and spread the mixture over the paste. Cut the assembly into small diamonds, and bake in a preheated 400° F. [200° C.] oven until lightly browned—about 20 minutes. Lift the cookies off the baking sheet while still warm.

EVA MARIA BORER
TANTE HEIDI'S SWISS KITCHEN

Linz Nut Cookies

Linzer Nussgebäck

To make about 50

3½ cups	flour	875 ml.
1⅔ cups	sugar	400 ml.
½ lb.	butter, cut into pieces and softened	¼ kg.
5	eggs, the yolks separated from the whites	5
7 oz.	almonds, blanched, peeled and ground, or hazelnuts, roasted, peeled and ground (about 1¾ cups [425 ml.])	200 g.
8 oz.	semisweet baking chocolate, grated	¼ kg.

Work the flour, ⅔ cup [150 ml.] of the sugar, the butter and the egg yolks into a dough and knead well. Roll out the dough to a thickness of ¼ inch [6 mm.]; place on a buttered baking sheet and bake in a preheated 350° F. [180° C.] oven for 10 minutes until half-done.

Meanwhile, stir the remaining sugar, the egg whites, ground nuts and chocolate over low heat until the mixture is thick and creamy. When the half-cooked pastry has cooled, coat it with this mixture. Return the pastry to the 350° F. oven and bake until the topping is firm—about 10 minutes. Remove the pastry from the oven and let it cool before cutting it into 2-inch [5-cm.] squares.

ELEK MAGYAR
KOCHBUCH FÜR FEINSCHMECKER

Almond Date Bars

Gorikhivnyk

To make 24

1 cup	sifted flour	¼ liter
2 tbsp.	granulated sugar	30 ml.
	salt	
4 tbsp.	butter, cut into pieces	60 ml.
2	egg yolks	2
1 tbsp.	heavy cream	15 ml.
½ tsp.	vanilla extract	2 ml.
Almond and date topping		
2 cups	confectioners' sugar	½ liter
6	egg whites, stiffly beaten	6
½ lb.	almonds, blanched, peeled and chopped (about 2 cups [½ liter])	¼ kg.
½ lb.	pitted dates, finely chopped (about 1¼ cups [300 ml.])	¼ kg.
½ lb.	semisweet baking chocolate, grated	¼ kg.

Sift the flour with the granulated sugar and a pinch of salt. Cut in the butter. Combine the egg yolks, cream and vanilla. Add them to the flour and mix until the dough coheres. Pat the dough in a smooth layer into a buttered 9-by-12-inch [23-by-30-cm.] baking pan. Bake in a preheated 350° F. [180° C.] oven for 10 to 15 minutes, or until it is firm but not browned.

While the dough is baking, prepare the topping. Gradually beat the confectioners' sugar into the beaten egg whites. When the mixture is firm, fold in the almonds, dates and chocolate. Spread the topping over the partially baked dough. Reduce the oven temperature to 325° F. [160° C.] and continue baking for about 40 minutes, or until the topping is set. Cool the sheet in the pan, then cut it into 1½-by-3-inch [4-by-8-cm.] bars.

SAVELLA STECHISHIN
TRADITIONAL UKRAINIAN COOKERY

Frazer's Cheaters (Nut Squares)

For a bottom crust with the finest possible texture, rub the butter into the flour mixture with your hands, as demonstrated on pages 38-39.

The coconut can be omitted and the quantity of chopped pecans increased to 1½ cups [375 ml.].

To make 64

1 cup	flour	¼ liter
2 tbsp.	granulated sugar	30 ml.
1 tsp.	salt	5 ml.
8 tbsp.	butter, cut into pieces	120 ml.
	Pecan topping	
1 cup	coarsely chopped pecans	¼ liter
1 cup	grated coconut	¼ liter
2½ cups	firmly packed light brown sugar	625 ml.
2	eggs	2
2 tbsp.	flour	30 ml.

To make the dough, combine the flour, granulated sugar and salt in a mixing bowl. Using a pastry blender, cut in the butter. Mix the ingredients with your hands and press the dough over the bottom of a baking pan 8 inches [20 cm.] square. Bake in a preheated 350° F. [180° C.] oven for 10 minutes, then remove the pan from the oven. Increase the oven temperature to 375° F. [190° C.].

Make the topping by mixing together the nuts, coconut, brown sugar, eggs and flour. Spread this mixture over the bottom crust. Bake for 20 minutes. Cool, cut into 1-inch [2½-cm.] squares and remove the squares from the pan with a narrow spatula.

JEAN HEWITT
THE NEW YORK TIMES NEW ENGLAND HERITAGE COOKBOOK

Toffee Treats

To make about 30

½ lb.	butter, softened	¼ kg.
1 cup	firmly packed light brown sugar	¼ liter
1	egg yolk	1
1 tsp.	vanilla extract	5 ml.
2 cups	flour, sifted with ¼ tsp. [1 ml.] salt	½ liter
6 oz.	semisweet baking chocolate, melted	175 g.
½ cup	finely chopped nuts	125 ml.

Cream the butter and sugar until fluffy; beat in the egg yolk and vanilla. Blend in the flour. Pat the dough evenly into a buttered 10½-by-15½-inch [26-by-39-cm.] jelly-roll pan. Cover with the melted chocolate; sprinkle with the nuts.

Bake in a preheated 375° F. [190° C.] oven for 15 to 20 minutes, or until a knife inserted into the center comes out clean. Cut into 1½-by-3-inch [4-by-8-cm.] bars while still warm.

THE JUNIOR CHARITY LEAGUE OF MONROE, LOUISIANA
THE COTTON COUNTRY COLLECTION

Toffee Squares

These cookies will keep fresh for two weeks stored in an airtight container.

To make about 30

½ lb.	butter, softened	¼ kg.
1 cup	sugar	¼ liter
1	egg, the yolk separated from the white, and the white lightly beaten	1
2 cups	flour, sifted	½ liter
⅛ tsp.	salt	½ ml.
1 tbsp.	ground cinnamon	15 ml.
6 oz.	pecans, finely chopped (about 1½ cups [375 ml.])	175 g.

Cream the butter and sugar. Add the egg yolk, flour, salt and cinnamon. Mix until the mixture resembles coarse meal. Flour a baking sheet and spread the mixture onto it with your fingers or a spatula. The dough should be evenly distributed over the sheet and no more than ¼ inch [6 mm.] thick. Pour the egg white over the dough and smooth the surface with a brush. Cover the dough with the nuts. Bake in a preheated 375° F. [190° C.] oven for five minutes, then increase the heat to 400° F. [200° C.] and bake for 15 to 20 minutes more. Remove the baking sheet from the oven and, while the dough is still hot, cut it into 2-inch [5-cm.] squares. Do not remove the cookies from the sheet until they are cold.

MARION FLEXNER
OUT OF KENTUCKY KITCHENS

Pecan Cookies

To make about 30

½ lb.	butter, softened	¼ kg.
1 cup	sugar	¼ liter
1	egg, the yolk separated from the white, and the white lightly beaten	1
2 cups	flour	½ liter
½ tsp.	ground cinnamon	2 ml.
1 lb.	pecans, halved (about 4 cups [1 liter])	½ kg.

Cream the butter and sugar, then add the egg yolk, flour and cinnamon. Spread out the dough very thin on a large, buttered baking sheet and brush it with the egg white. Then place pecans over the top and bake in a preheated 350° F. [180° C.] oven for 15 minutes, or until golden brown. Cut the sheet into squares while still hot, making certain there is a pecan on each cookie.

JUNIOR LEAGUE OF MEMPHIS, INC.
THE MEMPHIS COOK BOOK

Pecan Squares

To make about 50

4	eggs	4
2 cups	firmly packed light brown sugar	½ liter
1½ cups	flour	375 ml.
1½ tsp.	baking powder	7 ml.
1 tsp.	vanilla extract	5 ml.
6 oz.	pecans, chopped (about 1½ cups [375 ml.])	175 g.

Beat the eggs with the sugar until the mixture is fluffy. Stirring constantly, cook the mixture in the top of a double boiler over simmering water for 20 minutes, or until it is thick. Remove it from the heat. Sift the flour and baking powder together and add to the egg mixture with the vanilla extract and the pecans. Spread the batter ½ inch [1 cm.] thick in a buttered and floured 12-by-18-inch [30-by-45-cm.] jelly-roll pan, and bake in a preheated 400° F. [200° C.] oven for 12 minutes. Cut into 2-inch [5-cm.] squares.

HARRIET ROSS COLQUITT (EDITOR)
THE SAVANNAH COOK BOOK

Black Walnut and Coconut Bars

To make about 20

8 tbsp.	butter, softened	120 ml.
½ cup	firmly packed light brown sugar	125 ml.
1 cup	flour, sifted	¼ liter

Walnut and coconut topping

2 tbsp.	flour	30 ml.
½ tsp.	baking powder	2 ml.
¼ tsp.	salt	1 ml.
½ cup	shredded coconut	125 ml.
1 cup	chopped black walnuts	¼ liter
2	eggs	2
1 cup	firmly packed light brown sugar	¼ liter
1 tsp.	vanilla extract	5 ml.

Cream the butter and brown sugar until pale and fluffy. Blend in the flour and spread the mixture into a buttered 9-inch [23-cm.] square baking pan. Bake in a preheated

375° F. [190° C.] oven for 15 minutes, or until lightly browned and firm to the touch.

To make the topping, sift together the flour, baking powder and salt, and add the coconut and nuts. Beat the eggs, add the sugar and vanilla extract, and continue beating until the mixture is fluffy. Combine the two mixtures and pour this batter over the baked crust. Bake at 375° F. for about 20 minutes, or until the topping is firm and golden brown. Cool and cut the cake into 1½-by-3-inch [4-by-8-cm.] bars.

THE SETTLEMENT COOK BOOK

Nut-filled Pastries
Bubana

The original version of this recipe calls for rosolio—an aromatic Italian liqueur not obtainable in North America. Sweet vermouth makes a suitable substitute.

This sweet is something similar to the Greek baklava.

To make about 30

1 cup	almonds, blanched and peeled	¼ liter
1 cup	pine nuts	¼ liter
1 cup	walnuts	¼ liter
½ cup	pistachios	125 ml.
½ cup	candied lemon peel	125 ml.
½ cup	candied orange peel	125 ml.
2	egg whites	2
¼ cup	honey, warmed	50 ml.
¼ cup	sugar	50 ml.
2 tbsp.	sweet vermouth	30 ml.
1 cup	seedless white raisins	¼ liter
1 tsp.	ground cinnamon	5 ml.
½ tsp.	ground mace	2 ml.
1 lb.	rough puff dough (recipe, page 166)	½ kg.
2	egg yolks, lightly beaten	2
2 tbsp.	sugar	30 ml.

Using the medium or coarse disk, pass the almonds, pine nuts, walnuts, pistachios and candied lemon and orange peels through a food grinder, or pound them to a thick paste in a large mortar. Bind the paste with the egg whites, honey, sugar and vermouth. Add the raisins, cinnamon and mace. Divide the rough puff dough into three pieces and roll each piece about ⅛ inch [3 mm.] thick. On a buttered baking sheet, assemble alternate layers of dough and filling—beginning and ending with dough layers. Brush the top with the egg yolks and sprinkle it with the sugar. Bake in a preheated 350° F. [180° C.] oven for about 30 minutes, or until the pastry is crisp and golden. Cut it into squares when cool.

GIUSEPPE MAFFIOLI
CUCINA E VINI DELLE TRE VENEZIE

Jamaican Squares

To make 36

1 cup	granulated sugar	¼ liter
¾ cup	flour	175 ml.
1 tsp.	baking powder	5 ml.
1 tsp.	ground cinnamon	5 ml.
½ tsp.	freshly grated nutmeg	2 ml.
¼ tsp.	ground cloves	1 ml.
1 cup	chopped dates	¼ liter
1 cup	chopped walnuts or pecans	¼ liter
2	eggs	2
1 tbsp.	rum	15 ml.
	confectioners' sugar	

In a bowl, blend together the granulated sugar, flour, baking powder, cinnamon, nutmeg and cloves. Mix the dates and nuts into the flour mixture. Beat the eggs with the rum and stir them into the dry ingredients. Spoon the batter into a buttered and floured 9-inch [23-cm.] square baking pan and smooth the top with a spatula. Bake in a preheated 350° F. [180° C.] oven for 25 to 30 minutes, or until the top is lightly browned. Remove the pan from the oven and immediately sprinkle the cake with confectioners' sugar. While still warm, cut the cake into 1½-inch [4-cm.] squares.

CAROL CUTLER
THE SIX-MINUTE SOUFFLÉ

Flapjacks

Demerara is a partially refined light brown sugar imported from England and obtainable in specialty food stores. Turbinado sugar most closely resembles this product and is obtainable from health-food stores.

These cookies may be stored in an airtight container for as long as one week.

To make about 10

6 tbsp.	Demerara or turbinado sugar	90 ml.
½ cup	rolled oats	125 ml.
6 tbsp.	butter, softened and creamed	90 ml.

Mix together the sugar and oats, and gradually work them into the creamed butter until thoroughly blended. With a round-bladed knife, press the mixture evenly into a buttered 7½-inch [19-cm.] square, shallow baking pan. Bake in a preheated 425° F. [220° C.] oven for about 15 minutes—or until golden brown; halfway through the baking time turn the pan around to ensure even cooking. Cool the sheet slightly in the pan, mark it into finger-shaped pieces with a sharp knife and run the knife around the edge of the pan to loosen them; when firm, break the cookies apart.

THE GOOD HOUSEKEEPING INSTITUTE
GOOD HOUSEKEEPING COOKERY BOOK

Rolled Cookies

Pitcaithly Bannock

Bannock is the Scottish name for any large, round flat cake. Pitcaithly is a village near Perth.

To make 1 or 2

2 cups	flour	½ liter
1 cup	cornstarch	¼ liter
½ cup	confectioners' sugar	125 ml.
¼ cup	superfine sugar	50 ml.
½ lb.	butter, softened and cut into pieces	¼ kg.
½ cup	almonds, blanched, peeled and cut into flakes	125 ml.
¼ cup	finely chopped candied citron peel	50 ml.

Sift the flour, cornstarch and sugars onto a board and knead the mixture gradually into the butter. This traditional mixing method takes a little longer than the creaming method. If you prefer the creaming method, just beat the sugars and butter until creamy, then mix in the flour and cornstarch.

Add almost all of the almonds to the mixture and roll out the dough into one or two rounds about ¾ inch [2 cm.] thick. Sprinkle the remaining almonds and the citron peel on top and press them in by rolling over them gently with a rolling pin. Now decorate the edges by pinching them with your finger and thumb.

Put the round on a buttered baking sheet and bake in a preheated 325° F. [160° C.] oven for 45 minutes to one hour, or until a pale golden color. If you have made two smaller rounds, use two baking sheets and bake for 30 to 45 minutes.

CATHERINE BROWN
SCOTTISH REGIONAL RECIPES

Coconut Shortbread

To open a coconut, puncture the three eyes at one end of the coconut shell, drain out the liquid and split the shell in half. Pry the white meat from the shell with a small knife, pare off the papery brown skin, then grate the meat. An average-sized coconut will yield 3 to 4 cups [¾ to 1 liter] of grated meat.

To make about 25

1 cup	flour	¼ liter
½ tsp.	baking powder	2 ml.
	salt	
4 tbsp.	butter, cut into pieces	60 ml.
¼ cup	sugar	50 ml.
⅔ cup	freshly grated coconut	150 ml.
1	egg yolk, mixed with 1 tbsp. [15 ml.] milk	1

Sift the flour, baking powder and a pinch of salt into a mixing bowl, and rub in the butter. Add the sugar, coconut and the egg-yolk mixture. Knead the dough lightly. Roll the dough about ¼ inch [6 mm.] thick and cut it into 3-inch [8-cm.] squares. Bake on a lightly buttered baking sheet in a preheated 350° F. [180° C.] oven for 20 minutes, or until delicately browned.

THE GIRL GUIDES' ASSOCIATION OF FIJI (EDITORS)
SOUTH SEA ISLANDS RECIPES

Little Alberts

Albertle

To make about 60

7 tbsp.	butter, softened	105 ml.
4	eggs	4
¾ cup	granulated sugar	175 ml.
1 tbsp.	vanilla sugar	15 ml.
1¾ cups	flour	425 ml.
1 cup	cornstarch	¼ liter
2 tbsp.	heavy cream	30 ml.
2 tsp.	baking powder	10 ml.

In a bowl, beat the butter until fluffy. Alternately beat in the eggs and sugars; then beat in all the other ingredients. Refrigerate the dough for at least one hour, or until it is firm. Roll out the dough to a thickness of ⅛ inch [3 mm.] and pattern the surface by pressing it with the small holes of a box grater. Cut out round cookies, each about 2 inches [5 cm.] across, and bake them in a preheated 350° F. [180° C.] oven until pale gold—12 to 15 minutes.

HANS KARL ADAM
DAS KOCHBUCH AUS SCHWABEN

Rum Butter Cookies

Vajas Piskóta

To make 15 to 20

8 tbsp.	butter, cut into pieces	120 ml.
1 cup	flour, sifted	¼ liter
2 tsp.	rum	10 ml.
½ tsp.	salt	2 ml.
3	egg yolks	3

Cut the butter into the flour until there are granules the size of peas. Combine the rum, salt and two of the egg yolks. Stir into the flour mixture. Knead the dough lightly, then cover and refrigerate it for one hour, or until firm. Roll the dough ¼ inch [6 mm.] thick and cut it into 2-inch [5-cm.] rounds. Place the rounds on a baking sheet. Beat the remaining egg yolk lightly and brush it over the cookies. Bake the cookies in a preheated 350° F. [180° C.] oven for about 10 minutes, or until golden.

INGE KRAMARZ
THE BALKAN COOKBOOK

Ice Cream Wafers

To make about 50

¾ cup	sifted flour	175 ml.
¼ tsp.	salt	1 ml.
⅓ cup	granulated sugar	75 ml.
½ tsp.	baking powder	2 ml.
6 tbsp.	butter, cut into pieces	90 ml.
1	egg yolk, beaten with ½ tsp. [2 ml.] vanilla extract	1
	confectioners' sugar	

Sift the dry ingredients together into a bowl. Cut in the butter until the mixture resembles coarse bread crumbs. Add the egg yolk and mix to form a cohesive dough. Cover the dough with plastic wrap and chill for at least one hour.

Sprinkle a board and rolling pin with confectioners' sugar. Roll out the dough a small amount at a time to a thickness of ⅛ inch [3 mm.]. Cut the dough into round cookies about 2 inches [5 cm.] in diameter and place them 1 inch [2½ cm.] apart on buttered baking sheets. Bake in a preheated 350° F. [180° C.] oven for about six minutes, or until the cookies are lightly browned. Dust the cookies with confectioners' sugar.

NELL B. NICHOLS (EDITOR)
FARM JOURNAL'S COUNTRY COOKBOOK

Sand Cookies

Sablés

Adding baking powder to this dough will make the cookies somewhat lighter in texture. The authors suggest varying the basic mixture by adding a little jam, chopped almonds or melted chocolate.

To make about 15

2 cups	flour	½ liter
¾ cup	confectioners' sugar	175 ml.
½ tsp.	salt	2 ml.
½ tsp.	baking powder (optional)	2 ml.
8 tbsp.	butter, cut into pieces	120 ml.
1	egg	1
1	egg yolk	1
1 tsp.	vanilla extract or grated lemon peel (optional)	5 ml.
	caramel-colored egg glaze (recipe, page 164)	

Put the flour, confectioners' sugar, salt, baking powder (if using) and butter into a mixing bowl. With your finger tips, rub the butter into the dry ingredients until it is evenly distributed and the mixture is crumbly. Add the egg, the egg yolk and the flavoring, if using. Mix, then knead the dough and shape it into a ball. Wrap the ball and refrigerate it for at least 30 minutes to firm the dough.

Place the ball on a lightly floured surface, dust the top with flour and then flatten the ball with a rolling pin to make a thick disk. Roll the dough to a thickness of about ⅛ inch [3 mm.], using a steady stroke and frequently rotating the expanding disk. Dust the dough and work surface with flour when necessary to prevent sticking.

With a round cutter, 4 inches [10 cm.] in diameter (or a triangular, heart-shaped or square cutter of similar size), cut out 10 to 12 cookies, leaving as few dough scraps as possible. If the central part of the dough is a bit thick, roll it again before cutting it.

Gather the dough scraps gently and place them one on top of another. Flour the work surface and scraps, and roll the dough to the same thickness as before. Cut out four or five more cookies.

Using a metal spatula, transfer each cookie to lightly buttered baking sheets, arranging them in staggered rows.

Paint each cookie with the caramel-colored egg glaze, taking care to keep the glaze off the baking sheets. When the first coat has set, glaze the cookies a second time. Then, using a four-tined table fork, scratch square, diamond or triangular designs onto the cookies.

Bake the cookies in a preheated 375° F. [190° C.] oven for about 12 minutes. Do not judge whether the cookies are done by the color of the tops, which will be dark from the glaze and will give a false impression. Instead, check the undersides, which should be golden at the end of cooking. Put the cookies on wire racks to cool as soon as they come out of the oven.

B. DESCHAMPS AND J. CL. DESCHAINTRE
PÂTISSERIE, CONFISERIE, GLACERIE: TRAVAUX PRATIQUES

Sand Cookies from Caen

Sablés de Caen

To make about 40

2 tbsp.	grated orange peel	30 ml.
2 cups	flour	½ liter
½ cup	sugar	125 ml.
	salt	
3	hard-boiled egg yolks, crumbled	3
½ lb.	butter, cut into pieces and softened	¼ kg.

Blanch the orange peel for three minutes in boiling water and drain it. In a bowl, mix the flour and sugar, a pinch of salt, the orange peel and the crumbled hard-boiled egg yolks. Little by little, incorporate the softened butter. Form the dough into a ball, cover the bowl with a cloth and let the dough rest for one to two hours.

Roll the dough to a thickness of ¼ inch [6 mm.]; cut it into rounds with a cutter or glass about 3 inches [8 cm.] in diameter. Place the rounds on lightly moistened baking sheets; with a knife point, make crisscross lines on top of each cookie. Bake the cookies in a preheated 350° F. [180° C.] oven for eight to 10 minutes, or until delicately browned.

CÉLINE VENCE
ENCYCLOPÉDIE HACHETTE DE LA CUISINE RÉGIONALE

Salers' Squares

Carrés de Salers

To make about 50

2½ cups	flour	625 ml.
1¼ cups	granulated sugar	300 ml.
5	eggs, lightly beaten	5
20 tbsp.	butter, softened	300 ml.
	confectioners' sugar	

Mix together all of the ingredients—except the confectioners' sugar—to make a smooth dough. Roll the dough out to a thickness of 1/16 to ⅛ inch [1½ mm. to 3 mm.]. Cut the dough into 3-inch [8-cm.] squares. Place them on buttered baking sheets and bake in a preheated 450° F. [230° C.] oven for 10 minutes, or until they are delicately browned. Sift confectioners' sugar over the squares at least twice while they are baking to give them a perfect glaze.

AMICALE DES CUISINIERS ET PÂTISSIERS AUVERGNATS DE PARIS
CUISINE D'AUVERGNE

Exquisite Cookies

Gâteaux Exquis

Crystallized orange blossoms are obtainable at some fine food stores. If not available, substitute orange-flower water for the plain water beaten with the egg yolks and increase the crushed macaroons to ⅓ cup [75 ml.].

To make about 30

1 lb.	rough puff dough (recipe, page 166)	½ kg.
2	egg yolks, beaten with 1 tbsp. [15 ml.] water	2
2 tbsp.	crystallized orange blossoms, crushed to a powder	30 ml.
2 tsp.	grated lime peel	10 ml.
¼ cup	finely crushed dry macaroons	50 ml.
¼ cup	almonds, blanched, peeled and slivered	50 ml.

Roll out the dough and cut it into ovals about 2 inches [5 cm.] long. Brush the tops with the beaten egg yolks. Mix the orange blossoms, grated lime peel, macaroons and almonds, and sprinkle the tops of the cookies with this mixture. Arrange the cookies on ungreased baking sheets and chill them for about one hour.

Place the cookies in a preheated 450° F. [230° C.] oven and, after two minutes, reduce the temperature to 400° F. [200° C.]. Continue to bake the cookies for 10 minutes, or until they are puffed and lightly browned. Cover the cookies with wax paper if the tops brown before the pastry is cooked.

LE MANUEL DE LA FRIANDISE

Maple Sugar Cookies

To make about 50

4 tbsp.	butter, softened	60 ml.
2 cups	crushed maple sugar (about 1 lb. [½ kg.])	½ liter
1 tsp.	vanilla extract	5 ml.
2	eggs	2
1 cup	sour cream	¼ liter
about 3 cups	flour, sifted	about ¾ liter
½ tsp.	salt	2 ml.
1 tsp.	baking soda	5 ml.

Cream the butter and maple sugar together until smooth and pale. Add the vanilla extract. Add the eggs and beat until fluffy. Add the sour cream and blend it into the mixture. Sift together the flour, salt and baking soda and add to the creamed mixture. Blend until the dough is smooth. Add more flour if necessary to make a medium-soft dough. Chill in the refrigerator for several hours. Turn the dough out onto a lightly floured board and roll it to a thickness of ⅛ inch [3 mm.]. Cut into rounds about 2 inches [5 cm.] in diameter and set 1 inch [2½ cm.] apart on buttered baking sheets. Bake the cookies in a preheated 375° F. [190° C.] oven for 10 minutes, or until golden brown.

MARY EMMA SHOWALTER
MENNONITE COMMUNITY COOKBOOK

Honey Kisses

Pierniczki Caluski

To make about 35

3 tbsp.	honey	45 ml.
½ tsp.	ground cloves	2 ml.
½ tsp.	ground cinnamon	2 ml.
3 tbsp.	water	45 ml.
2½ cups	flour	625 ml.
2 tbsp.	butter or lard, cut into pieces	30 ml.
1 cup	confectioners' sugar	¼ liter
1	egg	1
1 tbsp.	baking soda	15 ml.

Stirring constantly, cook the honey, cloves and cinnamon in a small, heavy saucepan set over low heat until the honey becomes brown—about five minutes. Stir in 1 tablespoon [15 ml.] of the water and let the honey cool. Sift the flour onto a pastry board, leaving a little aside to use for rolling the dough. With your hands, work the butter or lard into the flour until the mixture resembles small peas; mix in the confectioners' sugar. Add the honey and egg. Dissolve the baking soda in the remaining water, add and mix well.

Knead the dough until it is smooth. Divide the dough in half and roll out each half to a thickness of about ⅓ inch [1 cm.]. Cut out the cookies with a glass or cutter about 2 inches [5 cm.] in diameter. Arrange the cookies on buttered baking sheets, leaving space between them to allow them to spread during baking. Bake the cookies in a preheated 400° F. [200° C.] oven for 12 minutes, or until delicately browned.

ZOFIA CZERNY AND MARIA STRASBURGER
ŻYWIENIE RODZINY

Honey Crackers

These are good, but not sweet. For sweeter cookies, these should be iced with a mixture of 1 tablespoon [15 ml.] of fresh lemon juice and 1 cup [¼ liter] of confectioners' sugar.

To make about 30

2 cups	flour	½ liter
¼ tsp.	salt	1 ml.
½ tsp.	allspice	2 ml.
⅔ tsp.	baking soda	3 ml.
1 tsp.	grated lemon peel	5 ml.
1 tsp.	fresh lemon juice	5 ml.
2 tbsp.	honey	30 ml.
2	eggs	2

Mix the dry ingredients; add the lemon peel, lemon juice, honey and eggs. Beat well. Roll the dough ¼ inch [6 mm.] thick and cut it into 3-inch [7½-cm.] rounds. Bake on buttered baking sheets in a preheated 350° F. [180° C.] oven for 15 minutes, or until delicately browned.

LOIS LINTNER SUMPTION AND MARGUERITE LINTNER ASHBROOK
AROUND-THE-WORLD COOKY BOOK

Russian Sugar Cookies

To make about 70

½ lb.	butter, softened	¼ kg.
½ cup	granulated sugar	125 ml.
¼ tsp.	salt	1 ml.
3	eggs, beaten	3
3 tbsp.	sour cream	45 ml.
½ tsp.	grated lemon peel	2 ml.
1 tsp.	fresh lemon juice	5 ml.
3½ cups	flour, sifted with ⅛ tsp. [1 ml.] baking soda	875 ml.
	coarse sugar or coarsely crushed sugar tablets	

With a wooden spoon beat the butter, granulated sugar and salt until fluffy. Beat in the eggs, one at a time. Mix in the sour cream and the lemon peel and juice. Gradually mix in the flour. On a floured board, roll the dough to a thickness of ¼ inch [6 mm.]. Sprinkle it with coarse sugar. Using a knife, cut the dough with crossing diagonal lines to form diamond-shaped cookies and place these on buttered and floured baking sheets. Bake in a preheated 450° F. [230° C.] oven for eight minutes, until the cookies are just golden—not brown.

VIOLETA AUTUMN
A RUSSIAN JEW COOKS IN PERÚ

Sour-Cream Cookies

Sugar mixed with a little flour may be sifted over the dough before it is cut into cookies. Raisins may be pressed into each cookie before baking.

To make about 35

8 tbsp.	butter, or 4 tbsp. [60 ml.] butter and 4 tbsp. lard, softened	120 ml.
1 cup	sugar	¼ liter
2	eggs, beaten	2
½ cup	sour cream	125 ml.
2½ cups	flour	625 ml.
½ tsp.	baking soda	2 ml.
½ tsp.	salt	2 ml.
2 tsp.	grated nutmeg	10 ml.

Cream the butter, add the sugar, and cream again. Add the eggs and the sour cream. Sift 1 cup [¼ liter] of the flour with the remaining ingredients and stir into the creamed mixture. Work in the rest of the flour to form a smooth dough.

Roll out the dough ⅓ inch [1 cm.] thick and cut it into any desired shape. Place the shapes on buttered baking sheets and bake in a preheated 350° F. [180° C.] oven for 15 minutes, or until the cookies are lightly browned.

LOUISE BENNETT WEAVER AND HELEN COWLES LECRON
A THOUSAND WAYS TO PLEASE A HUSBAND

Calais Cookies

To make 40 to 160, depending on thickness

½ lb.	lard, softened	¼ kg.
1 cup	sugar	¼ liter
1	egg	1
½ cup	molasses, warmed	125 ml.
½ cup	cold water	125 ml.
4 cups	flour	1 liter
1 tsp.	ground ginger	5 ml.
1 tsp.	salt	5 ml.
1 tsp.	baking soda	5 ml.

Cream the lard and sugar. Drop in the egg and beat well. Stir in the molasses. Add the water. Sift the flour three times with the ginger, salt and baking soda, and add. Mix to a soft dough, kneading as little as possible.

Roll the dough ½ inch [1 cm.] thick for soft cookies, ¼ inch [6 mm.] thick for medium crisp cookies and ⅛ inch [3 mm.] thick for very crisp cookies. Cut the dough into rounds with a 2½-inch [6-cm.] cutter and place the cookies on baking sheets. Bake in a preheated 375° F. [190° C.] oven for about 10 minutes. If stored in airtight containers as soon as they cool, the crisp cookies remain crisp and the soft cookies remain soft.

IMOGENE WOLCOTT (EDITOR)
THE YANKEE COOK BOOK

Easter Cakes

Fugazzi

These cakes are a specialty of Bonifacio, a town in Corsica, and are traditionally eaten on Good Friday.

To make about 80		
8 cups	flour	2 liters
1½ cups	sugar	375 ml.
½ cup	oil	125 ml.
⅓ cup	dry white wine	75 ml.
⅓ cup	*pastis* or other anise-flavored liqueur	75 ml.
	salt	

Mix together the flour, sugar, oil, wine, *pastis* and a pinch of salt. Knead the mixture for a few moments until it forms a smooth dough. Roll out the dough to a thickness of about ¼ inch [6 mm.]. Cut it into rounds with a teacup (or a 3-inch [8-cm.] biscuit cutter). Nick the edges of the rounds with a knife, prick them with a fork and sprinkle them with sugar. Arrange the cookies on floured baking sheets and bake them in a preheated 350° F. [180° C.] oven for 20 to 30 minutes, or until lightly browned.

MARIE CECCALDI
CUISINE DE CORSE

Cardamom Butter Cookies

To make about 95		
½ lb.	butter, softened	¼ kg.
1¼ cups	sugar	300 ml.
2	eggs, lightly beaten	2
1 tsp.	vanilla extract	5 ml.
3 cups	sifted flour	¾ liter
1 tsp.	baking powder	5 ml.
½ tsp.	salt	2 ml.
1 tsp.	ground cardamom	5 ml.
½ tsp.	ground cinnamon	2 ml.
¼ tsp.	ground allspice	1 ml.

Cream the butter and sugar until light and fluffy. Stir in the eggs a little at a time, add the vanilla extract and beat well.

Sift together the remaining ingredients; stir them into the creamed mixture and mix well. Chill the dough for at least an hour, roll it out and cut it with a cookie cutter. Or, if you prefer, shape the dough into two cylinders and wrap them in wax paper; chill the cylinders, then cut them into thin slices.

Place the cookies on baking sheets and bake them in a preheated 350° F. [180° C.] oven for eight to 10 minutes, depending on the thickness of the cookies.

THE McCORMICK SPICES OF THE WORLD COOKBOOK

Springerle

The technique of making and printing springerle with the traditional carved rolling pin is demonstrated on page 67.

Arrack is a dry, pungent liqueur with a pronounced anise or licorice flavor.

To make about 50		
4	eggs	4
4 cups	confectioners' sugar	1 liter
2 tsp.	grated lemon peel	10 ml.
1 tbsp.	arrack or other anise-flavored liqueur	15 ml.
4 cups	flour	1 liter
2 tbsp.	anise seeds	30 ml.

Beat the eggs and sugar until thick—about 15 minutes; add the lemon peel and arrack. Slowly add the flour and knead the mixture to form a dough. Roll the dough ¼ inch [6 mm.] thick. Sprinkle a carved rolling pin with flour and press it firmly on the dough to make patterned cookies. Cut the cookies along the lines between the patterns. Butter a large baking sheet and sprinkle it with the anise seeds. Place the cookies on the sheet, cover them lightly with parchment or wax paper and let them dry overnight in a cool place—not the refrigerator.

The next day, uncover the cookies and bake them in a preheated 300° F. [150° C.] oven for 15 to 20 minutes. The cookies should be white on top and light brown on the bottom. Store in an airtight container for about three weeks to soften the cookies slightly before serving them.

HEDWIG MARIA STUBER
ICH HELF DIR KOCHEN

Anise Seed Shells

Coques à l'Anis

To make about 20

2 cups	flour	½ liter
1 cup	superfine sugar	¼ liter
2	egg whites, lightly beaten	2
2 tbsp.	anise seeds	30 ml.
	salt	

In a large bowl, mix together the flour, sugar, egg whites, **anise seeds** and a pinch of salt. Work all the ingredients **together** well to obtain a smooth dough. Flour a pastry board **or** other work surface and roll out the dough to a thickness of **about ⅓** inch [1 cm.]. Use a round cutter, 4 inches [10 cm.] in **diameter,** to cut out the cookies, then place them on a buttered **and** floured baking sheet. Bake the cookies in a pre-**heated** 325° F. [160° C.] oven for about 20 minutes, or until **they** are lightly colored.

LUCETTE REY-BILLETON
LES BONNES RECETTES DU SOLEIL

Poppy Seed Cookies

Ciastka Makowe

To make about 50

½ cup	poppy seeds	125 ml.
2 cups	flour	½ liter
7 tbsp.	butter, cut into pieces	105 ml.
⅔ cup	confectioners' sugar	150 ml.
2	egg yolks	2
about 3 tbsp.	sour cream	about 45 ml.
1	egg, beaten	1

Parboil the poppy seeds for five minutes, and let them soak in the cooking water until they swell and become soft enough to be crushed between the fingers—about two hours. Drain the seeds in a sieve.

Sift the flour onto a pastry board, setting a little aside to use when rolling out the dough. Add the butter to the sifted flour, chop finely with a knife and mix in the sugar and poppy seeds. Add the egg yolks and then just enough of the sour cream to make a soft dough that does not stick to the board. Gather the dough into a ball, wrap and refrigerate it for one hour, or until the dough is firm.

Divide the dough into two or three pieces and—one at a time—roll each piece to a thickness of ⅛ inch [3 mm.]. Cut out the cookies with a glass or a 2-inch [5-cm.] round biscuit cutter. Transfer the cookies to buttered baking sheets, spacing them well apart, and brush each cookie with beaten egg.

Bake the cookies in a preheated 400° F. [200° C.] oven for 12 minutes, or until they are golden brown.

ZOFIA CZERNY AND MARIA STRASBURGER
ŻYWIENIE RODZINY

Dutch Cinnamon Cookies

Janhagel

To make about 20

1¼ cups	flour	300 ml.
7 tbsp.	butter, cut into pieces	105 ml.
¼ cup	superfine sugar	50 ml.
¼ tsp.	salt	1 ml.
1 tsp.	ground cinnamon	5 ml.
2 tbsp.	beaten egg, mixed with ½ tbsp. [7 ml.] milk	30 ml.
3 tbsp.	granulated sugar	45 ml.
2 tbsp.	slivered almonds (optional)	30 ml.

Sift the flour, rub in the butter and add the superfine sugar, salt and cinnamon. Roll the dough out into a rectangle just under ¼ inch [6 mm.] thick. Butter a baking sheet and place the dough on it. Brush the dough with the egg and milk. Sprinkle on the granulated sugar and the almonds, if using, and press them in lightly with a rolling pin. Place the baking sheet in the center of a preheated 350° F. [180° C.] oven and bake until the cake is golden brown—about 20 minutes.

While it is still on the baking sheet, quickly cut the warm cake into rectangles about 1½ by 3 inches [4 by 8 cm.]. Remove the cookies from the baking sheet and cool them.

H. H. F. HENDERSON, H. TOORS AND H. M. CALLENBACH
HET NIEUWE KOOKBOEK

Cinnamon Cookies

Zimtkekse

To make about 70

4 cups	flour	1 liter
1¾ cups	confectioners' sugar, sifted	425 ml.
1 tsp.	ground cinnamon	5 ml.
20 tbsp.	butter, cut into pieces and softened	300 ml.
2 tbsp.	milk	30 ml.
1	egg	1
3 to 4 tbsp.	sweet white wine	45 to 60 ml.

Sift the flour, confectioners' sugar and cinnamon onto a board. Work in the butter, then add the milk, egg and white wine and knead the mixture into a dough. Roll the dough ⅛ inch [3 mm.] thick and cut it into 2-inch [5-cm.] squares or triangles. Place the cookies on buttered baking sheets and bake them in a preheated 375° F. [190° C.] oven until they are golden brown—about 15 minutes.

JOZA BŘÍZOVÁ AND MARYNA KLIMENTOVÁ
TSCHECHISCHE KÜCHE

Gingerbread

This recipe can be used to make the dough for the gingerbread house shown on pages 78-79, but you will need four times the quantities of ingredients given here.

If you intend to hang your gingerbread figures from the Christmas tree in the traditional way, use a skewer to make a little hole in the top of each figure before baking it. When the cookies are baked and cooled, thread a narrow ribbon through each hole and hang the figure on the tree.

To make about 35

⅔ cup	firmly packed light brown sugar	150 ml.
⅓ cup	molasses	75 ml.
1 tsp.	ground cinnamon	5 ml.
1 tsp.	ground ginger	5 ml.
⅛ tsp.	ground cloves	½ ml.
6 tbsp.	butter	90 ml.
1½ tsp.	baking powder	7 ml.
4 cups	flour, sifted	1 liter
	salt	
1	egg, lightly beaten	1
1 cup	confectioners' sugar glaze (recipe, page 164)	¼ liter

In a heavy-based pan over low heat, dissolve the sugar with the molasses, spices and butter. Slowly and carefully bring the mixture to a boil, cool it to room temperature, then mix in the baking powder. Place the flour in a bowl with a pinch of salt and make a well in the center. Pour in the cooled syrup mixture and the egg, and stir from the center to incorporate the flour. Turn the dough out onto a floured surface and knead, then wrap it in wax paper and refrigerate it for about 30 minutes.

Take out the dough and roll it about ⅛ inch [3 mm.] thick. Using assorted cutters, stamp out gingerbread men, animals, trees, etc., and place them on buttered baking sheets. Bake in a preheated 325° F. [160° C.] oven for eight to 10 minutes, then remove and cool on a wire rack. Finish the gingerbread men by piping confectioners' sugar glaze around the edges and filling in noses, mouths, eyes, hats and buttons with more glaze.

MARGARET WADE
CAKES AND BISCUITS

Swedish Gingernuts

To make about 70

⅔ cup	golden syrup	150 ml.
2 cups	superfine sugar	½ liter
14 tbsp.	butter, melted	210 ml.
1 cup	heavy cream	¼ liter
⅔ cup	chopped, candied orange peel	150 ml.
1 tbsp.	ground ginger	15 ml.
1 tbsp.	ground cinnamon	15 ml.
½ tsp.	ground cloves	2 ml.
2 tsp.	ground cardamom (optional)	10 ml.
1 tsp.	baking soda	5 ml.
about 4 cups	flour, sifted	about 1 liter

Heat the syrup and sugar together until the sugar dissolves. Pour the mixture into a large bowl and stir in the butter, cream, candied peel, ginger, cinnamon, cloves, cardamom, if using, and baking soda. Work the flour into the mixture, adding just enough to make a firm dough. Roll the dough about ¼ inch [6 mm.] thick. Cut it into 2-inch [5-cm.] rounds and arrange the rounds—spacing them well apart—on buttered baking sheets. Bake the cookies in a preheated 400° F. [200° C.] oven for about 15 minutes, or until lightly browned.

INGA NORBERG (EDITOR)
GOOD FOOD FROM SWEDEN

Mrs. Gurney's Ginger Snaps

To make about 50

1 cup	sugar	¼ liter
1 cup	golden syrup	¼ liter
½ lb.	butter, or 12 tbsp. [180 ml.] butter and 2 tbsp. [30 ml.] lard, melted	¼ kg.
2 tsp.	ground ginger	10 ml.
1 tsp.	baking soda	5 ml.
2 tbsp.	hot water	30 ml.
about 4 cups	flour	about 1 liter

Mix together the sugar, golden syrup, melted butter or butter and lard, and ginger. Dissolve the baking soda in the hot water and add to the ginger mixture. Work in just as much flour as will make a very stiff dough. Roll out on a floured board as thin as possible—about ⅛ inch [3 mm.] thick—and cut into small rounds. Bake on baking sheets in a preheated 350° F. [180° C.] oven for about 15 minutes, or until beginning to brown.

MAY BYRON
POT-LUCK

Shrewsbury Cakes

To make about 30

½ lb.	butter, softened	¼ kg.
¾ cup	superfine sugar	175 ml.
2 cups	flour	½ liter
1 tsp.	ground cinnamon	5 ml.
2 tsp.	caraway seeds	10 ml.
2	eggs	2
¼ tsp.	rose water	1 ml.

Beat the butter to a cream and mix it with the sugar, flour, cinnamon, caraway seeds, eggs and rose water. Roll the paste out ¼ inch [6 mm.] thick, cut the cakes into shapes and place them on baking sheets. Bake in a preheated 325° F. [160° C.] oven for 20 minutes, or until delicately browned.

ANNE COBBETT
THE ENGLISH HOUSEKEEPER

Original Moravian Christmas Cakes

For many years at Winston-Salem, North Carolina, a little paper-thin spiced cookie has been baked and stored in tins to delight the children at Christmas. The holidays would be incomplete without them. This recipe was given by an experienced Moravian cakemaker. The cakes will keep for weeks if placed in airtight containers.

To make about 200

12 tbsp.	butter, softened	180 ml.
12 tbsp.	lard, softened	180 ml.
2 cups	firmly packed light brown sugar	½ liter
about 15 cups	flour	about 3¾ liters
1 tbsp.	ground mace	15 ml.
2 tbsp.	ground cloves	30 ml.
2 tbsp.	ground cinnamon	30 ml.
4 cups	molasses, warmed	1 liter
2 tbsp.	grated lemon peel	30 ml.
¾ cup	brandy	175 ml.
2 tbsp.	baking soda	30 ml.
¼ cup	milk	60 ml.

In a large bowl, mix together the butter and lard, and cream them with the sugar. Add the flour to the bowl. Mix the mace, cloves and cinnamon with the molasses and add to the bowl. Mix all together, using your hands. Add the lemon peel and brandy. Dissolve the baking soda in the milk and add to the dough. The dough should be stiff but pliable. If necessary, add more flour. Roll the dough about ⅛ inch [3 mm.]

thick and cut it into cakes in the shape of stars, crescents, animals, etc. Bake on buttered baking sheets in a preheated 350° F. [180° C.] oven for 10 to 12 minutes, or until the cakes are crisp and well browned.

MARION BROWN
THE SOUTHERN COOK BOOK

Fig Newtons

To make about 20

5 tbsp.	unsalted butter, softened	75 ml.
2 tbsp.	sour cream	30 ml.
⅔ cup	firmly packed dark brown sugar	150 ml.
2	eggs	2
1 tsp.	vanilla extract	5 ml.
2 cups	flour	½ liter
2 tsp.	baking powder	10 ml.
½ tsp.	baking soda	2 ml.
¼ tsp.	ground cinnamon	1 ml.
½ tsp.	salt	2 ml.

Fig filling

2 cups	dried figs, preferably moist-pack black figs, heavy stems removed	½ liter
1¾ cups	water	425 ml.
⅓ cup	sugar	75 ml.
2 tsp.	grated lemon peel	10 ml.
¼ tsp.	salt	1 ml.

In a small bowl, beat the butter and sour cream until light. Gradually add the brown sugar, beating until the mixture is very light and thick. Incorporate the eggs one at a time; beat in the vanilla extract.

Sift together the flour, baking powder, baking soda, cinnamon and salt. Add gradually to the creamed mixture. Divide the dough into three equal parts, wrap each part in lightly floured plastic wrap, then refrigerate the dough for at least two hours.

Meanwhile, combine the figs and water in a heavy saucepan and simmer, covered, for 30 minutes, or until the fruit is soft. Add the sugar, lemon peel and salt, and simmer, covered, for 15 minutes longer. Press the mixture through the coarse disk of a food mill, then cool it.

On a well-floured board, roll one piece of chilled dough into a rectangle about 5 by 11 inches [12 by 28 cm.]. Spread one third of the fig filling along one side of the dough, covering an area roughly 2 inches [5 cm.] wide and 10 inches [25 cm.] long and leaving margins of about ½ inch [1 cm.] on the edges. Mound the filling slightly along its length, then moisten the exposed margins with water. Very gently, lift the uncovered dough with a spatula and fold it over the filling. Press it down, then trim the edges and shape the roll into a neat half cylinder about 11 inches [28 cm.] long and 2 to 2½ inches [5 to 6 cm.] wide. Place the filled roll on a large baking sheet that has been buttered lightly or covered with parchment paper.

Repeat the filling operation with the remaining two thirds of the dough and filling, then bake the three rolls in a preheated 350° F. [180° C.] oven for 25 minutes, or until they are lightly browned.

Cool the rolls briefly on a rack. Then with a sharp, serrated knife, trim off the ends of each roll and cut it into slices about 1½ inches [4 cm.] thick. Replace the slices on the rack. When the fig bars are completely cool, store them in airtight containers.

HELEN WITTY AND ELIZABETH SCHNEIDER COLCHIE
BETTER THAN STORE-BOUGHT

Small Currant Cookies

Kleine Johannisbeer-Kuchen

To make the currant purée called for in this recipe, simmer ½ pound [¼ kg.] or 1⅓ cups [325 ml.] of fresh currants with 2 tablespoons [30 ml.] of sugar and 2 teaspoons [10 ml.] of water until the fruit is soft and pulpy—about 15 minutes. Purée the mixture through a sieve or the fine disk of a food mill. If fresh currants are not obtainable, substitute melted currant jelly for the purée.

To make about 80

4 cups	flour	1 liter
20 tbsp.	butter, cut into pieces	310 ml.
⅓ cup	granulated sugar	75 ml.
2	sugar tablets, rubbed over the peel of a lemon, then crushed	2
9	hard-boiled egg yolks, sieved	9
3	egg whites, stiffly beaten	3
	confectioners' sugar	
1 cup	currant purée	¼ liter

Place the flour in a bowl, add the butter and cut it in until the mixture has the texture of coarse meal. Add the granulated sugar, lemon-flavored sugar and hard-boiled egg yolks, and work the ingredients together until the dough coheres. Roll the dough to a thickness of ⅓ inch [1 cm.]. Cut out rounds 3 inches [8 cm.] in diameter or ovals, if preferred. Transfer the cookies to baking sheets, prick each one here and there with the point of a knife, and bake them in a preheated 375° F. [190° C.] oven for 15 minutes, or until well colored. Set the cookies aside on the baking sheets.

Combine the beaten egg whites and 3 tablespoons [45 ml.] of confectioners' sugar. Using a pastry bag fitted with a small tube, pipe this meringue in a lattice pattern onto the cookies; pipe a rim around the edge of each cookie. Sprinkle the cookies with a little more confectioners' sugar and bake them in a 300° F. [150° C.] oven for 15 minutes, or until the meringue is golden. Transfer the cookies to wire racks to cool completely, then fill the spaces in the lattice pattern with currant purée.

SOPHIE WILHELMINE SCHEIBLER
ALLGEMEINES DEUTSCHES KOCHBUCH FÜR ALLE STÄNDE

Derbyshire Wakes Cakes

To make about 40

3 cups	flour	¾ liter
½ lb.	butter, cut into pieces	¼ kg.
1 cup	sugar	¼ liter
½ cup	dried currants	125 ml.
1 to 2 tsp.	caraway seeds	5 to 10 ml.
2 tsp.	grated lemon peel	10 ml.
½ tsp.	baking powder	2 ml.
1	egg, beaten	1

Rub the flour and butter together until thoroughly blended; add ¾ cup [175 ml.] of the sugar, the currants, caraway seeds (whose quantity must be judged according to taste, lest the distinctive, somewhat astringent flavor dominate), lemon peel and baking powder. Form into a firm paste by beating in the egg. Roll the dough about ¼ inch [6 mm.] thick and cut into rounds about the size of your palm. Place the rounds on buttered baking sheets. Scatter the surface with the remaining sugar and bake in a preheated 375° F. [190° C.] oven for about 10 minutes, until the cakes become crisp.

JOYCE DOUGLAS
OLD DERBYSHIRE RECIPES AND CUSTOMS

Currant Cookies

To make about 50

½ lb.	butter, cut into small pieces	¼ kg.
3 cups	flour	¾ liter
¾ cup	superfine sugar	175 ml.
1½ cups	dried currants	375 ml.
¼ tsp.	grated nutmeg	1 ml.
3	egg yolks, beaten	3

Rub the butter into the flour, add the sugar, currants and nutmeg, and bind the mixture with the egg yolks. Roll the dough out to a thickness of ¼ inch [6 mm.] and cut it into shapes with a cookie cutter or a glass. Place the cookies on baking sheets and bake them in a preheated 350° F. [180° C.] oven for 10 to 15 minutes, or until very pale brown.

MRS. AUBREY DOWSON (EDITOR)
THE WOMEN'S SUFFRAGE COOKERY BOOK

Karen's Oat Cookies

Karens Havremakroner

The oatmeal called for in this recipe is finely ground oat kernels—not the familiar rolled oats. Oatmeal is obtainable from health-food stores.

To make about 25

2 cups	fine oatmeal	½ liter
1 cup	superfine sugar	¼ liter
1 tsp.	ground cloves	5 ml.
1 tsp.	ground cinnamon	5 ml.
1 tsp.	baking powder	5 ml.
1¼ cups	flour	300 ml.
½ lb.	butter, melted	¼ kg.
5 tbsp.	heavy cream	75 ml.
1 cup	seedless white raisins, chopped	150 g.

Mix the oatmeal with the sugar. Sift the spices and baking powder with the flour, and stir them into the oatmeal mixture. Gradually beat in the butter and cream. Add the raisins. On a lightly floured board, roll the dough into a round about ¼ inch [6 mm.] thick. Cut the dough into plain or fluted rounds with a 2-inch [5-cm.] cookie cutter. Place the rounds about 1 inch [2½ cm.] apart on a buttered baking sheet and bake them in a preheated 375° F. [190° C.] oven until golden brown—about 12 to 15 minutes.

ELIZABETH CRAIG
SCANDINAVIAN COOKING

Cherry Cookies

These cookies can be made very elegant by icing them with a confectioners' sugar glaze that has been tinted with food coloring, and then placing half a candied cherry on each one.

Those who like caraway seeds can substitute a few for the cherries. If neither cherries nor caraway seeds are used, two of the plain cookies are very nice sandwiched together with a little jam. These make a very pretty dish if the tops are iced in different colors. In Kent, cookies sandwiched together in this way are called sweethearts.

To make about 60

½ lb.	butter, cut into pieces	¼ kg.
3 cups	flour	¾ liter
⅔ cup	superfine sugar	150 ml.
¾ cup	candied cherries, cut into pieces	175 ml.
	salt	
2	eggs, lightly beaten	2

Rub the butter quickly and lightly into the flour, add the sugar, the cherry pieces and a pinch of salt. Using a knife to mix the ingredients, bind the mixture with enough of the beaten eggs to form a cohesive dough. Gather the dough into one piece, turn it onto a floured board and roll it ⅛ inch [3 mm.] thick. Cut the dough with a round, fluted cookie cutter 2 inches [5 cm.] in diameter. Lay the cookies on buttered baking sheets and bake them in a preheated 350° F. [180° C.] oven until firm and lightly browned—10 to 15 minutes.

FLORENCE WHITE
GOOD ENGLISH FOOD

White Nuremberg Peppercakes

Weisse Nürnberger Pfefferkuchen

Rice paper is made by pressing a rice-flour paste between hot irons to form a very thin sheet. It is obtainable from confectionery-supply stores.

To make about 90

2 cups	sugar	½ liter
8	eggs	8
1 lb.	almonds, blanched, peeled and finely chopped (about 4 cups [1 liter])	½ kg.
4 cups	flour	1 liter
1 tbsp.	anise seeds, crushed to a powder and sieved	15 ml.
1 tsp.	ground cloves	5 ml.
1 tsp.	ground cardamom	5 ml.
1 tsp.	ground cinnamon	5 ml.
½ cup	finely chopped candied lemon peel	125 ml.
½ cup	finely chopped candied orange peel	125 ml.

Beat the sugar and eggs together until the mixture is very thick and pale in color and has increased to four times its original volume—about 20 to 40 minutes. Mix in the almonds, flour, spices and candied peels. Roll out the dough into sheets about ⅛ inch [3 mm.] thick. Cut them into rectangles or rounds, and place the cookies on baking sheets covered with floured parchment paper. Alternatively, place the sheets of dough on sheets of rice paper and cut out the dough and the rice-paper backing together; arrange the cookies on plain baking sheets.

Bake in a preheated 350° F. [180° C.] oven for 20 minutes, or until the cookies are lightly browned.

SOPHIE WILHELMINE SCHEIBLER
ALLGEMEINES DEUTSCHES KOCHBUCH FÜR ALLE STÄNDE

Pine Nut Cookies

Croquets aux Pignons

To make about 25

2	eggs	2
½ cup	superfine sugar	125 ml.
⅓ cup	flour	75 ml.
1 cup	pine nuts	¼ liter
2 tbsp.	butter, softened, or 1 tbsp. [15 ml.] heavy cream	30 ml.

Beat the eggs well, then add the sugar and continue to beat until the mixture is pale and thick—approximately seven to 10 minutes. Stir in the flour and pine nuts, and then add the butter or cream.

On a floured board, spread out the dough by hand to avoid crushing the pine nuts, and cut it into rounds with a glass. Place the rounds on buttered or oiled baking sheets and bake them in a preheated 400° F. [200° C.] oven for 30 minutes, or until delicately browned.

ÉLIANE AND JACQUETTE DE RIVOYRE
LA CUISINE LANDAISE

Parson's Hats

Pfaffenhütchen

To make about 25

6 tbsp.	butter, softened	90 ml.
⅓ cup	sugar	75 ml.
1	egg	1
½ tsp.	grated lemon peel	2 ml.
1 cup	almonds, blanched, peeled and ground	¼ liter
1 cup	flour	¼ liter
½ tsp.	baking powder	2 ml.
1	egg yolk, beaten	1
Hazelnut filling		
1 cup	hazelnuts, roasted, peeled and ground	¼ liter
⅓ cup	sugar	75 ml.
	water	

For the dough, cream the butter and sugar and beat in the egg, lemon peel and ground almonds. Sift together the flour and baking powder and fold them in.

For the filling, mix together the hazelnuts and sugar and add enough water to make a creamy mixture.

Roll the dough about ¼ inch [6 mm.] thick and cut it into 3-inch [8-cm.] rounds. Place a small amount of hazelnut filling in the center of each round, draw the edges up and pinch them together to form a pyramid. Place the cookies on a buttered baking sheet, brush them with the egg yolk and bake them in a preheated 400° F. [200° C.] oven for 15 minutes, or until they are browned.

ELIZABETH SCHULER
MEIN KOCHBUCH

Crisp Nut Cookies

Croquants du Périgord

These cookies are often made with 3 tablespoons [45 ml.] of anise seeds instead of nuts. The orange-flower water may be replaced by rum, vanilla extract or grated lemon peel.

To make about 20

4	eggs	4
1 cup	sugar	¼ liter
1¼ cups	flour	300 ml.
2 tbsp.	heavy cream	30 ml.
1 tsp.	orange-flower water	5 ml.
1 cup	walnuts, chopped, or hazelnuts, ground	¼ liter

Break the eggs into a bowl, add the sugar and beat them together until well blended. Add the flour and cream, and beat the mixture until it forms a firm, homogeneous dough. Add the orange-flower water and the nuts; knead the dough until it stiffens and pulls away from the sides of the bowl. Place the dough on a pastry board and knead it for two or three minutes. Let the dough rest for 10 minutes.

Roll out the dough 1 inch [2½ cm.] thick. Cut it into 4-by-1-inch [10-by-2½-cm.] sticks and place the sticks on a buttered or oiled baking sheet. Bake in a preheated 300° F. [150° C.] oven for 30 minutes, or until the cookies are crisp.

LA CUISINE DU PÉRIGORD

English Rout Biscuits

The technique of preparing confectioners' sugar glaze is shown on page 8.

English rout biscuits are modeled after a form of marzipan made with superfine sugar and egg yolks. The marzipan may be colored before use and can be shaped in a great variety of ways. A good selection is described here, but the cook's own ingenuity will probably add to the list.

To make about 30

1 cup	almonds, blanched, peeled and ground	¼ liter
½ cup	superfine sugar	125 ml.
¼ tsp.	almond extract	1 ml.
2 or 3	egg yolks	2 or 3

Combine the almonds with the superfine sugar and flavor with the almond extract. Then mix in enough egg yolk to form a pliable paste of modeling consistency. Avoid overworking the paste or it will become oily. Make it into little cookies as follows.

Cherry horns. Roll out some of the rout paste about ⅛ inch [3 mm.] thick and cut it into rounds using a 1½-inch [4-cm.] cutter. Brush the center of each round with egg yolk, lay half a candied cherry on top and roll the dough around the cherry to form a conical horn. Arrange the biscuits on a buttered and floured baking sheet, and set them aside for several hours to firm. Brush them with beaten egg yolk and bake in a preheated 450° F. [230° C.] oven just long enough to brown the edges—about five minutes.

Rout rings. Color some of the rout paste pink or green, and roll it about ¼ inch [6 mm.] thick. Then cut it into small rings using two round cutters of nearly the same size. Set aside to firm, brush with egg yolk and bake in the hot oven; finish with a little confectioners' sugar glaze *(recipe, page 164)* and four silver decorating balls placed at the four points of the compass.

Almond rout biscuits. Color some of the rout paste, roll it about ¼ inch thick and cut into small fancy cookies. Set aside to firm, brush with egg yolk and stick a split almond on top. Bake in the hot oven.

Chocolate sticks. Using colored rout paste, roll it about ¼ inch thick and cut it into neat sticks. Set aside to firm and—without brushing with egg yolk—bake in the hot oven. When cold, dip the tips in melted semisweet baking chocolate and then in chocolate vermicelli.

Walnut bonbons. Roll some colored rout paste into small balls. Stick a half walnut on either side. Set aside to firm, brush with egg yolk and bake in the hot oven.

Little loaves. Shape some plain rout paste into little balls, flatten them slightly and, with the back of a knife blade, mark a cross in the top of each loaf. Set aside to firm, brush with egg yolk and bake in the hot oven.

MARGARET BATES
TALKING ABOUT CAKES WITH AN IRISH AND SCOTTISH ACCENT

Puff-Pastry Slices with Almond Topping
Condé Grand Four

You can vary this recipe by sprinkling coarse sugar crystals or finely chopped pistachios over the almond topping.

To make about 40

3 or 4	eggs	3 or 4
½ cup	sugar	125 ml.
6 oz.	almonds, blanched, peeled and cut into very fine slivers (about 1½ cups [375 ml.])	175 g.
1 lb.	rough puff dough *(recipe, page 166)*, rolled and folded six times	½ kg.

For the topping, beat three of the eggs until smooth, then stir in all except 2 tablespoons [30 ml.] of the sugar, and the slivered almonds. Continue to stir until the mixture forms a thick paste that is easy to spread. If the paste is stiff, add a little more beaten egg.

Roll out the rough puff dough ½ inch [1 cm.] thick. Cut it into strips 1¼ by 3¼ inches [3 by 8.5 cm.]. Spread almond topping on each of the strips and sprinkle them with the remaining sugar. Arrange the strips on ungreased baking sheets and bake them in a preheated 425° F. [220° C.] oven for 15 minutes, or until golden.

ROSALIE BLANQUET
LE PÂTISSIER DES MÉNAGES

Bear's Paws or Chocolate Shells
Bärentätzle oder Schokoladenmuscheln

Traditionally, these are shaped by pressing wooden Speculaas molds with forms and figures carved into them onto the dough. The molds are obtainable at fine kitchen-supply stores. If they are not available, roll out the dough ¼ inch [6 mm.] thick and cut it with cookie cutters.

To make about 10

1 cup	granulated sugar	¼ liter
4	egg whites, stiffly beaten	4
2 oz.	semisweet baking chocolate, grated	60 g.
¼ cup	cocoa powder	50 ml.
3 tbsp.	strained fresh lemon juice	45 ml.
1 tbsp.	vanilla sugar	15 ml.
8 oz.	almonds, ground (about 2 cups [½ liter])	250 g.

Fold the granulated sugar into the beaten egg whites and then gradually fold in the other ingredients. Let the mixture rest for one hour. On a sugared and floured board, knead the dough until smooth. Roll the dough about ½ inch [1 cm.] thick. Press the molds into the dough, bearing down firmly to leave a clear impression in the dough.

Then cut the cookies apart with a floured knife, place them on buttered baking sheets and let them stand overnight. Bake in a preheated 400° F. [200° C.] oven for about 10 minutes, or until lightly browned.

HANS KARL ADAM
DAS KOCHBUCH AUS SCHWABEN

Chocolate Fleck Rings

This dough may also be used for jam-filled cookies. Cut as many cookie rounds as rings. Brush the rounds thinly with apricot or raspberry jam and cover them with the rings. Bake as below. While still hot, fill the centers of the rings with more jam. Dust the rings only with a mixture of equal quantities of cocoa powder and confectioners' sugar.

To make about 40

½ lb.	unsalted butter, softened	¼ kg.
1 cup	sugar	¼ liter
2 cups	flour	½ liter
⅛ tsp.	salt	½ ml.
3 tbsp.	finely chopped almonds	45 ml.
4	egg yolks	4
2 oz.	sweet baking chocolate, grated	60 g.
1 tbsp.	grated lemon peel	15 ml.
1 tbsp.	ground cinnamon	15 ml.
1	egg white, lightly beaten	1

Cream together the butter and sugar. Add the flour, salt, almonds, egg yolks and chocolate, and mix to form a smooth and soft dough. Add the grated peel and cinnamon.

On a floured board, roll the dough ⅛ inch [3 mm.] thick. Cut out rings with a 2-inch [5-cm.] doughnut cutter. Place the rings on a large buttered baking sheet and brush them with the egg white. Bake the rings in a preheated 350° F. [180° C.] oven for 10 to 15 minutes, or until crisp.

JULIETTE ELKON
THE CHOCOLATE COOKBOOK

Dutch "Shell Bark" Macaroons

To make about 40

2	eggs	2
1 tsp.	milk	5 ml.
½ cup	firmly packed light brown sugar	125 ml.
⅓ cup	granulated sugar	75 ml.
1¼ cups	flour, sifted with ½ tsp. [2 ml.] baking powder and ¼ tsp. [1 ml.] salt	300 ml.
1 cup	pecans, chopped	¼ liter

Beat the eggs lightly with the milk and add first the brown then the granulated sugar, the flour, and finally the nuts. Mix well. Roll the dough out to a thickness of ½ inch [1 cm.] and cut it into 2-inch [5-cm.] rounds. Place the rounds on buttered baking sheets and bake them in a preheated 350° F. [180° C.] oven for 15 minutes, or until well browned.

J. GEORGE FREDERICK
PENNSYLVANIA DUTCH COOKERY

Rolled Peanut Butter Cookies

To make about 25

½ cup	peanut butter	125 ml.
8 tbsp.	butter, softened	120 ml.
½ cup	granulated sugar	125 ml.
½ cup	firmly packed light brown sugar	125 ml.
1	egg, well beaten	1
1¼ cups	sifted flour	300 ml.
¼ tsp.	salt	1 ml.
½ tsp.	baking powder	2 ml.
¼ tsp.	baking soda	1 ml.

Cream the peanut butter and butter; add the granulated and brown sugars gradually; add the egg and mix well. Sift together the flour, salt, baking powder and baking soda, and add to the peanut-butter mixture. Mix well. Chill the dough for at least one hour, or until firm. Roll out the dough to a thickness of ¼ inch [6 mm.], cut out cookies and bake them in a preheated 350° F. [180° C.] oven for 10 to 15 minutes, or until lightly browned.

IMOGENE WOLCOTT (EDITOR)
THE YANKEE COOK BOOK

Cold-Dough Yeast Cookies

Kolache

To make 60 to 70

½ lb.	vegetable shortening, softened	¼ kg.
½ lb.	butter, softened	¼ kg.
5	eggs, beaten	5
¼ oz.	package active dry yeast, or ⅗ oz. [18 g.] cake fresh yeast, mixed with 1 cup [¼ liter] tepid milk	7 ½ g.
1 tsp.	vanilla extract	5 ml.
5 to 6 cups	flour	1 ¼ to 1 ½ liters
2 tsp.	baking powder	10 ml.
1 tsp.	salt	5 ml.
	confectioners' sugar	
	apricot jam, prune butter, or nut paste *(recipe, page 165)* made with almonds or walnuts	

Cream the shortening and butter together until very soft. Add the eggs to the creamed mixture and blend well. Add the yeast mixture and stir in the vanilla. Sift together 4 cups [1 liter] of the flour, the baking powder and salt, and stir into the batter. Knead the dough, adding the remaining flour a little at a time until the dough no longer sticks to your hands. Cover tightly and refrigerate overnight.

Break off a large handful of the dough and roll it in confectioners' sugar. On a lightly floured board, roll the dough to a large square or rectangle about ¼ inch [6 mm.] thick. Cut the dough into 2- to 3-inch [5- to 8-cm.] squares. Place a teaspoonful of apricot jam, prune butter or nut paste in the center of each square. Shape the dough into packages by folding two opposite corners of each square over the filling and pinching them together. Or shape pinwheels by slashing each square from the corners to the filling in the center, then lifting every other halved corner, pulling it to the center and pinching these four tips together above the filling. Repeat the rolling, cutting, filling and shaping processes to form the remaining cookies.

Place the cookies 3 inches [8 cm.] apart on ungreased baking sheets and bake in a preheated 350° F. [180° C.] oven for 20 to 25 minutes, or until golden brown. When the cookies have cooled a little, sprinkle them with sifted confectioners' sugar to give them a shiny coating.

THE GREAT COOKS' GUIDE TO COOKIES

Refrigerator Cookies

Ayrshire Shortbread

Rice flour is obtainable at health-food stores.

To make about 35

2 cups	all-purpose flour	½ liter
1 tbsp.	rice flour	15 ml.
8 tbsp.	butter, cut into pieces	120 ml.
½ cup	superfine sugar	125 ml.
1	egg yolk	1
2 tbsp.	heavy cream	30 ml.

Sift the all-purpose flour and rice flour together into a bowl. Rub in the butter and add the sugar. Make a well in the center and add the egg yolk and cream. Knead together lightly to make a fairly stiff dough. Divide the dough into three pieces and roll each piece into a cylinder about 1½ inches [4 cm.] in diameter. Wrap and refrigerate for several hours or overnight. Cut each cylinder into rounds ¼ inch [6 mm.] thick, place the rounds on buttered baking sheets and bake in a preheated 350° F. [180° C.] oven for 10 to 15 minutes, or until delicately browned.

CATHERINE BROWN
SCOTTISH REGIONAL RECIPES

Icebox Cookies

To make about 130

½ lb.	butter, softened	¼ kg.
2 cups	firmly packed light brown sugar	½ liter
2	eggs	2
3½ cups	flour	875 ml.
1 cup	chopped nuts	¼ liter
½ tsp.	salt	2 ml.
1 tsp.	baking soda	5 ml.

Cream the butter and sugar. Add the eggs and mix well. Sift the flour, add the nuts to this, then mix in the salt and baking soda. Combine with the creamed mixture. Shape into a long rectangular loaf and refrigerate overnight, or until very firm. Slice thin and bake the cookies in a preheated 350° F. [180° C.] oven for about eight minutes, or until they turn a dark golden color.

JUNIOR LEAGUE OF SPARTANBURG, INC.
SPARTANBURG SECRETS II

Orange Pecan Cookies

To make about 70

½ lb.	butter, softened	¼ kg.
½ cup	firmly packed light brown sugar	125 ml.
½ cup	granulated sugar	125 ml.
1	egg	1
2 tbsp.	fresh orange juice	30 ml.
1 tbsp.	grated orange peel	15 ml.
2¾ cups	flour, sifted with 1 tsp. [5 ml.] baking soda	675 ml.
½ cup	chopped pecans	125 ml.

Cream the butter and sugars together until smooth and fluffy. Add the egg, orange juice and orange peel. Add the sifted flour. Fold in the pecans. Blend all together. Form into one or two 1½-inch [4-cm.] cylinders, wrap in wax paper and chill in the refrigerator for at least one hour. Cut into ¼-inch [6-mm.] slices, place on baking sheets and bake in a preheated 350° F. [180° C.] oven for 10 to 12 minutes, or until lightly browned.

WILLIAM I. KAUFMAN AND SISTER MARY URSULA COOPER, O.P.
THE ART OF CREOLE COOKERY

Chinese Almond Cookies

Sablés aux Amandes

These can be kept for several weeks in an airtight container.

To make about 35

2 tsp.	baking powder	10 ml.
½ tsp.	baking soda (optional)	2 ml.
	water	
5 tbsp.	lard or butter, melted	75 ml.
1	egg, lightly beaten	1
½ tsp.	salt	2 ml.
1 tsp.	almond extract	5 ml.
⅔ cup	firmly packed light brown sugar	150 ml.
1⅔ cups	flour, sifted	400 ml.
¾ cup	almonds, blanched and peeled	175 ml.
1	egg yolk, lightly beaten	1

Dissolve the baking powder and the baking soda (if using) in 1 tablespoon [15 ml.] of water. In a large bowl, mix together thoroughly the lard or butter, egg, salt, diluted baking powder and almond extract. Gradually stir in the sugar and

flour. Knead the dough well. It should be fairly firm, but if it is too dry to cohere well, add a little water.

Divide the dough into two or three pieces and, on a lightly floured board, roll each piece into a cylinder about 1¾ inches [4½ cm.] in diameter. Wrap each cylinder in plastic wrap or aluminum foil and leave for 30 minutes in the freezer (or at least three hours in the refrigerator).

Cut the cylinders into rounds about ¼ inch [6 mm.] thick, using a knife that you should flour lightly from time to time. Arrange the rounds on oiled baking sheets, leaving about ¾ inch [2 cm.] between the rounds. Place one or two blanched almonds horizontally on each round and press them gently into the dough. Then brush each round lightly with the beaten egg yolk.

Bake the cookies in a preheated 350° F. [180° C.] oven for about 25 minutes, or until they are golden brown.

NGUYEN NGOC RAO
LA CUISINE CHINOISE À L'USAGE DES FRANÇAIS

Dead Men's Bones

Totenbeinli

To make about 70

6 tbsp.	butter, softened	90 ml.
1 cup plus 2 tbsp.	superfine sugar	280 ml.
3	eggs	3
9 oz.	almonds, blanched, peeled and chopped (about 2¼ cups [550 ml.])	275 g.
½ tbsp.	ground cinnamon	7 ml.
	salt	
3 cups	flour, sifted	¾ liter
1	egg yolk, lightly beaten	1

Beat the butter with the sugar until white and creamy. Add one egg at a time, beating well, then add the almonds, cinnamon, a pinch of salt and finally the flour. Knead the dough well and shape it into a long rectangle about 1½ inches [4 cm.] thick and 2½ to 3 inches [6 to 8 cm.] wide. Refrigerate the dough for one hour, or until firm. Cut the rectangle crosswise into ¼-inch [6-mm.] slices, place them on baking sheets and brush them with the egg yolk. Bake in a preheated 400° F. [200° C.] oven for 20 minutes, until just golden.

EVA MARIA BORER
TANTE HEIDI'S SWISS KITCHEN

Refrigerator Cookies

To make about 70

¾ lb.	butter, melted	350 g.
1 cup	granulated sugar	¼ liter
1 cup	firmly packed dark brown sugar	¼ liter
3	eggs	3
1 cup	finely chopped black walnuts	¼ liter
4½ cups	flour	1125 ml.
2 tsp.	baking soda	10 ml.
1 tsp.	salt	5 ml.
½ tsp.	grated nutmeg	2 ml.
½ tsp.	ground cloves	2 ml.
1 tsp.	ground cinnamon	5 ml.

In a large bowl, cream the butter and sugars. Add the eggs one at a time, mixing thoroughly. Stir in the nuts. Sift together the remaining ingredients and blend them into the mixture. Shape the dough into a cylinder 2 inches [5 cm.] in diameter, wrap, and refrigerate it overnight.

The next morning, cut the dough into slices ¼ inch [6 mm.] thick and place them on buttered baking sheets. Bake the cookies in a preheated 425° F. [220° C.] oven for eight minutes, or until lightly browned.

DOROTHY C. FRANK
COOKING WITH NUTS

Sesame Roundels

Petits Fours au Sésame

These cookies can be kept for several weeks in an airtight container at room temperature.

To make about 35

1 cup	sesame seeds	¼ liter
2 tsp.	baking powder	10 ml.
½ tsp.	baking soda (optional)	2 ml.
5 tbsp.	lard or butter, melted and cooled	75 ml.
1	egg, lightly beaten	1
½ tsp.	salt	2 ml.
½ cup	firmly packed light brown sugar	125 ml.
1¾ cups	flour, sifted	425 ml.

Toast the sesame seeds in a dry skillet over medium heat, stirring them constantly until they are lightly browned.
Dissolve the baking powder and baking soda, if using, in

1 tablespoon [15 ml.] of water. In a large bowl, mix together the lard or butter, the egg, the salt and the dissolved baking powder. Gradually stir in the sugar, the flour and, finally, the sesame seeds. Mix everything thoroughly, then knead the dough for a minute or two. If the dough feels dry, incorporate a little water.

On a lightly floured board, form the dough into a cylinder about 1½ inches [4 cm.] in diameter. Wrap it in plastic wrap or aluminum foil and freeze it for 30 minutes (or refrigerate it for at least three hours).

Unwrap the cylinder and use a lightly floured knife to cut it into rounds about ¼ inch [6 mm.] thick. Arrange the rounds on lightly oiled baking sheets, leaving about ¾ inch [2 cm.] between them. Bake in a preheated 350° F. [180° C.] oven for 20 minutes, or until the cookies are light golden.

NGUYEN NGOC RAO
LA CUISINE CHINOISE À L'USAGE DES FRANÇAIS

Black and White Cookies

Marmorplätzchen

To make about 90

½ lb.	butter, softened	¼ kg.
1 cup	granulated sugar	¼ liter
1 tbsp.	vanilla sugar	15 ml.
2	eggs	2
2 tbsp.	rum	30 ml.
½ tsp.	baking powder	2 ml.
4 cups	flour	1 liter
3 tbsp.	cocoa powder	45 ml.
1	egg white, lightly beaten	1

Cream the butter, granulated sugar and vanilla sugar until fluffy. Beat in the eggs and add the rum. Sift the baking powder with the flour and quickly work them into the butter-and-sugar mixture. Divide the dough in half and color one half by beating into it the cocoa powder. Wrap and refrigerate both portions for at least one hour, or until firm.

For spirals, roll out the light and dark portions of the dough separately into equal-sized rectangles about ¼ inch [6 mm.] thick. Brush the light dough with egg white and place the dark dough on top. Brush the dark dough with egg white, and—starting at one of the long sides—roll the two rectangles up together jelly-roll fashion.

For checkerboards, set about a quarter of the light dough aside, then shape each remaining portion of dough into two thin cylinders about 24 inches [60 cm.] long. Coat all of the cylinders with egg white. Place a dark cylinder beside a light one. Place the other two cylinders on top, reversing the colors. Press them all together. Roll out the remaining light mixture into a 24-inch-long rectangle about ⅛ inch [3 mm.]

thick, coat it with egg white and roll it around the cylinders.

For tree-trunk slices, roll the light portion of the dough into a rectangle 24 inches long and about ¼ inch thick. Form the dark mixture into a cylinder 24 inches long, coat it with egg white and roll it up in the light dough.

Wrap the shaped roll in foil and refrigerate it for an hour to firm it. Cut the roll into slices ¼ inch thick. Bake the cookies in a preheated 375° F. [190° C.] oven for eight to 10 minutes, or until the cookies are firm to the touch.

HEDWIG MARIA STUBER
ICH HELF DIR KOCHEN

Molded and Hand-shaped Cookies

Almond Toast

Mandelbrot

To make about 25

1 cup	whole almonds	¼ liter
2 cups	sifted flour	½ liter
2½ tsp.	baking powder	12 ml.
½ tsp.	salt	2 ml.
¼ tsp.	grated nutmeg	1 ml.
6 tbsp.	unsalted butter, softened	90 ml.
⅔ cup	sugar	150 ml.
1 tsp.	almond extract	5 ml.
½ tsp.	vanilla extract	2 ml.
2	eggs	2

Spread the almonds on a baking sheet and toast them in a preheated 300° F. [150° C.] oven for 15 minutes. Remove the almonds from the oven and increase the oven heat to 375° F. [190° C.].

Sift together the flour, baking powder, salt and nutmeg. Set aside. In a mixing bowl, cream the butter until it is light. Gradually cream in the sugar until the mixture is light and fluffy. Add the almond and vanilla extracts, then beat in the eggs, one at a time. Stir in the flour mixture (on lowest speed, if you are using a mixer). Mix in the almonds thoroughly.

Smooth foil over a baking sheet measuring at least 11 by 17 inches [28 by 42 cm.]. Spoon two strips of batter crosswise onto the sheet, equidistant from each other and the ends of the sheet; they should measure about 9 inches [23 cm.] in

length and 3½ inches [9 cm.] in width. Smooth them and even the sides with a flexible spatula dipped in cold water.

Bake the strips for 15 to 20 minutes, or until they are pale golden. Slide the foil off the sheet and place the strips on a rack to cool for 15 minutes. Reset the oven heat to 300° F.

With a very sharp serrated knife, cut the almond toast carefully into slices ¾ inch [2 cm.] thick and lay them flat, very close together, on the baking sheet.

Return the cookies to the oven for 15 minutes, then turn them over and bake for 15 minutes longer, or until they are golden. Cool the almond toast on a rack. Pack in an airtight container; it will keep for a month.

HELEN WITTY AND ELIZABETH SCHNEIDER COLCHIE
BETTER THAN STORE-BOUGHT

Hazelnut Cookies

Croquets aux Noisettes Sauvages

To make about 60

1¼ lb.	honey (about 3⅓ cups [825 ml.])	600 g.
7 oz.	hazelnuts, ground (about 1¾ cups [425 ml.])	200 g.
½ tsp.	ground cinnamon	2 ml.
12	whole cloves, crushed to a powder	12
5 cups	flour, sifted	1¼ liters
¼ cup	rum	50 ml.
1	egg, beaten	1

Heat the honey until liquid, without letting it boil, and pour it into a bowl. Add the hazelnuts, cinnamon, cloves, flour and rum, and mix together. Divide the mixture in two.

Roll each piece of dough into a cylinder about 3 inches [8 cm.] in diameter. Place each cylinder on a buttered and floured baking sheet. Flatten the cylinders to resemble loaves of bread. Glaze the dough with the egg, and scratch the surface with the tines of a fork to decorate the loaves. Place the loaves in a preheated 375° F. [190° C.] oven, immediately reduce the heat to 350° F. [180° C.] and bake them for 20 minutes, or until the loaves are golden and a knife inserted into the center comes out dry.

Cut the loaves into ½-inch [1-cm.] slices while they are still warm. Cool them thoroughly before storing the slices in an airtight container.

AMICALE DES CUISINIERS ET PÂTISSIERS AUVERGNATS DE PARIS
CUISINE D'AUVERGNE

Zwieback

These crisp toasts are marvelous with café au lait or at tea-time. They will keep almost indefinitely.

To make 90 to 100

½ cup plus 1 tsp.	sugar	130 ml.
two ¼ oz.	packages active dry yeast	two 7½ g.
¼ cup	tepid water	50 ml.
2 cups	milk	½ liter
12 tbsp.	unsalted butter	180 ml.
1 tsp.	salt	5 ml.
¼ tsp.	ground cinnamon	1 ml.
⅛ tsp.	grated nutmeg	½ ml.
¼ tsp.	ground mace	1 ml.
3	eggs, beaten	3
1 cup	light or medium rye flour	¼ liter
5 to 6 cups	unbleached flour	1¼ to 1½ liters

Stir together 1 teaspoon [5 ml.] of the sugar, the yeast and the tepid water in a small bowl. The mixture will rise to several times its original volume while you continue.

In a saucepan, heat the milk, the remaining sugar, 8 tablespoons [120 ml.] of the butter and the salt just until the butter melts. Then cool to 100° F. [38° C.], or until the mixture feels barely warm. Combine the milk mixture and the yeast mixture in a large bowl. Stir in the cinnamon, nutmeg and mace, beat in the eggs, then the rye flour.

A cupful at a time, beat in as much as possible of the unbleached flour. When the dough is too stiff to stir, turn it out onto a pastry board dusted with flour and knead in the remaining flour, or as much as necessary to make a smooth, elastic, medium dough, not too stiff. Knead thoroughly for five to 10 minutes. Gather the dough into a ball.

Lightly butter a large bowl and turn the ball of dough about in the butter to coat all surfaces. Cover the bowl with plastic wrap and let the dough rise until it has doubled in bulk—about one and one half hours. Punch the dough down, cover and let it rise again until doubled—about 45 minutes.

Turn the dough out onto a floured pastry board, knead it a few strokes to expel air and divide it into five equal parts. Rolling the pieces under the palms of your hands, form each part into a cylindrical loaf about 10 inches [25 cm.] long.

Lay the loaves crosswise on two generously buttered 11-by-17-inch [28-by-43-cm.] baking sheets, leaving 2 inches [5 cm.] between the loaves and a 1-inch [2½-cm.] margin at each end. Melt the remaining butter. Brush the tops and sides of the loaves with the butter. Let the loaves rise again in a warm place until they have almost doubled in bulk.

Bake the loaves in the center of a preheated 350° F. [180° C.] oven until they are firm and golden and sound hollow when the bottoms are tapped—about 30 minutes. Cool them on wire racks.

When the loaves are almost cool, reheat the oven to 200° F. [100° C.]. Slicing diagonally, cut the loaves into slices about ½ inch [1 cm.] thick—about 18 to a loaf. Lay the slices, close together, on baking sheets or cake racks and place them in the oven; when the slices are dry throughout, increase the oven temperature to 300° F. [150° C.] and let the slices brown delicately, watching closely lest they over-brown. Cool the zwieback on wire racks.

HELEN WITTY AND ELIZABETH SCHNEIDER COLCHIE
BETTER THAN STORE-BOUGHT

Jawbreakers

Sciappa Denti

Eau de vie, literally, "water of life," is a colorless French brandy. To toast the nuts, spread them on a baking sheet and bake in a preheated 350° F. [180° C.] oven for 10 minutes, turning them often so that they color evenly.

To make about 100

8 cups	flour	2 liters
¼ oz.	package active dry yeast, or ⅗ oz. [18 g.] cake fresh yeast, mixed with 3 tbsp. [45 ml.] tepid water	7½ g.
½ lb.	butter, softened	¼ kg.
6	eggs, the yolks separated from the whites, the yolks lightly beaten, and the whites stiffly beaten	6
2 cups	milk, warmed	½ liter
4 cups	sugar	1 liter
2 tbsp.	*eau de vie* or other brandy	30 ml.
1 cup	almonds, blanched, peeled, toasted and finely chopped	¼ liter
2 tbsp.	grated orange peel	30 ml.
	egg-yolk glaze, made by beating 2 yolks with 2 tbsp. [30 ml.] water	

Place the flour in a large bowl and make a well in the center. Add the yeast, butter, the six lightly beaten egg yolks, milk, sugar, brandy, almonds and grated peel. Mix well, then fold in the egg whites. Cover the bowl with a cloth and let the dough rest for 30 minutes. Divide the dough into six pieces and form them into cylinders about 8 inches [20 cm.] long and 2 inches [5 cm.] thick. Place the cylinders on oiled baking sheets and bake in a preheated 350° F. [180° C.] oven for 10 minutes. Brush the cylinders with the egg-yolk glaze and bake for an additional five minutes, or until golden brown. Cut the cylinders diagonally into ½-inch [1-cm.] slices, place the slices flat on the baking sheet and bake for a further 10 minutes, or until they are dry and crisp.

MARIA NUNZIA FILIPPINI
LA CUISINE CORSE

Madeleines

Baking powder will help the batter rise, but it may be omitted for thinner cookies. The vanilla bean may be replaced by 1 teaspoon [5 ml.] of vanilla extract, added with the butter.

To make about 40 to 140, depending on the size of the molds

1	vanilla bean	1
1 cup	sugar	¼ liter
5	eggs	5
2 tsp.	grated lemon or orange peel	10 ml.
1¾ cups	flour, sifted	425 ml.
1 tsp.	baking powder	5 ml.
12 tbsp.	butter, melted and cooled until tepid	180 ml.

Split open the vanilla bean and scrape out the seeds. (Reserve the pod for use as a sugar flavoring.) Whisk together the vanilla seeds, sugar and eggs for 10 to 15 minutes, or until the mixture triples in volume and is almost white in color. Add the lemon peel. Sift the flour and baking powder together, sprinkle them onto the egg mixture, and fold them in gently but thoroughly—however, do not overwork the batter. Fold in the tepid butter.

Let the batter rest in a cool place, not the refrigerator, for at least 15 minutes; it can wait for several hours. Brush madeleine molds with softened butter and flour them. Fill the molds three quarters full with the batter. Bake in a preheated 375° F. [190° C.] oven for 10 to 12 minutes, or until the cookies spring back when pressed with a finger.

LA CUISINE D'ÈVE ET OLYMPE

Russian Cookies

To make about 80

10	eggs, the yolks separated from the whites, and the whites stiffly beaten	10
1 cup	superfine sugar	¼ liter
1½ cups	flour	375 ml.
1 cup	ground almonds	¼ liter
1 tsp.	anise seeds	5 ml.

In a heatproof bowl set over simmering water, whisk the egg yolks and sugar together until they form a thick batter; lightly stir in the egg whites, then the flour, almonds and anise seeds. Pour the batter into two buttered loaf pans, filling them to a depth of about 2 inches [5 cm.]. Bake in a preheated 350° F. [180° C.] oven until the loaves are lightly browned—30 minutes. Unmold them onto racks to cool. Then cut them into ¼-inch [6-mm.] slices. Place the slices on baking sheets and bake at 350° F. until they are lightly colored—seven or eight minutes on each side.

FRANCATELLI'S THE MODERN COOK

Lace Molasses Wafers

The technique of shaping curved cookies is demonstrated on pages 34-35.

To make 50 to 60

½ cup	molasses	125 ml.
½ cup	sugar	125 ml.
8 tbsp.	butter	120 ml.
1 cup	flour	¼ liter
½ tsp.	baking powder	2 ml.
¼ tsp.	baking soda	1 ml.

Slowly heat the molasses, sugar and butter to the boiling point. Boil for one minute and remove from the heat. Sift together the flour, baking powder and baking soda and add to the molasses mixture. Stir well. Set the pan in a vessel of hot water to keep the batter from hardening. Drop quarter teaspoonfuls of the batter 3 inches [8 cm.] apart on buttered baking sheets or inverted baking pans. Bake in a preheated 350° F. [180° C.] oven until brown—about 10 minutes. Cool slightly, then lift off the wafers carefully with a thin knife. If desired, roll the wafers around the handle of a wooden spoon to shape them into tubes while they are still warm.

IMOGENE WOLCOTT (EDITOR)
THE YANKEE COOK BOOK

Brandy Snaps

To make about 20

4 tbsp.	butter	60 ml.
¼ cup	sugar	50 ml.
2 tbsp.	molasses	30 ml.
½ cup	flour	125 ml.
	salt	
½ tsp.	ground ginger	2 ml.
½ tsp.	fresh lemon juice	2 ml.
1 tsp.	brandy	5 ml.
½ cup	heavy cream, whipped	125 ml.

Melt the butter, sugar and molasses; let the mixture cool. Sift in the flour, a pinch of salt and the ginger. Mix in the lemon juice and brandy. Drop the batter by the tablespoonful onto well-buttered baking sheets—spacing the mounds 4 inches [10 cm.] apart. Bake in a preheated 325° F. [160° C.] oven for seven to eight minutes, or until the cookies are brown. Remove the baking sheets from the oven and, after waiting for about one minute, roll each cookie gently around the handle of a wooden spoon to shape it into a tube. Transfer the cookies to a plate and let them cool completely. Fill the tubes with the whipped cream just before serving them.

HOPE J. NORMAN AND LOUISE A. SIMON (EDITORS)
LOUISIANA ENTERTAINS

Brown Sugar Brandy Snaps
Gauffres

Bake these cookies in small batches so that they do not cool and become brittle before they can be shaped. The technique of shaping curved cookies is shown on pages 34-35.

These are delicious filled with whipped cream flavored with finely chopped crystallized ginger.

To make about 90

8 tbsp.	lard or butter	120 ml.
2⅔ cups	firmly packed light brown sugar	650 ml.
1 tbsp.	brandy	15 ml.
4 cups	flour	1 liter
¼ tsp.	grated nutmeg	1 ml.
6	eggs, beaten	6
1 tbsp.	water	15 ml.

In a saucepan, melt the lard or butter over low heat, add the sugar and cook until the sugar dissolves. Remove the pan from the heat and stir in the remaining ingredients to form a soft, dropping batter. Drop the batter—about 2 teaspoonfuls [10 ml.] at a time—onto buttered baking sheets, leaving several inches between the rounds for each cookie to spread to saucer size. Bake in a preheated 400° F. [200° C.] oven for 10 minutes, or until the cookies are firm to the touch. As each batch is baked, remove the cookies one by one and wrap them quickly around a stick or the handle of a wooden spoon to form tubes. They will dry and almost instantly become crisp and shiny; they should be pale toffee-colored and full of air holes.

DOROTHY HARTLEY
FOOD IN ENGLAND

Roof Tiles
Tejas

The technique of shaping curved cookies is demonstrated on pages 34-35.

To make about 25

½ cup	sugar	125 ml.
1 cup	flour	¼ liter
2	egg whites, stiffly beaten	2
¾ cup	heavy cream, whipped	175 ml.

Sift the sugar and flour together. Fold them into the egg whites, then stir in the cream. With a spoon, form small mounds of the mixture—spaced well apart—on baking sheets lined with parchment paper. Bake in a preheated 350° F. [180° C.] oven for two minutes, then increase the heat to 400° F. [200° C.] and continue to cook for eight minutes, or until the cookies are just beginning to brown. Remove the cookies from the oven and, while they are still hot, bend them into curved shapes that resemble Spanish roof tiles.

MARIA DEL CARMEN CASCANTE
MANUAL MODERNO DE PASTELERIA CASERA

Italian Roof Tiles
Tegoline

The technique of shaping curved cookies is demonstrated on pages 34-35.

To make about 40

½ cup	almonds, blanched and peeled	125 ml.
1 cup	superfine sugar	¼ liter
8 tbsp.	butter, cut into small pieces and softened	120 ml.
2	eggs	2
2	egg whites	2
2 tbsp.	grated orange peel	30 ml.
1 cup	flour	¼ liter

In a mortar, pound the almonds with 1 tablespoon [15 ml.] of the sugar until they form a very fine powder.

Line two baking sheets with parchment paper. Butter the paper and flour it, shaking off the excess.

Put the softened butter pieces in a bowl and work them with a wooden spoon until the butter is like cream. Add the rest of the sugar and work the mixture for a few minutes. Add the eggs, egg whites, powdered almonds, orange peel and flour, making sure that each ingredient is well blended before adding the next. Pour some of the batter into a pastry bag fitted with a plain tube about ½ inch [1 cm.] in diameter. Squeeze the bag lightly to form strips about 3 inches [8 cm.] long on one of the lined baking sheets, spacing the strips well apart. Reserve the remaining batter. Put the baking sheet into a preheated 425° F. [220° C.] oven and let the cookies bake for a few minutes.

Meanwhile, rub a little vegetable oil onto a rolling pin. When the edges of the cookies have begun to brown but the centers are still white—and before the cookies are firm—take the baking sheet out of the oven. Keeping the sheet on top of the warm oven so that the cookies do not cool, lift them off one by one with a knife and press them around the rolling pin so that they curve. Pipe, bake and shape the remaining batter similarly. Cool the cookies before serving them.

FERNANDA GOSETTI
IN CUCINA CON FERNANDA GOSETTI

Wood Shavings

Copeaux

These cookies keep for a long time in an airtight container.

To make about 35

1 cup	almonds, blanched, peeled and chopped	¼ liter
1 cup	superfine sugar	¼ liter
2 cups	flour	½ liter
½ tsp.	vanilla extract	2 ml.
about 6	egg whites	about 6

In a mortar, pound the almonds to a paste, adding the sugar gradually. Stir in the flour and vanilla extract, and enough egg whites to make a soft dough.

Oil two baking sheets, or butter them with clarified butter. With a pastry bag, pipe strips of dough about 4 inches [10 cm.] long and ½ inch [1 cm.] wide onto the sheets—spacing them well apart. Set the rest of the dough aside. Bake in a preheated 400° F. [200° C.] oven for eight to 10 minutes, or until the edges of the cookies are lightly browned.

Keeping the baking sheets warm beside the oven, detach the cookies one by one and roll them around a small stick to give them a corkscrew shape. Pipe, bake and shape the rest of the dough similarly.

MANUEL PRATIQUE DE CUISINE PROVENÇALE

Russian Cigarettes

Cigarettes Russes

This recipe may be used for both the cigarette cookies and the tile cookies shown on pages 34-35. For tile cookies with almonds, add 1½ cups [375 ml.] of sliced almonds to the batter and drop the batter onto the baking sheet by spoonfuls. Spread the batter thin with a fork dipped in water to evenly distribute the almonds.

As a precaution, first pipe and bake one test cookie. If it is not crisp when rolled, add 1 tablespoon [15 ml.] of melted butter to the batter. If it is too brittle, add 1 to 2 tablespoons [15 to 30 ml.] of additional flour.

To make about 40

10 tbsp.	butter, softened	150 ml.
1¾ cups	confectioners' sugar	425 ml.
6	egg whites	6
1¼ cups	flour	300 ml.
1 tbsp.	heavy cream	15 ml.
1 tsp.	vanilla extract	5 ml.

Cream the butter and sugar and gradually beat in three of the egg whites. Add one heaping teaspoonful of flour and mix well. Gradually beat in the remaining egg whites. Stir in the remaining flour, then add the cream and vanilla and mix well. Put about one quarter of the batter into a pastry bag fitted with a ⅜-inch [9-mm.] plain tube and pipe mounds the size of walnuts onto a buttered baking sheet—spacing the mounds well apart. Rap the baking sheet sharply on the table to flatten the mounds, then bake the cookies in a preheated 450° F. [230° C.] oven for four to five minutes, or until they brown around the edges.

Loosen the cookies from the baking sheet with a metal spatula, but leave them on the sheet. Place one cookie upside down on a table and roll it quickly around the handle of a wooden spoon or dowel to shape it into a cigarette. Remove the cookie at once; set it on a rack to cool and roll up the remaining cookies as quickly as possible. If they become too stiff to roll, put them back into the oven for one minute to soften them. Pipe, bake and shape the remaining cookies in the same manner.

ANNE WILLAN
FRENCH COOKERY SCHOOL

Cream Horns

Hohlippen

This recipe is adapted from a 19th Century cookbook. The conical metal mold called for is about 5½ inches [14 cm.] long and 1¼ inches [3 cm.] across at its mouth. Such molds are obtainable where kitchen and baking supplies are sold.

To make about 30

5	eggs	5
1½ cups	sugar	325 ml.
2 tsp.	grated lemon peel	10 ml.
¾ cup	flour	175 ml.
1 cup	heavy cream, whipped	¼ liter
1 tsp.	vanilla extract	5 ml.

Beat together the eggs, 1¼ cups [300 ml.] of the sugar and the lemon peel until thick and light—about 15 minutes. Fold in the flour. Roll out the dough about ⅛ inch [3 mm.] thick and cut it into rectangles about 4 inches [10 cm.] long and 3 inches [8 cm.] wide. Lay about one quarter of the rectangles on a buttered baking sheet and bake them in a preheated 350° F. [180° C.] oven for about 10 minutes, or until they are a light yellow color.

Separate them from the baking sheet one at a time and twist them as quickly as possible around a conical metal mold to form them into cornucopias. Leave them in a warm place to get crisp and dry. Bake and shape the rest of the rectangles similarly.

Flavor the whipped cream with the vanilla and the remaining sugar, and fill the cornucopias with the cream.

LADY HARRIET ST. CLAIR (EDITOR)
DAINTY DISHES

Small Cornets

Petits Cornets

The conical metal mold called for in this recipe is about 5½ inches [14 cm.] long and 1¼ inches [3 cm.] across at its mouth. Such molds are obtainable where kitchen and baking supplies are sold. The author suggests filling the cornets with butter cream; whipped cream is also appropriate.

To make about 40		
8 tbsp.	butter, softened	120 ml.
½ cup	superfine sugar or ¾ cup [175 ml.] confectioners' sugar	125 ml.
	vanilla extract	
5	egg whites	5
1 cup	flour	¼ liter

Cream the butter and sugar together, then add two or three drops of vanilla extract. Gradually beat in the egg whites. The mixture usually curdles at this stage but will become smooth after the flour is added. Fold in the flour. Pour about one quarter of the batter into a pastry bag fitted with a ¼-inch [6-mm.] plain tube and pipe very small mounds of the batter onto a well-buttered baking sheet. Leave ample room between the mounds for them to spread into rounds about 1½ to 2 inches [4 to 5 cm.] across. Bake in a preheated 400° F. [200° C.] oven for 10 minutes, until light golden brown. While they are still hot remove one round at a time from the sheets and shape it quickly into a horn by pressing it around a conical metal mold. Pipe, bake and shape the remaining horns—using one quarter of the batter for each batch.

WILLIAM BARKER
THE MODERN PÂTISSIER: A COMPLETE GUIDE TO PASTRY COOKERY

Walnut Shortbread

To make 18		
2 cups	flour	½ liter
4 tbsp.	cornstarch	60 ml.
about ½ cup	superfine sugar	about ¼ liter
	vanilla extract	
½ lb.	butter, cut into small pieces	¼ kg.
⅓ cup	walnuts, chopped	75 ml.

Place the flour, cornstarch and ⅓ cup [75 ml.] of the superfine sugar in a bowl. Add a few drops of vanilla extract and the butter. Crumble the butter with your fingers and gradu-

ally work all of the ingredients into one piece. Toward the end of this process, add the chopped walnuts.

Turn the mixture onto a floured board and shape it into three round cakes, each about 7 inches [18 cm.] in diameter. Place the cakes in buttered layer-cake pans. Cut each cake into six triangular pieces and, using a fork, prick the cakes all over. Bake in a preheated 350° F. [180° C.] oven for 20 minutes, or until the cakes just begin to brown. Dust them with superfine sugar while they are still hot and let the cakes cool in their baking pans.

MARGARET BATES
TALKING ABOUT CAKES WITH AN IRISH AND SCOTTISH ACCENT

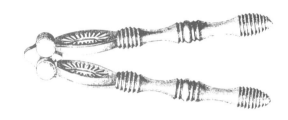

Shortbread

Rice flour is obtainable at health-food stores.

If the dough becomes rather soft in the making, it will be well to allow the shortbread to stand until quite cool before baking, otherwise it is apt to lose its form.

A strip of candied peel may be put on the top, if wished, or any other decoration that is desired.

To make 1		
1 cup	all-purpose flour	¼ liter
⅓ cup	rice flour	75 ml.
¼ cup	superfine sugar	50 ml.
8 tbsp.	butter, cut into pieces	120 ml.
½ tsp.	vanilla or almond extract	2 ml.

Sift all the dry ingredients into a bowl and rub in the butter. Add the flavoring and then knead all into one lump without using any liquid. Turn out the dough onto a board sprinkled with rice flour and form it into a smooth round, 8 inches [20 cm.] in diameter. If a shortbread mold is obtainable, shape the cake in that; if not, pinch around the edges with your fingers or mark the edges with a knife. Then place the shortbread on a buttered baking sheet and prick it all over with a fork. Bake in a preheated 350° F. [180° C.] oven for about 20 minutes, or until the shortbread is pale golden and feels firm to the touch. Allow it to cool slightly before removing it from the baking sheet.

FLORENCE B. JACK
COOKERY FOR EVERY HOUSEHOLD

Dorset Shortbread

To make about 35

3 cups	flour	¾ liter
½ cup	confectioners' sugar, sifted	125 ml.
½ lb.	butter, cut into pieces	¼ kg.
¼ cup	Demerara or turbinado sugar	50 ml.

Mix together all of the ingredients except the Demerara sugar. With your hands, roll the mixture into a cylinder about 2 inches [5 cm.] in diameter. Roll the cylinder in Demerara sugar to coat it thinly. Cut ¼-inch [6-mm.] slices and place them on a baking sheet. Bake the cookies in a preheated 350° F. [180° C.] oven for 10 to 15 minutes, or until they are pale golden brown.

DORSET FEDERATION OF WOMEN'S INSTITUTES
WHAT'S COOKING IN DORSET

Candlemas Cookies from St. Victor

Navettes de St. Victor

These boat-shaped cookies—thought to represent the boat in which Mary Magdalene sailed from Jerusalem to Provence in the First Century A.D.—are traditionally eaten in Marseilles on February 2, the celebration of Candlemas Day. The Abbey of St. Victor is a Marseilles church, outside of which these cookies are sold.

To make about 30

6 cups	flour	1½ liters
5 tbsp.	butter, cut into pieces and softened	75 ml.
1⅔ cups	superfine sugar	400 ml.
2 tsp.	grated lemon peel	10 ml.
2 tbsp.	orange-flower water	30 ml.
2	eggs	2
1 cup	water	¼ liter

Put the flour on a work surface, make a well in the center, and in the well put the butter, sugar, lemon peel, orange-flower water, eggs and water. Knead everything together to form a smooth dough.

Flour the work surface, divide the dough into 10 pieces and roll each piece into a cylinder about ½ inch [1 cm.] in diameter. Cut each cylinder into three pieces and curve each piece into a boat shape, pointed at both ends. Place the cookies on a buttered baking sheet and allow them to rest for two hours.

Bake in a preheated 400° F. [200° C.] oven for 15 minutes. These cookies keep for a long time in an airtight container.

FLORENCE DE ANDREIS
LA CUISINE PROVENÇALE D'AUJOURD'HUI

Sighs from Cudillero

Suspiros de Cudillero

Suspiro, or "sigh," is the generic name for this kind of cookie, which is as light as a sigh. Cudillero is a town in northwestern Spain.

To make about 50

½ lb.	butter, softened	¼ kg.
¾ cup	sugar	175 ml.
2	egg whites	2
4 cups	flour	1 liter

Put the butter in a bowl and add the sugar, little by little, beating until the mixture is creamy. Then add the egg whites and stir in the flour, a little at a time, mixing all the ingredients thoroughly. Shape the mixture into balls about the size of walnuts. Flatten them a little and place them on lightly buttered baking sheets. Bake in a preheated 325° F. [160° C.] oven for about 12 minutes or until golden. Remove the cookies from the oven and sprinkle them with sugar.

MARIA LUISA GARCÍA
EL ARTE DE COCINAR

Gipsy Creams

The oatmeal called for in this recipe is finely ground oat kernels—not the familiar rolled oats. It is obtainable at health-food stores. Golden syrup is a mild molasses syrup imported from England and sold at some specialty food stores.

To make about 20

4 tbsp.	butter, softened	60 ml.
4 tbsp.	lard, softened	60 ml.
¼ cup	sugar	50 ml.
1 cup	flour	¼ liter
1 tsp.	baking soda	5 ml.
½ cup	oatmeal	125 ml.
3 tbsp.	water	45 ml.
1 tsp.	golden syrup or jam	5 ml.
½ cup	uncooked butter icing (recipe, page 164), flavored with chocolate	125 ml.

Cream the butter and lard with the sugar until fluffy; mix in the flour, baking soda and oats, and gather the mixture into a stiff dough with the water and syrup or jam. Knead the dough lightly and shape it into small balls; set the balls on buttered baking sheets, allowing room for spreading, and bake in a preheated 350° F. [180° C.] oven for 30 minutes, or until the cookies are golden and firm to the touch. When cold, sandwich the cookies in pairs with the icing.

LIZZIE BOYD (EDITOR)
BRITISH COOKERY

Hussar's Kisses

Huszárcsók

To make 20 to 30

12 tbsp.	butter, softened	180 ml.
½ cup	sugar	125 ml.
1½ cups	flour	375 ml.
2 tsp.	grated lemon peel	10 ml.
1	egg, the yolk separated from the white, and the white lightly beaten	1
½ cup	almonds, blanched, peeled and finely chopped	125 ml.
½ cup	thick jam	125 ml.

Blend the butter and sugar together, then beat in the flour, lemon peel and finally the egg yolk. Roll the dough into small balls. Dip each ball in the egg white and roll it in the chopped almonds. Place the balls on a buttered baking sheet. Make a depression in each ball and bake in a preheated 375° F. [190° C.] oven until lightly browned—12 to 15 minutes. Fill the depressions in the cookies with the jam.

INGE KRAMARZ
THE BALKAN COOKBOOK

Lady's Kisses

Baci di Dama

You can substitute Marsala or Lachryma Christi wine for the liqueur. The cookies may be sandwiched with jam instead of chocolate.

To make about 35

7 oz.	almonds, blanched and peeled (about 1¾ cups [425 ml.])	200 g.
1¾ cups	flour	425 ml.
1 cup	sugar	¼ liter
14 tbsp.	butter, melted	210 ml.
2 tbsp.	semisweet liqueur such as amaretto or port	30 ml.
2 oz.	semisweet baking chocolate, melted	60 g.

Crush the almonds fine in a mortar. Mix the almonds with the flour and sugar, and make a well in the center. Pour the butter and the liqueur into the well, and mix the ingredients to form a smooth dough. Shape the dough into balls the size of walnuts, place them on buttered baking sheets and flatten them with your fingers. Bake in a preheated 425° F. [220° C.] oven for 15 minutes, or until the cookies are delicately browned. When the cookies are cool, make "kisses" by joining them together in pairs with the melted chocolate.

LAURA GRAS PORTINARI
CUCINA E VINI DEL PIEMONTE E DELLA VALLE D'AOSTA

Best Peanut Butter Cookies

To make 60

½ cup	firmly packed dark brown sugar	125 ml.
½ cup	granulated sugar	125 ml.
8 tbsp.	butter, softened	120 ml.
1 cup	peanut butter	¼ liter
1	egg	1
1½ cups	sifted flour	375 ml.
½ tsp.	salt	2 ml.
½ tsp.	baking soda	2 ml.
½ tsp.	vanilla extract	2 ml.

Cream the brown sugar, granulated sugar and butter together. Beat in the peanut butter, then add the egg. Combine the flour, salt and soda, sift them into the peanut-butter mixture, then blend the dough well. Add the vanilla extract. Roll the dough into small balls and place them about 2 inches [5 cm.] apart on buttered baking sheets. Flatten the balls with a fork. Bake the cookies in a preheated 350° F. [180° C.] oven for 12 to 15 minutes, or until they are slightly brown on the edges.

THE JUNIOR CHARITY LEAGUE OF MONROE, LOUISIANA
THE COTTON COUNTRY COLLECTION

Little Horns

Cachitos

Brazil nuts and a few drops of almond extract may be used instead of almonds.

To make about 25

1 lb.	almonds, blanched, peeled and ground (about 4 cups [1 liter])	½ kg.
1¾ cups	confectioners' sugar, sifted	425 ml.
2	egg whites	2
1 tbsp.	apricot jam	15 ml.
½ tsp.	vanilla extract	2 ml.
	salt	
¼ cup	walnuts, ground	50 ml.

Mix together all of the ingredients, except for 2 teaspoons [10 ml.] of the egg whites and all of the walnuts. Working on a floured board, form the mixture into balls 1½ inches [4 cm.] in diameter, roll them into cigar shapes, then curve them to make horns. Brush the tops with the reserved whites and sprinkle them with the walnuts. Arrange the cookies on a large buttered and floured baking sheet. Bake in a preheated 350° F. [180° C.] oven for 18 minutes, until light brown.

VIOLETA AUTUMN
A RUSSIAN JEW COOKS IN PERÚ

Brandy Cookie Twists

Koulourakia

To make about 150

1 lb.	butter, softened	½ kg.
2 cups	sugar	½ liter
5 tsp.	baking powder	25 ml.
2 tsp.	baking soda	10 ml.
2 tbsp.	brandy	30 ml.
about 20 cups	flour	about 5 liters
12	eggs, beaten	12
2	egg yolks, beaten	2

Cream the butter and sugar together until pale and fluffy; add the baking powder and baking soda to the creamed mixture; add the brandy. Add the flour alternately with the eggs; use as much flour as needed to make a pliable dough.

To shape each cookie, break off a ball of dough about the size of a walnut; roll it into a 4-inch [10-cm.] cylinder, bend the cylinder in half, and wrap the halves around each other to form a braid or twist. Place the cookies on ungreased baking sheets. Brush the tops of the cookies with the egg yolks and bake in a preheated 425° F. [220° C.] oven for 10 to 12 minutes, or until they are lightly browned and firm.

THE HELLENIC WOMAN'S CLUB
COME COOK WITH US: A TREASURY OF GREEK COOKING

Almond Crescents from Provence

Croissants de Provence

For a finer-textured cookie, substitute 1⅓ cups [325 ml.] of confectioners' sugar for the granulated sugar.

To make about 25

½ lb.	almonds, blanched and peeled, 6 oz. [175 g.] ground (about 1½ cups [375 ml.], the rest chopped or slivered	¼ kg.
¾ cup	sugar	175 ml.
1 tbsp.	apricot jam, sieved	15 ml.
	vanilla extract	
2	egg whites, lightly beaten	2
3 tbsp.	milk	45 ml.

In a bowl, mix together the ground almonds and ⅔ cup [150 ml.] of the sugar. Stir in the jam and a drop or two of vanilla extract. Little by little, incorporate two thirds of the egg white and stir to form a fairly thick dough that can be worked by hand.

On a floured work surface, divide the dough into pieces the size of walnuts and roll each piece into a cylinder about 3

inches [8 cm.] long. Brush the surface of each cookie with the remaining egg white, then roll it in the chopped or slivered almonds. Curving the ends to form crescents, place the cookies on a large buttered baking sheet. Bake the crescents in a preheated 375° F. [190° C.] oven for 10 to 12 minutes, or until they are pale golden.

Meanwhile, dissolve the remaining sugar in the milk. When the crescents are baked, transfer them to wire racks and paint them with the sugared milk to give them a shiny surface. Let them cool before serving them.

DOMINIQUE WEBER
LES BONNES RECETTES DES PROVINCES DE FRANCE

Almond Cookies

Fregolata

To make about 35

9 oz.	almonds, blanched and peeled (about 2¼ cups [550 ml.])	275 g.
1½ cups	sugar	375 ml.
2½ cups	flour	625 ml.
⅛ tsp.	salt	½ ml.
2 tsp.	grated lemon peel	10 ml.
2	eggs, lightly beaten	2
4 tbsp.	butter, diced and softened	60 ml.
2 tbsp.	light or heavy cream	30 ml.

Chop the almonds coarse in a blender, adding sugar as you go along. This is best done by dividing the almonds into eight batches and chopping each batch with 1 tablespoon [15 ml.] of sugar—8 tablespoons [120 ml.] in all. In a bowl, combine the almonds, flour, salt and lemon peel, and mix well. Stir in the remaining sugar, the eggs and butter. Mix with a spoon, then knead the dough with your hands, adding 1 tablespoon of cream at a time to make the dough easy to handle.

Break off pieces of dough and roll them with your hands into cylinders ¾ inch [2 cm.] in diameter. Cut these cylinders into pieces 1½ inches [4 cm.] long. Place the cookies on buttered and floured baking sheets. Bake in a preheated 350° F. [180° C.] oven for 20 to 25 minutes, or until barely golden. Do not overbake the cookies or they will be hard.

NIKA HAZELTON
THE REGIONAL ITALIAN KITCHEN

Almond Bites

Ossa da Mordere

To make 50 to 60

7 oz.	almonds, blanched and peeled (about 1¾ cups [375 ml.])	200 g.
6	egg whites	6
1 cup	superfine sugar	¼ liter
6 cups	flour	1½ liters
1 tsp.	grated lemon peel	5 ml.

Using a mortar and pestle, crush 1 cup [¼ liter] of the almonds to a fine powder. Cut the remaining almonds into halves and set them aside.

In a bowl, beat the egg whites and sugar until very firm; add the flour, crushed almonds and grated lemon peel. Work the ingredients together to form a smooth dough. Divide the dough into balls about 1 inch [2½ cm.] in diameter, flatten the balls, put half an almond on top of each one and place them on buttered baking sheets.

Bake in a preheated 350° F. [180° C.] oven until the cookies start to turn brown—about 20 minutes. Let the cookies cool before lifting them with a spatula.

LAURA GRAS PORTINARI
CUCINA E VINI DEL PIEMONTE E DELLA VALLE D'AOSTA

Almond-Coconut Cookies

Panellets

The technique of opening and grating a coconut is explained in the editor's note for Coconut Shortbread, page 113.

To make about 70

2 lb.	almonds, blanched, peeled and ground (about 8 cups [2 liters])	1 kg.
3	small potatoes, boiled, peeled and mashed (about 1 cup [¼ liter])	3
3 cups	granulated sugar	¾ liter
2 tbsp.	vanilla sugar	30 ml.
1⅓ cups	freshly grated coconut	325 ml.
¼ cup	anis or other anise-flavored liqueur	50 ml.
¼ cup	brandy	50 ml.
	orange or lemon extract	
½ lb.	pine nuts or whole almonds (about 2 cups [½ liter])	¼ kg.

Mix the ground almonds with the mashed potatoes, adding the granulated sugar and vanilla sugar. Divide the dough into two parts. To one part add the grated coconut and the liqueur. Add the brandy and three drops of the orange or lemon extract to the other half. Form the dough into little cookies about 1½ inches [4 cm.] across. Decorate each cookie by covering the top with pine nuts or sticking two whole almonds into the top. Place the cookies on buttered baking sheets. Bake in a preheated 400° F. [200° C.] oven for about six minutes, or until they are very lightly browned.

IRVING DAVIS
A CATALAN COOKERY BOOK

Moroccan Almond Cookies

Ghoriba aux Amandes

To make 70 to 90

3 lb.	almonds, blanched and peeled (about 12 cups [3 liters])	1½ kg.
5	eggs	5
7 cups	confectioners' sugar, sifted	1¾ liters
2 tsp.	grated lemon peel	10 ml.
1½ tbsp.	vanilla sugar	22½ ml.
1 tbsp.	baking powder	15 ml.

Pass the blanched almonds twice through the fine disk of a food grinder or pulverize them—a small batch at a time—in a food processor.

Beat the eggs with 6 cups [1½ liters] of the confectioners' sugar until the mixture turns pale. Stir in the lemon peel and vanilla sugar. Add this mixture to the almonds. Mix well and add the baking powder. The resulting dough should be firm but still malleable.

Grease your hands lightly with butter. Take a small piece of dough and shape it into a ball slightly bigger than a walnut. Flatten the ball and dip one side of it in the remaining confectioners' sugar. Place it on a lightly buttered baking sheet, with the sugared side facing upward. Repeat, placing the cookies well apart, until all of the dough has been used up. Bake the cookies in a preheated 350° F. [180° C.] oven for 15 to 20 minutes, or until delicately browned.

AHMED LAASRI
240 RECETTES DE CUISINE MAROCAINE

Lemon Praline Cookies

To make about 65

12 tbsp.	butter, softened	180 ml.
2 cups	firmly packed light brown sugar	½ liter
2	eggs, beaten	2
2 tsp.	grated lemon peel	10 ml.
1 tbsp.	fresh lemon juice	15 ml.
2 cups	flour	½ liter
1 cup	pecans, chopped	¼ liter

Cream the butter. Add the sugar, and cream thoroughly. Add the eggs, lemon peel and lemon juice. Blend well. Add the flour and nuts. Mix well. Shape into balls about 1 inch [2½ cm.] in diameter, place the balls on buttered baking sheets and flatten them to a thickness of ⅛ inch [3 mm.]. Bake in a preheated 375° F. [190° C.] oven for eight to 10 minutes, or until nicely browned.

WILLIAM I. KAUFMAN AND SISTER MARY URSULA COOPER, O.P.
THE ART OF CREOLE COOKERY

Linzer Cookies

To make about 50

8 tbsp.	butter, softened	120 ml.
½ cup	sugar	125 ml.
1	egg yolk	1
1 tsp.	grated lemon peel	5 ml.
1 tbsp.	fresh lemon juice	15 ml.
1 tsp.	grated unsweetened baking chocolate	5 ml.
1 cup	flour	¼ liter
½ cup	hazelnuts, blanched, peeled and ground	125 ml.
½ cup	almonds, ground	125 ml.
1 tsp.	ground cinnamon	5 ml.
¼ tsp.	ground cloves	1 ml.
1 cup	red raspberry jam	¼ liter

Cream the butter and sugar well. Beat in the egg yolk, lemon peel and juice, and add the chocolate. Mix together the flour, ground nuts and spices. Add them to the butter mixture and stir gently. Wrap and refrigerate for at least one hour, or until the dough is firm. Flouring your hands, break off small pieces of the dough and roll them into 1-inch [2½-cm.] balls. Place the balls on lightly buttered baking sheets—spacing them about 2 inches [5 cm.] apart. With your finger, make a shallow indentation in each ball. Bake the cookies in a preheated 375° F. [190° C.] oven for 10 to 12 minutes, or until the cookies are lightly browned on the bottom and slightly firm to the touch. Cool the cookies, then fill the indentations with a dab of raspberry jam.

JOYCE PIOTROWSKI
THE CHRISTMAS COOKIE COLLECTION

Bride's Cookies

Pastelitos de Boda

These are the best known of all polvorones, or Mexican sugar cookies, but there are many variations. Other kinds of nuts can be used—almonds, hazelnuts or peanuts—or the nuts may be replaced by an extra ½ cup [125 ml.] of flour, or a mixture of ¼ cup [50 ml.] of flour and 1 teaspoon [5 ml.] of ground cinnamon. The cinnamon cookies are rolled twice in

2 cups [½ liter] of confectioners' sugar sifted together with 2 teaspoons [10 ml.] of ground cinnamon—once while the cookies are warm from the oven and again when they are cold.

To make about 25

2 cups	flour	½ liter
¾ cup	sifted confectioners' sugar	175 ml.
1 cup	pecans, finely chopped	¼ liter
	salt	
1 tsp.	vanilla extract	5 ml.
½ lb.	butter, softened	¼ kg.

Mix together the flour, ½ cup [125 ml.] of the sugar, the nuts and a pinch of salt. Stir in the vanilla extract. Work the butter into the mixture until it forms a cohesive ball, then shape the dough into small patties. Lightly oil a large baking sheet and place the patties on it. Bake them in a preheated 350° F. [180° C.] oven for 30 minutes, or until the patties are delicately brown.

Lift the cookies off the baking sheet and cool them slightly on a wire rack. Dust them thickly with the remaining confectioners' sugar.

ELISABETH LAMBERT ORTIZ
THE COMPLETE BOOK OF MEXICAN COOKING

Brazil-Nut Crisps

To make about 40

2	eggs	2
2¼ cups	firmly packed light brown sugar	550 ml.
2 cups	cake flour	½ liter
¼ tsp.	salt	1 ml.
½ tsp.	baking powder	2 ml.
6 oz.	Brazil nuts, coarsely chopped (about 1½ cups [375 ml.])	175 g.
1 tsp.	vanilla extract	5 ml.

Beat the eggs until very light. Add the sugar gradually, beating all the time. Sift the flour with the salt and baking powder. Add the nuts, flour and vanilla extract to the egg mixture. Chill for several hours. Cut off chunks of dough and roll them between your hands into ½-inch [1-cm.] cylinders about 2 inches [5 cm.] long. If the dough sticks to your hands, keep your hands wet with cold water or dry with confectioners' sugar. The cold water seems to work best for those with moist hands, the confectioners' sugar for those with dry hands. Place the cookies on buttered baking sheets (not too close together since they will spread) and bake them in a preheated 350° F. [180° C.] oven for about 15 minutes, or until well browned. They keep well.

VIRGINIA PASLEY
THE CHRISTMAS COOKIE BOOK

Chocolate Almond Wreaths

Obwarzanki Czekoladowe

To make 20

2	egg whites	2
3 oz.	semisweet baking chocolate, grated	90 g.
1¼ cups	almonds, ground	300 ml.
⅔ cup	superfine sugar	150 ml.
⅓ cup	flour	75 ml.
1 cup	confectioners' sugar glaze (recipe, page 164)	¼ liter

Make a dough by adding the egg whites to the chocolate, almonds, sugar and flour. Divide the dough into 20 pieces. On a pastry board, roll each piece under the palms of your hands to form a rope and join the ends to shape the rope into a wreath 2½ inches [6 cm.] in diameter. Place the wreaths on a buttered baking sheet and bake in a preheated 275° F. [140° C.] oven for about 30 minutes, or until firm. When cool, coat the wreaths with the glaze.

MARJA DISSLOWA
JAK GOTOWAĆ

Chocolate Confectioners' Sugar Cookies

Kourambiethes me Socolata

To toast the nuts, spread them on a baking sheet and bake in a preheated 350° F. [180° C.] oven for 10 minutes, turning them over frequently so that they will toast evenly.

To make about 50

1 lb.	unsalted butter, softened	½ kg.
5 cups	confectioners' sugar	1¼ liters
1	egg yolk	1
2 tbsp.	brandy	30 ml.
1 tsp.	ground cloves	5 ml.
1 tsp.	grated nutmeg	5 ml.
1 oz.	milk chocolate, chilled and grated	30 g.
2 tbsp.	cocoa powder	30 ml.
¾ cup	almonds, toasted and chopped	175 ml.
5 to 6 cups	sifted flour	1¼ to 1½ liters

Beat the butter until fluffy. Add 4 cups [1 liter] of the confectioners' sugar and cream the mixture well. Beat in the

egg yolk. Add the brandy, cloves, nutmeg, grated chocolate, cocoa powder and almonds, mixing well. Gradually add enough flour to produce a soft dough. Shape the dough into crescents or bars about 2½ inches [6 cm.] long. Place on ungreased baking sheets and bake the cookies in a preheated 350° F. [180° C.] oven for about 10 minutes, or until they are lightly browned. While still hot, sprinkle the cookies with the remaining confectioners' sugar.

THE HELLENIC WOMAN'S CLUB
COME COOK WITH US: A TREASURY OF GREEK COOKING

Easter Cookies

Ma'moul

These are the Easter speciality of Lebanon. The flour may be replaced by semolina, or half of each may be used.

To make about 15

½ lb.	butter, melted and cooled	¼ kg.
4 cups	flour	1 liter
3 tbsp.	orange-flower water	45 ml.
3 tbsp.	rose water	45 ml.
2 to 4 tbsp.	water (optional)	30 to 60 ml.
	confectioners' sugar	
Nut filling		
½ lb.	walnuts, almonds or pistachios, chopped (about 2 cups [½ liter])	¼ kg.
1 cup	superfine sugar	¼ liter
3 tbsp.	orange-flower or rose water	45 ml.

Add the melted butter to the flour with the orange-flower water and the rose water. Then add a little water, if necessary, to make a firm but pliable dough. Set the dough aside to rest for two hours.

To make the filling, mix the nuts with the superfine sugar and orange-flower or rose water.

Break off pieces of dough the size of eggs, and shape each piece into a hollow cone. Place a bit of the filling in each cone, close the cone and flatten it. Using a fork, score the sides of the cone with a crisscross pattern. Place the cones on a lightly oiled baking sheet and bake them in a preheated 350° F. [180° C.] oven for 20 minutes, or until the cookies are crisp and delicately browned. Sprinkle the warm cookies with confectioners' sugar.

FAYEZ AOUN
280 RECETTES DE CUISINE FAMILIALE LIBANAISE

Venetian "Bean" Cookies

Fave alla Veneziana

Grappa is a pungent brandy made in Italy distilled from the pulp that remains after the grapes have been pressed and the juice squeezed out.

These cookies are traditionally sold in the patisseries of Venice during November. In Trieste, similar cookies are made from the same paste but are shaped like hazelnuts.

To make about 50

10 oz.	pine nuts (about 2½ cups [625 ml.])	300 g.
1 cup	superfine sugar	¼ liter
5	egg yolks	5
⅓ cup	grappa or Cognac	75 ml.
1 oz.	semisweet baking chocolate, finely grated	30 g.
½ tsp.	vanilla extract	2 ml.

Pound the nuts to a paste with the sugar. Add the egg yolks, grappa or Cognac, chocolate and vanilla extract. Divide the paste into small pieces and mold them into the shape of broad beans, each about 1 inch [2½ cm.] in diameter. Place the cookies on buttered and floured baking sheets and bake them in a preheated 350° F. [180° C.] oven for 15 minutes, or until they just begin to brown.

RANIERI DA MOSTO
IL VENETO IN CUCINA

Walnut Cigars

Bourak'r-râna

To make about 40

6 cups	flour	1½ liters
1 tbsp.	granulated sugar	15 ml.
	salt	
1 lb.	butter, melted and cooled	½ kg.
	water (optional)	
	Walnut paste	
1 lb.	walnuts, finely chopped (about 4 cups [1 liter])	½ kg.
2 cups	superfine sugar	½ liter
about 1 cup	orange-flower water	about ¼ liter

To prepare the dough, sift the flour onto a board and make a well in the center. Sprinkle in the sugar and a pinch of salt, and then pour in the melted butter. Mix and knead into a smooth dough—adding water, a few drops at a time, if necessary. Shape the dough into a ball, cover it and set it aside.

To prepare the walnut paste, stir together the walnuts and sugar. Add just enough orange-flower water to make the paste cohere. Divide the paste into four or five pieces and roll each piece into a rope about ½ inch [1 cm.] in diameter.

Roll the dough into a 16-inch [40-cm.] square about ⅛ inch [3 mm.] thick. Cut it into strips 4 inches [10 cm.] long and 1½ inches [4 cm.] wide. Lay a 3-inch [8-cm.] rope of walnut paste along the length of each strip. Roll the dough over on itself to form a cigar-shaped roll enclosing the paste. Seal the ends of the cigar by flattening them with your finger and cutting off the excess dough close to the paste with a pastry wheel or knife.

Place the cigars on oiled baking sheets and bake them in a preheated 325° F. [160° C.] oven for about 25 minutes, or until they begin to turn golden brown.

FATIMA-ZOHRA BOUAYED
LA CUISINE ALGÉRIENNE

Wine Sipping Cookies

Biscottini alla Romagnola

These cookies keep well in an airtight container.

To make about 65

2 cups	unbleached all-purpose flour	½ liter
4 cups	fine corn flour	1 liter
¾ tsp.	salt	4 ml.
¾ lb.	unsalted butter, melted and cooled	350 g.
¾ cup	sugar	175 ml.
1 tsp.	vanilla extract	5 ml.
1 cup	milk, beaten with 1 egg	¼ liter
¼ cup	seedless golden raisins, soaked in warm water for 15 minutes, drained and dried	50 ml.
⅓ cup	pine nuts or slivered almonds	75 ml.

Sift the two flours together with the salt onto a pastry board or other smooth work surface. Make a well in the center of the flours, and pour in the melted butter, sugar and vanilla extract. Work the ingredients together with your fingers, gradually adding the milk mixture. When the dough is smooth, work in the raisins and pine nuts or almonds.

Break off small pieces of dough and roll them into balls about the size of cherry tomatoes. Place the balls on buttered baking sheets and press each one down to flatten it slightly.

Bake in a preheated 400° F. [200° C.] oven for about 20 minutes, or until the color of light toast.

MARGARET AND G. FRANCO ROMAGNOLI
THE NEW ITALIAN COOKING

Peppernuts

Pfeffernüsse

To make about 50

2 tbsp.	butter, softened	30 ml.
1¼ cups	sifted confectioners' sugar	300 ml.
3	eggs, the yolks separated from the whites, the yolks well beaten, and the whites stiffly beaten	3
1 tsp.	grated lemon peel	5 ml.
2 cups	sifted flour	½ liter
½ tsp.	baking soda	2 ml.
½ tsp.	salt	2 ml.
2 tsp.	ground cinnamon	10 ml.
2 tsp.	ground cardamom	10 ml.
½ tsp.	ground cloves	2 ml.
½ tsp.	grated nutmeg	2 ml.
⅛ tsp.	ground black pepper	½ ml.
½ lb.	candied citron, finely chopped (about 2 cups [½ liter])	¼ kg.
½ tsp.	anise seeds	2 ml.
	confectioners' sugar glaze (recipe, page 164), made with milk instead of water	

Cream the butter. Add the sugar, then the egg yolks and lemon peel. Sift the dry ingredients together three times and mix them with the citron and anise seeds. Add the flour mixture to the creamed ingredients. Fold in the egg whites. Refrigerate the dough for one hour. Form the dough into small balls, place them on parchment or wax paper and let them stand at room temperature overnight.

Mix together the glaze ingredients and brush the top and sides of the balls with the glaze. Place the balls on buttered baking sheets. Bake in a preheated 375° F. [190° C.] oven for 15 minutes, or until firm and delicately browned.

ANNETTE LASLETT ROSS AND JEAN ADAMS DISNEY
THE ART OF MAKING GOOD COOKIES PLAIN AND FANCY

Hunting Nuts

The original version of this recipe calls for treacle, a dark, heavy syrup produced from molasses; it is rarely obtainable in America. Molasses makes a suitable substitute.

To make 50 to 60

1 cup	molasses	¼ kg.
1⅓ cups	firmly packed light brown sugar	325 ml.
12 tbsp.	butter	180 ml.
4 cups	flour	1 liter
2 tsp.	grated fresh ginger	10 ml.

Melt the molasses, brown sugar and butter in a saucepan and allow the mixture to cool. Add the flour and ginger. Mix all the ingredients together well. Roll small pieces of the dough into balls the size of walnuts. Bake them on ungreased baking sheets in a preheated 325° F. [160° C.] oven for 20 minutes, or until the cookies are dry to the touch.

MARY JEWRY (EDITOR)
WARNE'S MODEL COOKERY

Easter Milk Cookies

Kâk bi Halîb

The mahlab called for in this recipe is a Middle Eastern flavoring made from the kernels of black cherries. It is obtainable from stores specializing in Middle Eastern foods. Almond extract makes a suitable substitute.

These cookies are traditionally offered to visitors during the Easter holiday.

To make about 25

4 cups	flour	1 liter
¼ tsp.	ground *mahlab*	1 ml.
¼ tsp.	dried marjoram leaves	1 ml.
¼ tsp.	ground anise	1 ml.
¼ oz.	package active dry yeast	7½ g.
2 tbsp.	olive oil	30 ml.
7 tbsp.	butter, melted	105 ml.
1 cup	sugar	¼ liter
about ¾ cup	tepid milk	about 175 ml.

Make a well in the flour and add the *mahlab*, marjoram and anise, the yeast and, a little at a time, the olive oil and butter. Dissolve the sugar in the milk and add to the mixture. Work the dough well with your finger tips, as you would bread dough. Let the dough rest for about two hours.

Shape the dough into flat cookies about 3 inches [8 cm.] in diameter and ½ to ¾ inch [1 to 1½ cm.] thick. (You can stamp a design on them with a wooden mold.) The cookies may also be made in bracelet shapes the thickness of a finger. Place in a preheated 400° F. [200° C.] oven, then reduce the heat to 350° F. [180° C.] and bake for 15 minutes, or until the cookies are nicely browned.

FAYEZ AOUN
280 RECETTES DE CUISINE FAMILIALE LIBANAISE

Venetian Honey Cookies

Fenekia or Melomakarona

These marvelous cookies fragrant with spices were brought to Greece by Venetian bakers when Venice ruled the western Greek islands from the 14th to the 17th Centuries.

To make about 50

1	egg yolk	1
¼ cup	strained fresh orange juice	50 ml.
2 tbsp.	whiskey	30 ml.
½ cup	sugar	125 ml.
½ tsp.	grated orange peel	2 ml.
20 tbsp.	butter, melted and cooled, or 1¼ cups [300 ml.] oil	300 ml.
3½ cups	flour, or a mixture of 1½ cups [375 ml.] semolina and 1½ cups flour	875 ml.
2 tsp.	baking powder	10 ml.
¼ tsp.	baking soda	1 ml.
⅛ tsp.	salt	½ ml.
½ tsp.	ground cloves	2 ml.
1 tsp.	ground cinnamon	5 ml.
½ cup	chopped walnuts or almonds (optional)	125 ml.
½ cup	ground walnuts or almonds	125 ml.
Honey coating		
2 cups	honey	½ liter
1 cup	water	¼ liter

In a bowl, combine the egg yolk, orange juice, whiskey, sugar and orange peel, and blend together. Gradually add the but-

ter or oil and continue blending until the mixture is as thick as mayonnaise. Sift the flour or semolina and flour with the baking powder, baking soda, salt and spices. Mix the dry ingredients into the egg mixture, and knead the dough until smooth. It will be stiff.

Pick up a tablespoonful of dough in your hand and squeeze it slightly to form an egg shape. For a filled cookie, press a few pieces of the chopped nuts into the center of the dough before shaping it. Place the cookies on ungreased baking sheets and press the top of each one slightly with a fork to make a crisscross design. Bake in a preheated 350° F. [180° C.] oven for 20 minutes, or until lightly browned.

Bring the honey and water to a boil, then let it simmer gently. As soon as the cookies are baked, dip each one in this syrup for a few seconds and place it on a wire rack to drain. Sprinkle the cookies with the ground nuts and let them cool.

THERESA KARAS YIANILOS
THE COMPLETE GREEK COOKBOOK

Moroccan Sesame Seed Cookies

Ghoriba dial Jeljlane

To make about 40

2½ cups	sesame seeds	625 ml.
1¾ cups	flour	425 ml.
1¼ cups	superfine sugar	300 ml.
1 tbsp.	baking powder	15 ml.
2 tsp.	grated lemon peel	10 ml.
5	eggs	5
	olive oil	
	confectioners' sugar	

In a heavy skillet toast the sesame seeds over medium heat for two to three minutes—stirring them frequently so that they brown evenly. Remove the seeds and set them aside. Then sprinkle the flour into the skillet and brown it lightly. In a bowl, mix the sesame seeds and flour with the sugar, baking powder and grated lemon peel. Place the mixture on a work surface, form a well in the center and break the eggs into it. Blend the ingredients and knead them vigorously together to form a soft but cohesive dough.

Grease your hands with the oil, pick up a ball of dough the size of a walnut and flatten the ball by pressing it down in the confectioners' sugar. Continue in the same way until all of the dough is used up. Place the cookies—sugared sides facing upward—on lightly oiled baking sheets. Bake in a preheated 350° F. [180° C.] oven for about 20 minutes, or until the cookies are firm and lightly browned.

AHMED LAASRI
240 RECETTES DE CUISINE MAROCAINE

Pressed and Piped Cookies

Pressed Sour-Cream Cookies

To make about 50

2 cups	flour	½ liter
½ tsp.	baking powder	2 ml.
¼ tsp.	baking soda	1 ml.
¼ tsp.	grated nutmeg	1 ml.
8 tbsp.	butter, softened	120 ml.
1 cup	sugar	¼ liter
1	egg, lightly beaten	1
½ tsp.	lemon extract	2 ml.
⅓ cup	sour cream	75 ml.

Sift together the flour, baking powder, baking soda and nutmeg; set aside. Cream together the butter and sugar. Add the egg, lemon extract and sour cream. Gradually blend in the sifted ingredients. Press from a cookie press onto ungreased baking sheets. Bake in a preheated 375° F. [190° C.] oven for 10 to 15 minutes, or until the cookies are brown around the edges.

JUNIOR LEAGUE OF HOUSTON, INC.
HOUSTON JUNIOR LEAGUE COOKBOOK: FAVORITE RECIPES

Pressed Spice Cookies

Sprutad Krydda Kakor

To make about 60

½ lb.	butter, softened	¼ kg.
1½ cups	sugar	375 ml.
1 tbsp.	molasses	15 ml.
1	egg, beaten	1
2½ cups	flour	625 ml.
1 tsp.	baking soda	5 ml.
1 tsp.	ground cinnamon	5 ml.
1 tsp.	ground ginger	5 ml.
1 tsp.	ground cloves	5 ml.

Cream the butter; add the sugar, molasses and beaten egg. Sift together the flour, baking soda, cinnamon, ginger and cloves, and add to the creamed mixture. Push the dough through a cookie press onto buttered baking sheets and bake in a preheated 375° F. [190° C.] oven for about 10 minutes, or until firm and golden brown.

ALICE B. JOHNSON
THE COMPLETE SCANDINAVIAN COOKBOOK

Cream-Cheese Press Cookies

To make about 60

2½ cups	sifted flour	625 ml.
¼ tsp.	salt	1 ml.
1 cup	butter, softened	¼ liter
4 oz.	cream cheese, softened	125 g.
1 cup	sugar	¼ liter
1	large egg yolk	1
2 tsp.	grated lemon peel	10 ml.
1 tsp.	fresh lemon juice	5 ml.

Sift the flour with the salt. Cream the butter with the cheese until thoroughly blended. Add the sugar, egg yolk, lemon peel and lemon juice. Beat until light and fluffy. Blend in the flour mixture. Press the dough through a cookie press fitted with any desired shaping disk onto ungreased baking sheets. Bake the cookies in a preheated 350° F. [180° C.] oven for about 10 to 12 minutes, or until delicately browned.

DOLORES CASELLA
A WORLD OF BAKING

Spritz Cookies, Sweet Thumbs and Sand Rosettes

Sprits, Zoete Duimpjes, Zandrozetten

The technique of using a cookie press to make spritz cookies is shown on page 23.

To make about 35

8 tbsp.	butter, softened	120 ml.
½ cup	firmly packed light brown sugar	125 ml.
1	vanilla bean, seeds removed and pod reserved for another use, or 2 tsp. [10 ml.] grated lemon peel	1
½ tsp.	salt	2 ml.
1	egg white	1
1 cup	flour	¼ liter
1 tsp.	baking powder	5 ml.

Cream the butter with the sugar, vanilla seeds or grated lemon peel, and salt. Add the egg white, beat until smooth and then add the flour and baking powder. Put the dough into a cookie press or pastry bag.

Press the dough onto buttered baking sheets in straight or wavy ribbons, small rosettes or ribbed waves about 1½ inches [4 cm.] long; space the cookies about ¾ inch [2 cm.] apart. Bake in a preheated 325° F. [170° C.] oven for 20 to 25 minutes, or until firm and delicately browned. Remove the cookies immediately from the baking sheet (they soon become brittle) and cool them on a flat surface.

F. M. STOLL AND W. H. DE GROOT
HET HAAGSE KOOKBOEK

Chocolate Spritz

To make 50 to 60

½ lb.	butter, softened	¼ kg.
1 cup	sugar	¼ liter
1	egg, plus 1 egg yolk	1
2 oz.	unsweetened baking chocolate, melted	60 g.
1 tsp.	vanilla extract	5 ml.
2½ cups	flour	625 ml.
1 tsp.	baking powder	5 ml.
	chocolate sprinkles (optional)	

Chocolate icing

1 oz.	unsweetened baking chocolate, melted	30 g.
1½ cups	confectioners' sugar	375 ml.
1 tsp.	vanilla extract	5 ml.
about ½ cup	cream or milk	about 125 ml.

Beat the butter and sugar together until creamy. Mix in the egg, egg yolk, chocolate and vanilla. In a separate bowl, stir together the flour and baking powder. Add to the creamed mixture. Beat well. Spoon enough of the dough into a cookie press to fill it three quarters full. Press out the dough in any desired shape on ungreased baking sheets. Bake in a preheated 375° F. [190° C.] oven for six to eight minutes, or until just set. Remove the cookies from the oven and transfer them immediately to wire racks to cool.

While the cookies are cooling, make the chocolate icing. In a bowl, combine all the ingredients except the cream or milk, and mix them until smooth. Add enough cream or milk to make a thin icing. Drizzle a small amount over each cookie. Top each iced cookie with chocolate sprinkles, if desired.

LOU SEIBERT PAPPAS
COOKIES

Ladyfingers

Biscuits à la Cuiller

To make about 30

3	eggs, the yolks separated from the whites, and the whites stiffly beaten	3
⅓ cup	granulated sugar	75 ml.
	orange-flower water	
⅔ cup	flour	150 ml.
	sifted confectioners' sugar	

Whisk the egg yolks and granulated sugar until pale and fluffy. Add several drops of orange-flower water, then fold in the flour and egg whites. Using a pastry bag fitted with a ⅜-inch [9-mm.] plain tube, pipe 4-inch [10-cm.] strips of the mixture onto buttered baking sheets, leaving plenty of space for them to spread. Sprinkle the strips with confectioners' sugar and bake them in a preheated 325° F. [160° C.] oven for 20 minutes, or until they are very lightly colored and feel firm. Take care that the ladyfingers do not brown.

GINETTE MATHIOT
JE SAIS FAIRE LA PÂTISSERIE

Ladies' Wafers

Palets de Dame

To make the variation shown on page 31, press several dried currants or raisins onto each cookie before baking.

To make 80 to 90

½ lb.	butter, softened	¼ kg.
1¾ cups	confectioners' sugar	425 ml.
6	eggs	6
1 tsp.	vanilla extract	5 ml.
2½ cups	flour	625 ml.
1 cup	apricot jam, melted and sieved	¼ liter
	confectioners' sugar glaze (recipe, page 164), flavored with rum	

Cream the butter, add the sugar and beat until fluffy. Beat in the eggs one by one, then add the vanilla and finally the flour. Using a pastry bag, pipe small balls of the batter onto buttered and floured baking sheets—spacing the balls well apart. Bake in a preheated 350° F. [180° C.] oven for about 10 minutes, or until lightly browned.

Brush the cookies with the apricot jam, then coat them with the confectioners' sugar glaze. Return the cookies to the oven for about four minutes to set the glaze.

M. VITALIS
LES BASES DE LA PÂTISSERIE, CONFISERIE, GLACERIE

Vercelli Spice Sticks

Bicciolani di Vercelli

To make about 60

3½ cups	all-purpose flour	875 ml.
¾ cup	corn flour	175 ml.
2 tsp.	grated lemon peel	10 ml.
¾ cup	sugar	175 ml.
1 tsp.	ground coriander	5 ml.
½ tsp.	ground cinnamon	2 ml.
	ground cloves	
	grated nutmeg	
	ground white pepper	
5	eggs, lightly beaten	5
¾ lb.	butter, melted and cooled	350 g.

Mix together the all-purpose flour, corn flour, lemon peel, sugar, coriander, cinnamon and a pinch each of the cloves, nutmeg and pepper. Make a well in the center and add the eggs and melted butter. Combine the ingredients to make a smooth dough. Let the dough rest in a cool place—not the refrigerator—for six hours.

Divide the dough into eight to 10 pieces and press them one by one into a pastry bag fitted with a leaf tube. Pipe strips of dough each about 4 inches [10 cm.] long directly onto buttered and floured baking sheets. Leave some space between the sticks—as they will swell during cooking. Bake the sticks in a preheated 425° F. [220° C.] oven for 10 minutes, or until they are golden brown.

LAURA GRAS PORTINARI
CUCINA E VINI DEL PIEMONTE E DELLA VALLE D'AOSTA

Spoon Cookies

Löffelbiskuits

To make about 50

6	egg yolks	6
½ cup	granulated sugar	125 ml.
1 tsp.	grated lemon peel	5 ml.
5	egg whites, stiffly beaten	5
5 tbsp.	cornstarch, sifted	75 ml.
1 cup	sifted flour	¼ liter
	confectioners' sugar, sifted	

Beat the egg yolks with 1 teaspoon [5 ml.] of the granulated sugar and the grated lemon peel until they are frothy. Slowly sift the remaining sugar into the beaten egg whites, beating all the time. Fold the cornstarch into the whites and then add the yolk mixture. Finally, add the flour. Place this firm

cookie batter in a pastry bag fitted with a large tube. Pipe the batter onto baking sheets covered with parchment paper, forming strips about 4 to 5 inches [10 to 13 cm.] long and widened slightly at both ends to resemble spoons. Space the strips well apart. Sprinkle them with confectioners' sugar and bake in a preheated 350° F. [180° C.] oven for eight to 10 minutes, or until the cookies are golden.

ARNE KRÜGER AND ANNETTE WOLTER
KOCHEN HEUTE

Rum Cookies

Palais de Dames

To make rum and currant cookies, simply add 1 cup [¼ liter] of dried currants.

To make about 80

⅓ cup	rum	75 ml.
5	eggs	5
½ lb.	unsalted butter, softened	¼ kg.
1¼ cups	superfine sugar	300 ml.
1 cup	flour, sifted	¼ liter
2	eggs yolks, beaten with 1 tbsp. [15 ml.] water	2

Place all of the ingredients except the egg-yolk mixture in a large bowl and beat well until thoroughly blended. Put the dough in a pastry bag fitted with a plain or decorative tube and pipe small round cookies onto buttered baking sheets. Let the cookies stand for one hour.

Brush the cookies lightly with the egg-yolk mixture and bake in a preheated 300° F. [150° C.] oven for 25 minutes, or until browned.

ROSALIE BLANQUET
LE PÂTISSIER DES MÉNAGES

Orange Pipes

Cannoli all'Arancia

To make about 30

10 tbsp.	butter, cut into small pieces and softened	150 ml.
1¼ cups	confectioners' sugar, sifted	300 ml.
4 tbsp.	grated orange peel	60 ml.
1 tbsp.	vanilla sugar	15 ml.
1½ tbsp.	orange liqueur	22½ ml.
2¼ cups	flour	550 ml.
3	egg whites, stiffly beaten	3

Place the butter in a bowl and work it with a wooden spoon until it is like cream. Add the confectioners' sugar, orange peel, vanilla sugar and liqueur. When these ingredients are thoroughly mixed together, sift in the flour. Finally, add the stiffly beaten egg whites.

Put the batter into a pastry bag with a plain tube about ½ inch [1 cm.] across. Squeeze the batter onto buttered and floured baking sheets to form small disks or ovals about 2½ inches [6 cm.] long. Leave about 2 inches [5 cm.] between the shapes so that they do not stick together while baking; they will spread out considerably. When you have used up all of the batter, put the sheets into a preheated 475° F. [250° C.] oven for a few minutes. As soon as the cookies start to color at the edges (but are still white in the center), take the sheets out of the oven. Keep them on top of the oven so that they stay hot. Lift each cookie off in turn with a knife and press it around the handle of a wooden spoon to shape it into a tube. Cool the cookies on a wire rack.

FERNANDA GOSETTI
IN CUCINA CON FERNANDA GOSETTI

Cats' Tongues with Almonds

Langues-de-Chat aux Amandes

To make about 40

5 tbsp.	butter, softened	75 ml.
¼ cup	granulated sugar	50 ml.
2 tbsp.	vanilla sugar	30 ml.
2	eggs	2
⅔ cup	flour	150 ml.
½ cup	chopped almonds	125 ml.

Beat the butter until creamy and add the sugars. Beat together very thoroughly until light and fluffy. Add the eggs, one at a time, beating continuously. Add the flour and stir until the batter is smooth. Using a pastry bag and a ¼-inch [6-mm.] tube, pipe the batter into small sticks, spaced well apart on buttered and floured baking sheets. Sprinkle the sticks with the chopped almonds.

Bake in a preheated 350° F. [180° C.] oven for five to six minutes, or until the cookies are firm. Immediately remove the cookies from the baking sheets and let them cool on a wire rack. When the cookies are cold, store them in an airtight container.

JACQUELINE GÉRARD
BONNES RECETTES D'AUTREFOIS

Cats' Tongues

Langues-de-Chat

To make 90 to 100

½ lb.	butter, softened	¼ kg.
3 cups	confectioners' sugar	¾ liter
1 tsp.	vanilla extract	5 ml.
10	egg whites	10
4 cups	sifted flour	1 liter

Cream the butter, add the sugar and beat the mixture well. Add the vanilla extract. Little by little, add the egg whites, then fold in the flour. Using a pastry bag with a small plain round tube, pipe strips of dough about 3 inches [8 cm.] long onto lightly buttered baking sheets—leaving about 2 inches [5 cm.] between the strips. Bake in a preheated 425° F. [220° C.] oven for seven to eight minutes, or until the edges of the cookies are delicately browned. Remove the cookies immediately from the baking sheets with a metal spatula and place them on a rack to crisp.

M. VITALIS
LES BASES DE LA PÂTISSERIE, CONFISERIE, GLACERIE

Crisp Chartres Cookies

Croquignoles de Chartres

Adding a teaspoonful of egg white to the almonds when you are pounding them in a mortar prevents the nuts from becoming too oily.

To make about 60

⅔ cup	almonds, blanched and peeled	150 ml.
5	eggs, 1 beaten	5
1 cup	sugar	¼ liter
2½ cups	flour, sifted	625 ml.
	salt	
1 tsp.	grated lemon peel	5 ml.
4 tbsp.	butter, melted and cooled	60 ml.

In a mortar, pound to a paste the almonds and 1 teaspoon [5 ml.] of the white of one egg. Add the sugar and two of the eggs. Beat the mixture, incorporating two more eggs, a little at a time. Stir in the flour, a pinch of salt, the lemon peel and the butter.

Using a pastry bag, pipe the batter onto buttered baking sheets to form little balls, no bigger than cherries. Brush with the beaten egg. Bake in a preheated 325° F. [160° C.] oven for 15 minutes, or until they just begin to brown.

DOMINIQUE WEBER
LES BONNES RECETTES DES PROVINCES DE FRANCE

Almond Petits Fours

Petits Fours aux Amandes

For a demonstration of piping techniques, see page 22.

The cookies of each shape should be as uniform in size as possible so that they bake evenly. They can be stored for one to two weeks in an airtight container.

To make 12 to 14		
6 oz.	almonds, blanched, peeled and ground (about 1 ½ cups [375 ml.])	175 g.
¾ cup	sugar	175 ml.
1 tsp.	apricot jam (optional)	5 ml.
2	egg whites, lightly beaten	2
½ tsp.	vanilla extract	2 ml.

Decorations

	almonds, blanched, peeled and split into halves; candied cherries or orange peel, cut into pieces; candied angelica, cut into diamonds; raisins	

Glaze

1 tbsp.	confectioners' sugar	15 ml.
2 tbsp.	milk or water	30 ml.

Mix the ground almonds and sugar, add the apricot jam, if using, and stir in enough egg white to make a paste that is soft enough to pipe but still holds its shape. Beat in the vanilla extract. Using a pastry bag fitted with a large star tube, pipe the paste into flowers, rosettes or figure 8s onto baking sheets lined with parchment paper. Decorate each cookie with one or more of the decorations and bake them in a preheated 350° F. [180° C.] oven for 15 to 20 minutes, or until they begin to brown. Leave them on the baking sheet.

To prepare the glaze, heat the sugar with the milk or water until it dissolves and brush the mixture over the petits fours while they are still hot. Lift one end of the parchment paper slightly, immediately pour a glass of water under the paper and stand back: The hot baking sheet will turn the water into steam, making it easy to remove the petits fours. Leave them for a few moments; then remove them from the paper and set them on a rack to cool.

FAYE LEVY
LA VARENNE TOUR BOOK

Meringues and Macaroons

Crispy Meringue Drops

Croquignoles Fins

To make about 30		
½ cup	superfine or vanilla sugar	125 ml.
2	egg whites	2

Whisk the sugar and egg whites together until the meringue is of such a consistency that it can be placed on paper without running. Using a spoon, form very small mounds of the meringue on baking sheets lined with parchment paper. Place the meringues immediately in a preheated 275° F. [140° C.] oven and bake for about one and one half hours, or until the *croquignoles* are quite dry inside. Check by breaking one of them open. Let them cool, then store them in a dry place. *Croquignoles* do not keep long.

ROSALIE BLANQUET
LE PÂTISSIER DES MÉNAGES

French Puffs

Petits Soufflés à la Française

These cookies may be colored pink, green or yellow by adding a few drops of food coloring to the dough.

To make about 25		
2	egg whites	2
¾ cup	superfine sugar	175 ml.
1 cup	flour, sifted	¼ liter
	rose water	

In a small bowl, beat the egg whites and ½ cup [125 ml.] of the sugar until they form stiff peaks. Stir in the flour and knead the mixture for several minutes. Add a little rose water and the remaining sugar, and knead for a few more minutes. The dough should be fairly firm, very supple and shiny. With a teaspoon, place mounds of the dough the size of large olives on a baking sheet. Set the cookies in a warm place, such as an oven with the heat turned off, for five to six hours to dry their top surfaces. Then bake the cookies in a preheated 275° F. [140° C.] oven. The cookies will keep their original shape, but will rise about ⅔ inch [2 cm.]. Take them out when they are a delicate pinkish gold—about 10 minutes; even after baking, they will be quite pale.

ANTONIN CARÊME
LE PÂTISSIER ROYAL PARISIEN

Meringue Fingers

Doigt de Dame

The technique of making these cookies, using puréed straw-
berries, is shown on pages 62-63.

To make strawberry or raspberry meringue fingers, cook
the sugar syrup to the hard-crack stage, 300° F. [150° C.] on a
candy thermometer. Add about ¼ cup [50 ml.] of puréed fresh
strawberries or raspberries to bring the temperature of the
syrup down to 250° F. [120° C.], before combining it with the
egg whites. Omit any other flavoring.

To make 50 to 60

1 cup	sugar	¼ liter
⅓ cup	water	75 ml.
4	egg whites, stiffly beaten	4
1 tbsp.	finely grated semisweet baking chocolate, or 1 tsp. [5 ml.] coffee extract or vanilla extract	15 ml.

Dissolve the sugar in the water and boil the syrup to the
hard-ball stage, 250° F. [120° C.] on a candy thermometer.
Whisking continuously, pour the syrup into the stiffly beat-
en egg whites. When the mixture is again at the stiff-peak
stage, whisk in the chocolate, or coffee or vanilla extract.

Using a pastry bag with a small tube, pipe 3-inch-long [8-
cm.] strips of the meringue onto buttered and floured baking
sheets. Bake in a preheated 200° F. [100° C.] oven for about
three hours, or until the meringues are thoroughly dried.

M. VITALIS
LES BASES DE LA PÂTISSERIE, CONFISERIE, GLACERIE

Dutch Meringue Cookies

Schuimpje

To make about 50

1⅔ cups	superfine sugar	400 ml.
⅓ cup	water	75 ml.
4	egg whites	4
1 tbsp.	vanilla sugar	15 ml.
	red food coloring	
1 tbsp.	raspberry jam, sieved	15 ml.
1 tsp.	coffee extract	5 ml.
2 tsp.	cocoa powder	10 ml.

Dissolve 1⅓ cups [325 ml.] of the superfine sugar in the
water and bring it to a boil. Without stirring, boil until the
syrup reaches 240° F. [116° C.] on a candy thermometer—
the soft-ball stage. Beat the egg whites with the remaining
superfine sugar until they form stiff peaks. Add a thin trick-
le of the syrup and beat it in. Repeat until all of the syrup is

used and the meringue mixture is smooth and firm. Divide
the meringue into four parts. Leave one uncolored and mix
in the vanilla sugar. Color the second pink with two drops
of red food coloring and flavor with the raspberry jam. Flavor the third with the coffee extract and the fourth with
the cocoa powder.

Using a pastry bag with a star tube, pipe small, pointed
rosettes of meringue onto buttered and floured baking
sheets. Place in a preheated 200° F. [100° C.] oven for one
hour to dry out the cookies.

C. A. H. HAITSMA MULIER-VAN BEUSEKOM (EDITOR)
CULINAIRE ENCYCLOPÉDIE

Date Cookies

To make about 24

2	egg whites	2
1 cup	confectioners' sugar	¼ liter
1 cup	chopped dates	¼ liter
1 cup	chopped walnuts	¼ liter

Beat the egg whites until stiff. Cut in the confectioners' sugar, dates and nuts—do not stir. Drop spoonfuls of the mixture onto buttered baking sheets and bake in a preheated
300° F. [150° C.] oven for 45 minutes, or until the cookies are
firm and dry to the touch.

MRS. DON RICHARDSON (EDITOR)
CAROLINA LOW COUNTRY COOK BOOK
OF GEORGETOWN, SOUTH CAROLINA

Cinnamon Stars

Zimtsterne

To make about 20

6	egg whites, stiffly beaten	6
2 cups	superfine sugar	½ liter
2 tsp.	grated lemon peel	10 ml.
2 tsp.	ground cinnamon	10 ml.
1 lb.	almonds, ground (about 4 cups [1 liter])	½ kg.

Combine the egg whites, sugar and lemon peel, and beat
continuously until stiff and shiny—15 minutes by hand,
seven minutes with a standing electric mixer. Beat in the
cinnamon. Divide the mixture in half and mix the almonds
thoroughly into one half to make a dough. On a floured
board, roll out the almond dough ¼ inch [6 mm.] thick and
use a cookie cutter about 3 inches [8 cm.] wide to cut out
stars. Coat the cookies with the remaining egg-white mixture. Place on buttered baking sheets and bake in a preheated 325° F. [160° C.] oven for 15 minutes, or until stiff and dry.

HENRIETTE DAVIDIS
PRAKTISCHES KOCHBUCH

Spilamberto Macaroons

Amarretti di Spilamberto

The original version of this recipe calls for bitter almonds, which are not sold in America. Almond extract makes a suitable substitute.

	To make about 120	
1 lb.	almonds, blanched and peeled (about 4 cups [1 liter])	½ kg.
½ tsp.	almond extract	2 ml.
2½ cups	superfine sugar	625 ml.
5	egg whites, stiffly beaten	5

Pound the almonds finely in a mortar, adding the almond extract and 1 tablespoon [15 ml.] of the sugar. Fold the almonds into the egg whites, then fold in 2 cups [½ liter] of the remaining sugar. Put teaspoonfuls of the dough onto baking sheets lined with parchment paper, spacing the mounds at regular intervals. Sprinkle with the rest of the sugar. Bake in a preheated 350° F. [180° C.] oven for 20 minutes.

GIORGIO GIUSTI (EDITOR)
CENTONOVANTADUE RICETTE DELL' 800 PADANO

Dutch Macaroons

Edible rice paper is made by pressing a rice-flour paste between hot irons to form a very thin sheet. It is obtainable from confectionery-supply stores.

The distinctive feature of Dutch macaroons is the lovely smile down the center of each one. This is obtained by an interesting trick. After shaping, the macaroons are left in a warm place until they form a thick skin. This is then cut through from end to end with a sharp knife. When the macaroons are in the oven, the center mixture bubbles through the cuts giving them a most attractive and appetizing appearance. If wished, two of these macaroons may be sandwiched together with uncooked butter icing *(recipe, page 164)*, flavored with coffee.

	To make about 25	
1⅓ cups	confectioners' sugar, sifted	325 ml.
½ cup	almonds, blanched, peeled and ground	125 ml.
	almond extract	
2 to 3 tbsp.	egg whites, lightly beaten	30 to 45 ml.

Combine the confectioners' sugar with the ground almonds. Flavor with a few drops of almond extract and stir in enough

of the beaten egg whites to give the mixture a thick, creamy consistency. The mixture should flow level without spreading. Place it in a large pastry bag fitted with a ¼-inch [6-mm.] plain tube, and pipe small oval shapes onto a baking sheet lined with rice paper or parchment paper. Put the cookies aside in a warm place for one to two days until a thick skin has formed on each one. Then, using a sharp knife, make a clean cut from end to end of each cookie. Bake the cookies in a preheated 325° F. [160° C.] oven for 15 minutes, or until they are golden.

MARGARET BATES
TALKING ABOUT CAKES WITH AN IRISH AND SCOTTISH ACCENT

Macaroons, in the Style of Nice

Macarons ou Amaretti Niçois

The original version of this recipe calls for flavoring the mixture with bitter almonds, which are not obtainable in America. Almond extract makes a suitable substitute.

	To make about 35	
½ lb.	almonds, blanched and peeled (about 2 cups [½ liter])	¼ kg.
2 to 3 tbsp.	lightly beaten egg whites	30 to 45 ml.
¼ tsp.	almond extract	1 ml.
1¼ cups	granulated sugar	300 ml.
	pine nuts	
	confectioners' sugar	

In a mortar, pound the almonds and 1 teaspoonful [5 ml.] of the egg whites together to form a smooth paste. With the pestle, mix in the almond extract and half of the granulated sugar, then incorporate 2 teaspoons [10 ml.] of the egg whites. Blend in the remaining granulated sugar and 1 tablespoon [15 ml.] of the egg whites. If the mixture is sticky and clings to the mortar, add another tablespoon of egg whites. Mix thoroughly once again. Cover two baking sheets with parchment paper and spoon the mixture onto the paper, using about 2 teaspoonfuls to form each mound and spacing the mounds an inch [2½ cm.] or so apart. Bake the macaroons in a preheated 425° F. [220° C.] oven for 10 minutes, or until they are firm to the touch. Remove them from the oven, decorate them with pine nuts and sprinkle them with confectioners' sugar. Return the macaroons to the oven for a moment to set the toppings, but take them out quickly. Cool the macaroons before removing them from the paper.

JOSÉPHINE BESSON
LA MÈRE BESSON "MA CUISINE PROVENÇALE"

Macaroons

Macarons

To make 12

1 cup	almonds, blanched, peeled and ground	¼ liter
1 cup	granulated sugar	¼ liter
	vanilla extract	
2	egg whites	2
	confectioners' sugar	

Place the ground almonds in a heavy bowl. Pounding them with a wooden pestle, gradually add the granulated sugar. It is not enough simply to mix the sugar and almonds: Some of the oil from the almonds must be extracted by pounding.

Add a drop or two of vanilla extract and, little by little, the egg whites. The dough should be firm enough to knead by hand. Divide the dough into 12 balls of equal size.

Oil a sheet of parchment paper and place it on a baking sheet. Place the balls on the paper—setting them well apart—and flatten them a little. Brush the surface of the macaroons with water. Sprinkle each one with a pinch of confectioners' sugar. Bake in the top third of a preheated 350° F. [180° C.] oven for 15 to 18 minutes, or until lightly browned. Slide the sheet of paper onto a well-dampened cloth towel. As soon as the paper is moist, remove the macaroons; be careful not to let them absorb any moisture.

JACQUELINE GÉRARD
BONNES RECETTES D'AUTREFOIS

Bitter-Almond Macaroons

Macarons Soufflés aux Amandes Amères

The original version of this recipe calls for bitter almonds, which are not sold in America. Almond extract makes a suitable substitute.

To make about 80

1 lb.	almonds, blanched and peeled (about 4 cups [1 liter])	½ kg.
3 cups	superfine sugar	¾ liter
about 3	egg whites	about 3
1 tsp.	almond extract	5 ml.

Slice the almonds thinly crosswise. Mix them with ½ cup [125 ml.] of the sugar and ½ tbsp. [7 ml.] of egg white; spread them out on a large baking sheet and toast in a preheated 250° F. [120° C.] oven—stirring them occasionally—until the almonds are dry and pale golden—about 30 minutes.

Set the almonds aside to cool. Meanwhile, beat the remaining sugar and two egg whites together in a bowl for 15 minutes. Gradually add the cooled almonds and the almond extract and stir until they are completely coated with the egg-white mixture.

To test the dough, place a teaspoonful on a baking sheet and bake in a preheated 250° F. oven for 20 minutes. If the surface collapses, add a little sugar to the dough; if the surface is too hard and the macaroon is too stiff, add a little egg white. If the test macaroon keeps its shape, you can go ahead with the rest of the mixture. Dampen your hands and roll spoonfuls of the dough between your palms to form balls the size of nutmegs—about 1 inch [2½ cm.] in diameter. Place them on buttered baking sheets. When they are all shaped, dip your finger tips in water and press the surface of each macaroon lightly.

Place the baking sheets in the oven and do not open the door for 20 minutes. When the macaroons are a beautiful light golden color and firm to the touch, remove them from the oven. When cold, remove them from the baking sheets.

ANTONIN CARÊME
LE PÂTISSIER ROYAL PARISIEN

Mirrors

Miroirs

To make about 30

10 oz.	almonds, blanched and peeled (about 2½ cups [625 ml.]), ½ cup [125 ml.] finely chopped	300 g.
2½ cups	sugar	625 ml.
6	egg whites, stiffly beaten	6
	Cream filling	
1 cup	almonds, blanched, peeled and ground	¼ liter
3	eggs	3
½ cup	sugar	125 ml.
8 tbsp.	butter, softened	120 ml.
¼ cup	rum	50 ml.

To form the mirror frames, first grind the whole almonds and sugar together in a mortar until the nuts are powdered, then sieve the mixture. Fold in the egg whites. Using a pastry bag with a medium-sized plain tube, pipe oval rings about 1½ inches [4 cm.] long onto buttered and floured baking sheets. Sprinkle these frames with the chopped almonds to give them a gritty surface.

Whisk together all of the filling ingredients. Pipe the filling into the centers of the frames. Bake in a preheated 325° F. [160° C.] oven for 15 minutes, or until the mirrors are firm and delicately browned.

MANUEL PRATIQUE DE CUISINE PROVENÇALE

Fried Cookies

Fried Cookies from Lyons

Les Bugnes comme à Lyon

To make about 40

2¾ cups	flour	675 ml.
1 tsp.	salt	5 ml.
½ cup	superfine sugar	125 ml.
4 tbsp.	butter, softened	60 ml.
3	eggs	3
1 tbsp.	baking powder	15 ml.
	rum	
2 tsp.	grated lemon peel	10 ml.
	oil for deep frying	

Place the flour on a board, make a well in the center, and put in the salt and half of the sugar. Add the butter, eggs and baking powder, and knead together. Add a few drops of rum and the lemon peel to flavor the dough, which should be fairly firm.

Let the dough rest for one hour, then roll it out about ⅛ inch [3 mm.] thick. Cut it into 1-by-2-inch [2½-by-5-cm.] rectangles and deep fry them in oil heated to 350° F. [180° C.] on a deep-frying thermometer until golden brown—about five minutes. Drain the cookies and sprinkle them with the remaining sugar. The cookies should be very crisp.

RAYMOND THUILIER AND MICHEL LEMONNIER
LES RECETTES DE BAUMANIÈRE

Polish Chrust

To make about 50

6	egg yolks	6
¼ tsp.	salt	1 ml.
⅓ cup	granulated sugar	75 ml.
¼ cup	heavy cream	50 ml.
⅛ tsp.	ground mace	½ ml.
2 to 2½ cups	sifted flour	500 to 625 ml.
	shortening for deep frying	
	vanilla sugar	

Beat the egg yolks with the salt and granulated sugar until light and fluffy. Stir in the cream and mace. Add enough flour to make a soft dough. Do not knead the dough. Kneading will result in hard, tough cookies. Divide the dough in two and chill.

On a well-floured cloth, roll the dough as thin as possible, one portion at a time. Cut into strips 1 by 3 inches [2½ by 8 cm.]. Make a slit down the center of each strip. Pull one end of the strip through the slit.

Heat shortening in a deep skillet to 375° F. [190° C.] on a deep-frying thermometer. Fry a few strips at a time in the shortening, turning them once. They are done when lightly brown on both sides. Drain on paper towels. When cool, dust the cookies with vanilla sugar.

PAULA PECK
THE ART OF FINE BAKING

Fried Pastries

Faramayas

This recipe comes from Galicia, a region in northwest Spain just north of Portugal.

To make about 50

2 cups	flour	½ liter
	salt	
¼ cup	superfine sugar	50 ml.
2 tsp.	grated lemon peel	10 ml.
4 tbsp.	butter, cut into pieces and softened	60 ml.
2 tbsp.	brandy	30 ml.
1 tbsp.	water	15 ml.
	oil for deep frying	
	confectioners' sugar	

Sift the flour and a pinch of salt, and blend in the superfine sugar and lemon peel. Lightly rub in the butter, then add the brandy and water, and knead just enough to form a cohesive dough. Cover the dough with a damp cloth and leave it in a cool place—not the refrigerator—for about two hours.

Roll the dough to a thickness of about ⅛ inch [3 mm.] and cut it into 2-inch [5-cm.] squares. Leave the squares on a floured baking sheet in a cool place or on a marble top for half an hour. In hot oil about 1½ inches [4 cm.] deep, fry the squares—a batch at a time—until golden brown. Drain them well and dust them with plenty of confectioners' sugar. The cookies may be eaten hot or cold.

ANNA MACMIADHACHÁIN
SPANISH REGIONAL COOKERY

Fried Ribbon Cookies

Crostoli da Friuli

Grappa is a pungent Italian brandy distilled from the pulp that remains after the grapes have been pressed and their juice squeezed out.

To make 50 to 60

2	eggs	2
¼ cup	granulated sugar	50 ml.
2 tsp.	grated lemon peel	10 ml.
½ tsp.	salt	2 ml.
3 tbsp.	grappa or rum	45 ml.
2 to 4 tbsp.	milk, warmed	30 to 60 ml.
2½ cups	flour	625 ml.
5 tbsp.	butter, melted	75 ml.
	oil for deep frying	
	confectioners' sugar	

Break the eggs into a bowl. Add the granulated sugar, lemon peel, salt and grappa or rum, and beat thoroughly until the mixture is light. Stir in 2 tablespoons [30 ml.] of the milk. Put the flour into another bowl and make a well in the middle. Pour in the egg mixture and the butter. Stir to mix well, making a dough that is on the soft side. If necessary, add the remaining milk, a little at a time.

On a lightly floured board, roll out the dough to a thickness of about ⅛ inch [3 mm.]. Cut the dough into strips ½ inch [1 cm.] wide and 7 inches [18 cm.] long. Tie the strips loosely into knots.

Heat the oil to 375° F. [190° C.] on a deep-frying thermometer. Fry a few cookies at a time until they are golden and rise to the surface of the oil. Remove them with a slotted spoon and drain them thoroughly on towels. Sprinkle the cookies with confectioners' sugar before serving them on a plate lined with a table napkin.

NIKA HAZELTON
THE REGIONAL ITALIAN KITCHEN

Rice Flour Cookies

Rice flour is obtainable at Asian markets and health-food stores. Jaggery is an unrefined coarse brown Indian sugar made from palm-tree sap and sold in chunks. Ghee is the Indian version of clarified butter, or butter with its easily burned milk solids removed. Both are obtainable at stores specializing in Indian foods, or you can make your own ghee. Start with at least one third more butter than is specified in the recipe—in this case, 8 tablespoons [120 ml.]. Melt the butter over low heat without browning it; spoon off the foam. Let stand off the heat until the milk solids settle; then strain the clear liquid through a sieve lined with four layers of dampened cheesecloth. Discard the milk solids.

To make about 40

2 cups	rice flour	½ liter
1 tbsp.	poppy seeds	15 ml.
10	whole cardamoms, the pods removed and the seeds crushed to a powder	10
	salt	
2 cups	finely grated jaggery or firmly packed light brown sugar	½ liter
2 cups	water	½ liter
6 tbsp.	*ghee*	90 ml.
	heavy cream, whipped	

Mix the flour, poppy seeds, ground cardamom and a pinch of salt in a saucepan. Make a syrup by boiling the sugar and water for a few minutes. Now pour the syrup onto the flour mixture and stir well until a thick, doughy mixture is formed. Cover the dough and set it aside to rest overnight.

The next day, knead the dough and form it into small balls about ¾ inch [2 cm.] in diameter. Flatten each ball to make cookies. Melt 2 tablespoons [30 ml.] of the *ghee* in a skillet and fry the cookies, a few at a time, until golden on both sides—about five minutes. Add more *ghee* to the skillet as necessary. Drain the cookies on paper towels and serve with the whipped cream.

JACK SANTA MARIA
INDIAN SWEET COOKERY

Wine Cookies

Tostones de Monja

To make about 70

4 cups	flour	1 liter
¾ cup	olive oil	175 ml.
¾ cup	muscatel wine	175 ml.
	oil for deep frying	
	confectioners' sugar mixed with ground cinnamon	

Combine the flour, olive oil and wine, and knead the mixture until it forms an elastic dough. Roll the dough about ¼ inch [6 mm.] thick with a rolling pin and cut it into 3-inch [8-cm.] rounds with a biscuit cutter. Deep fry the rounds, a small batch at a time, in hot oil for about two to three minutes. The rounds should turn over by themselves when one side has been well fried; if not, turn them with tongs. Drain the rounds on paper towels, dust them with the confectioners' sugar mixture and serve them hot.

MARÍA MESTAYER DE ECHAGÜE (MARQUESA DE PARABERE)
CONFITERÍA Y REPOSTERÍA

Snowballs

Schneeballen

To make the turnovers shown on page 53, cut the rolled dough into 2½-inch [6-cm.] rounds and use ½ teaspoon [2 ml.] of fig filling (recipe, page 165) for each turnover.

Raspberry syrup is imported from Germany and Switzerland and is obtainable at specialty food stores. If not available, substitute raspberry jam or jelly.

To make about 40

2 cups	flour	½ liter
2 tbsp.	granulated sugar	30 ml.
4 tbsp.	unsalted butter, cut into pieces and chilled	60 ml.
4	egg yolks	4
¼ cup	sour cream	50 ml.
1 tbsp.	rum	15 ml.
	oil for deep frying	
	vanilla confectioners' sugar	
	raspberry syrup (optional)	

Mix the flour and granulated sugar together on a pastry board and make a well in the center. Drop the butter pieces into the well and cut them into the flour mixture. Add the egg yolks, sour cream and rum, and—with a table knife—fold the flour mixture over them. With your hands, knead the dough until it is smooth and moderately soft. Refrigerate the dough for about one hour.

Divide the dough into three parts. On a lightly floured board, roll one part at a time to a thickness of about ⅛ inch [3 mm.]. With a pastry wheel or a knife, cut the dough into 2-by-4-inch [5-by-10-cm.] strips. Make a diagonal slit about ¾ inch [2 cm.] long in the center of each strip, then pull one end of the strip through the slit as far as it will go.

Heat the oil to a temperature of 375° F. [190° C.] on a deep-frying thermometer. Deep fry several cookies at a time until they are golden brown on both sides. Immediately remove them with a slotted spoon and place them on paper towels to drain. Roll, cut and fry the remaining dough.

While they are still hot, sprinkle the cookies with vanilla confectioners' sugar. Serve them warm or cold; if desired, top each serving with raspberry syrup.

LILLY JOSS REICH
THE VIENNESE PASTRY COOKBOOK

Rye Drops

The sour milk called for in this recipe can be made by adding 1½ tablespoons [22½ ml.] of fresh lemon juice or vinegar to

1½ cups [375 ml.] of fresh milk. Rye flour is obtainable at health-food stores.

To make 30

2 tbsp.	granulated sugar	30 ml.
2	eggs, beaten until thick	2
1 tsp.	baking soda	5 ml.
1 ½ cups	sour milk	375 ml.
1 cup	rye flour	¼ liter
1 cup	all-purpose flour	¼ liter
¼ tsp.	salt	1 ml.
¾ tsp.	ground cinnamon	4 ml.
	oil or fat for deep frying	
	confectioners' sugar mixed with ground cinnamon	

Add the granulated sugar to the beaten eggs. Stir the soda into the sour milk and combine the mixture with the eggs. Sift together the flours, salt and cinnamon, and add them. The dough should be stiff enough to drop off the end of a spoon. Drop the dough by small teaspoonfuls into hot oil or fat, and deep fry each batch for three to four minutes, or until puffed and browned. Drain the cookies on paper towels and roll them in the confectioners' sugar mixture before serving.

ANNETTE LASLETT ROSS AND JEAN ADAMS DISNEY
THE ART OF MAKING GOOD COOKIES PLAIN AND FANCY

Date Lozenges

Magrout'l-farina

To make about 35

1 lb.	dates, peeled, halved and pitted	½ kg.
	ground cinnamon	
	oil	
6 cups	flour	1 ½ liters
	salt	
½ lb.	butter, melted and cooled	¼ kg.
about 1 cup	water	about ¼ liter

Honey topping		
⅓ cup	honey, warmed	75 ml.
1¾ cups	sesame seeds, or almonds, blanched, peeled and ground	425 ml.

Put the dates through a food grinder or the coarse disk of a food mill. Add a pinch of cinnamon and knead the mixture well, moistening your hands with oil from time to time. Shape this paste into a ball and set aside.

To prepare the dough, sift the flour and a pinch of salt onto a board, make a well in the center and pour in the melted butter. Mix well. Knead the mixture, adding water a little at a time, until the dough is cohesive and fairly firm. Roll the dough into a rectangular sheet ⅛ inch [3 mm.] thick. Shape the date paste into a cylinder the length of the dough sheet and place it on one long edge of the dough. Roll the paste up in the dough. Flatten the roll slightly with a ruler. Cut the roll into lozenges ½ inch [1 cm.] thick. Prick each lozenge with a fork.

In a large, heavy skillet, heat a 1-inch [2½-cm.] layer of oil to 325° F. [160° C.] on a deep-frying thermometer. Immerse the lozenges—a small batch at a time—in the oil and fry them until golden brown—about three minutes. Drain the lozenges on paper towels, then set them on a wire rack placed over a baking sheet. While they are still warm, pour the warmed honey over the lozenges and sprinkle them with the sesame seeds or ground almonds.

FATIMA-ZOHRA BOUAYED
LA CUISINE ALGÉRIENNE

Deep-fried Pretzel-shaped Sweets

Jalebis

Rice flour is obtainable at health-food stores.

To make about 60

3 cups	all-purpose flour	¾ liter
¼ cup	rice flour	50 ml.
¼ tsp.	baking powder	1 ml.
2 cups	tepid water	½ liter
	vegetable oil for deep frying	

Syrup

4 cups	sugar	1 liter
3 cups	cold water	¾ liter
⅛ tsp.	cream of tartar	½ ml.
2 tsp.	yellow food coloring	10 ml.
⅛ tsp.	red food coloring	½ ml.
1 tsp.	rose water	5 ml.

In a deep bowl, make a smooth batter of the all-purpose and rice flours, baking powder and tepid water. Let the batter rest unrefrigerated and uncovered for 12 hours.

Just before frying the *jalebis,* prepare the syrup. Combine the sugar, cold water and cream of tartar in a large saucepan. Stir over medium heat until the sugar dissolves. Increase the heat to high and—timing it from the moment the syrup boils—cook the mixture briskly, undisturbed, for five minutes. The syrup is done when it reaches a tempera-

ture of 220° F. [105 C.] on a candy thermometer. Remove the pan from the heat, stir in the colorings and the rose water. Pour the syrup into a bowl and set it aside.

Pour the vegetable oil into a deep pan to a depth of 2 to 3 inches [5 to 8 cm.]. Heat the oil until it reaches a temperature of 350° F. [180° C.] on a deep-frying thermometer. To make the *jalebis,* spoon 1½ cups [375 ml.] of the batter into a pastry bag fitted with a plain tube ³⁄₁₆ inch [4½ mm.] in diameter. Squeezing it directly into the hot oil, loop a stream of batter back and forth four or five times to form a sort of pretzel made up of alternating figure 8s and circles, one over the other. Each *jalebi* should be about 3 inches [8 cm.] long and 2 inches [5 cm.] wide.

In batches of five or six, fry the *jalebis* for two minutes, or until golden on both sides. As they brown, transfer them to the syrup for a minute, then place them on a plate. Serve warm or at room temperature.

FOODS OF THE WORLD/THE COOKING OF INDIA

Crackers

Baked "Potato Chips"

Potato flour—or potato starch—is made from cooked, dried and ground potatoes.

Some chips brown before others (the ones on the outside edge of the pan seem to do this). Remove them as they brown and bake the remainder a few more minutes. Watch the chips carefully during the last 10 minutes of baking; they can change from golden brown to burned in seconds.

To make about 30

1¼ cups	tepid water	300 ml.
¼ cup	potato flour	50 ml.
	salt	

Pour ¾ cup [175 ml.] of the tepid water into a medium-sized bowl. Mixing constantly with a fork or wire whisk, sprinkle the potato flour very gradually into the water. When the batter is free of lumps, add ½ teaspoon [2 ml.] of salt; gradually mix in the remaining water. The batter will have the consistency of thin mashed potatoes. Drop the batter by large teaspoonfuls onto buttered nonstick baking sheets—spacing the rounds about 2 inches [5 cm.] apart. Sprinkle the chips with additional salt. Bake in a preheated 375° F. [190° C.] oven for 15 minutes. Reduce the heat to 325° F. [160° C.] and continue to bake for about eight to 12 minutes longer, or until the chips are crisp and brown. Remove them from the sheets at once.

JANET KAPLAN
CRACKERS AND SNACKERS

Norwegian Flatbread

Flattbröd

In the demonstration on pages 86-87, barley flour is substituted for the rye flour. The dough is given a resting period after kneading to make it easier to roll out. If you are in a hurry, this step can be omitted.

Flatbread has been made in Norway for centuries. Vast quantities were prepared to be stored for the winter months and, in the old days, a table was specially kept for making the flatbread—the table was often hung up under the beams of the farm kitchen and lowered for the performance.

Flatbread can be made with almost any mixture of flours and with root vegetables, too, in the proportion of one fifth flour to four fifths sieved, cooked vegetables.

To make 8		
3 cups	rye flour	¾ liter
2 cups	whole-wheat flour	½ liter
½ tsp.	salt	2 ml.
about 1½ cups	tepid water	about 375 ml.

Sift the flours and salt into a bowl. With a wooden spoon, stir in sufficient tepid water to form a fairly soft dough. Turn out the dough onto a floured surface and knead well for about 15 minutes, or until a little of the dough can be rolled into a cylinder and bent in half without cracking. Place the dough in a buttered bowl, cover the bowl with a damp cloth towel and let the dough rest for at least two hours.

Divide the dough into eight equal pieces and roll each piece into a round approximately 10 inches [25 cm.] in diameter. Prick each round all over with a fork. Heat a lightly oiled griddle or large skillet and, when it is very hot, place one of the rounds on it. Cook the bread until brown spots begin to form on the underside, then turn the bread over and brown the other side. Reduce the heat and continue turning the bread until it becomes crisp. Repeat this process with all of the rounds. If preferred, the rounds may be placed on baking sheets, pricked well and baked in a preheated 425° F. [220° C.] oven for about 20 minutes until they are slightly brown and crisp.

LORNA WALKER AND JOYCE HUGHES
THE COMPLETE BREAD BOOK

Uncle Max's Rye Crackers

Rye flour is obtainable at health-food stores.

The batter thickens upon standing. If you bake the crackers in two batches, you may need to add 1 to 2 teaspoons [5 to 10 ml.] of extra water to the second batch.

To make about 40		
1 cup	rye flour	¼ liter
1 cup plus 3 tbsp.	water	295 ml.
2 tbsp.	butter, melted	30 ml.
	salt	
	caraway seeds	

Place the flour in a bowl and gradually add the water, mixing well with a fork. Add the melted butter and ½ teaspoon [5 cm.] of salt. Drop the batter by the teaspoonful onto well-buttered nonstick baking sheets—spacing the rounds about 2 inches [5 cm.] apart. Sprinkle the crackers lightly with caraway seeds and additional salt. Bake in a preheated 350° F. [180° C.] oven for 20 to 30 minutes, or until the crackers are lightly browned and crisp around the edges. Remove them from the baking sheet at once. As they cool, the centers of the crackers will become crisp. When the crackers are cold, pack them in an airtight container.

JANET KAPLAN
CRACKERS AND SNACKERS

Oat Crackers

To make about 140		
⅔ cup	rolled oats	150 ml.
3 cups	whole wheat flour	¾ liter
⅓ tsp.	baking soda	2 ml.
¼ cup	honey, warmed	50 ml.
1 tsp.	salt	5 ml.
8 tbsp.	butter, softened	120 ml.
about ¾ cup	buttermilk, warmed	about 175 ml.

Mix all of the ingredients, except the buttermilk, and combine them thoroughly. Add enough buttermilk to make a firm but workable dough. Divide the dough in half. Roll out one half at a time, between sheets of wax paper, to a thickness of ¼ inch [6 mm.]. Cut the dough into 1- to 1½-inch [2½- to 4-cm.] squares. Prick each one with a fork. Lightly oil a baking sheet and place the crackers on it. Bake them in a preheated 325° F. [160° C.] oven for about 25 minutes, or until lightly browned.

FAYE MARTIN
RODALE'S NATURALLY DELICIOUS DESSERTS AND SNACKS

Donegal Oatcake

The oatmeal called for in this recipe is finely ground whole oat kernels—not the familiar rolled oats. Oatmeal is obtainable at health-food stores.

According to local tradition, Donegal oatcake was toasted on an iron stand called a bread iron or harnen (hardening) stand. The oatcake was put on the stand to toast very slowly for several hours at some distance from the open peat fire. The process is really more of a drying out than a toasting.

Oatcake keeps well and can be reheated—always at a minimum temperature—as often as you please. The only disadvantages of oatcake are the speed with which it disappears and the crumbs left scattered all over the table and the floor after an oatcake meal.

Eat the oatcake for breakfast or tea with cold creamy butter. It is wonderfully good also with fresh cream cheese.

To make 1 or 2		
5 cups	fine oatmeal	1 ¼ liters
2 tsp.	salt	10 ml.
2 to 4 tbsp.	butter or lard, cut into pieces	30 to 60 ml.
about 1 ½ cups	boiling water	about 375 ml.

Put the oatmeal in one mixing bowl, the salt and butter or lard in another. Over the latter pour the boiling water. Stir until the fat and salt are dissolved. Pour this mixture into the oatmeal. A little more water may be needed to mix the oatmeal into a pliable cake, which at this stage resembles nothing so much as a mud pie. This is now left overnight, or at least for several hours, until it is dry enough to press out, very thin and flat, into an ungreased baking pan, at least 8 by 12 inches [20 by 30 cm.]. After a little practice at making oatcake, you will find that it can be pressed out almost as thin as cardboard and then two pans will be needed.

Before baking the oatcake, leave it again to dry out for an hour or two. Press it once more and even out the top with a thin-bladed metal spatula.

Put the pan or pans on the bottom shelf of the slowest possible oven—250° to 275° F. [120° to 140° C.]—and leave them for a minimum of three hours, or longer if it happens to be convenient. Too high a temperature will ruin the oatcake; the longer the drying out at a very low temperature, the better it will be. Break the oatcake into wedges to serve it.

ELIZABETH DAVID
ENGLISH BREAD AND YEAST COOKERY

Orford's Water Biscuits

To make about 20		
2 cups	flour	½ liter
½ tsp.	salt	2 ml.
1 tsp.	baking powder	5 ml.
4 tbsp.	lard, cut into pieces	60 ml.
3 to 4 tbsp.	cold water	45 to 60 ml.
	coarse salt	

Sift the flour with the salt and baking powder, and rub in the lard. Moisten the mixture with enough water to make a firm dough. On a lightly floured board, roll the dough ⅛ inch [3 mm.] thick, prick it all over with a fork and stamp out 3- or 4-inch [8- or 10-cm.] rounds. Sprinkle the rounds with coarse salt and bake them in a preheated 350° F. [180° C.] oven for 10 to 15 minutes, until the edges are pale golden in color.

CONSTANCE SPRY AND ROSEMARY HUME
THE CONSTANCE SPRY COOKERY BOOK

Scotch Oatcakes

The oatmeal called for in this recipe is finely ground oat kernels—not the familiar rolled oats. Oatmeal is obtainable from health-food stores.

The scraps that are left over from cutting should be put back into the bowl and made up again.

To make 4 to 6		
⅔ cup	fine oatmeal	150 ml.
	salt	
	baking soda	
1 tsp.	butter or rendered bacon fat, melted	5 ml.
about ⅓ cup	hot water	about 75 ml.

Put the oatmeal, with a pinch of salt and baking soda, into a bowl, add the butter or fat and enough water to make a soft paste. Turn this out onto a board that has been well sprinkled with oatmeal. Flatten the dough with your hand or roll with a rolling pin until it is very thin. Rub with more oatmeal and cut into a round with a saucepan lid. Then cut the round into four or six wedge-shaped pieces and slide these cakes carefully onto a hot griddle. Cook them over medium heat until they begin to curl up, then toast them in front of a fire or under a broiler for one to two minutes; alternatively, put them on a baking sheet in a preheated 350° F. [180° C.] oven for a few minutes until they are dry and crisp.

FLORENCE B. JACK
COOKERY FOR EVERY HOUSEHOLD

Peanut Crackers

Rice flour is obtainable in health-food stores.

To make 36

1 cup	rice flour	¼ liter
¾ cup plus 1 tbsp.	water	190 ml.
¾ cup	salted peanuts, coarsely chopped	175 ml.
	salt	
2 tbsp.	butter, melted	30 ml.

Place the flour in a bowl and gradually add the water, mixing well so that there are no lumps. Fold in the salted peanuts and ¼ tsp. [1 ml.] of salt. Add the melted butter and mix very well. Check the consistency of the batter by placing a teaspoonful on a baking sheet. The batter should spread to make a cracker approximately 2 inches [5 cm.] in diameter. Add 1 teaspoon of additional water or flour if necessary.

Drop the batter by the teaspoonful onto buttered nonstick baking sheets about 2 inches apart. Sprinkle with additional salt. Bake in a preheated 375° F. [190° C.] oven for 25 to 30 minutes, or until the crackers are golden brown and crisp. Remove them from the sheets immediately.

JANET KAPLAN
CRACKERS AND SNACKERS

Rye Crackers

Rye flour is obtainable at health-food stores.

To make about 30

¼ oz.	package active dry yeast or ⅗ oz. [18 g.] cake fresh yeast mixed with ½ cup [125 ml.] tepid water	7½ g.
1 cup	stone-ground rye flour	¼ liter
1 tsp.	caraway seeds	5 ml.
½ tsp.	salt	2 ml.

In a bowl, combine the yeast mixture, flour, caraway seeds and salt, and knead the ingredients together until they form a cohesive ball of dough. Put the dough on a large buttered baking sheet and with a rolling pin roll it to a thickness of about ⅛ inch [3 mm.].

Cover the dough with a clean dry towel and leave it in a warm place for one hour. The dough will rise slightly, but not enough to be noticeable. With a sharp knife, score the dough into rectangles and place the baking sheet in a cold oven. Set the heat for very low (under 250° F. [120° C.]) and bake for 15 minutes. Increase the heat to 350° F. [180° C.] and bake the crackers until crisp and done—perhaps another 15 minutes.

STAN AND FLOSS DWORKIN
NATURAL SNACKS AND SWEETS: THE GOOD GOODIES

Bath Oliver Crackers

The technique of rolling and folding dough is demonstrated on page 90.

This cracker, excellent against indigestion, owes its name to Dr. Oliver, a famous physician of Bath, and the friend of Pope, Warburton and other 18th Century notabilities. When on his deathbed (1749), the doctor called for his coachman and gave him the recipe for such crackers, also 10 sacks of flour and 100 sovereigns. The fortunate fellow started a shop, where the crackers were made and sold, on Green Street, Bath.

To make about 30

4 tbsp.	butter	60 ml.
½ cup	milk	125 ml.
¼ oz.	package active dry yeast or ⅗ oz. [18 g.] cake fresh yeast	7½ g.
3 cups	flour, sifted with a pinch of salt	¾ liter

Stir the butter and milk in a saucepan over low heat until the butter is melted; cool until tepid and add the yeast. Let the mixture stand for 10 minutes, or until the yeast foams. Mix the flour in very smoothly; knead the dough well, wrap it in a warmed cloth, put it into a bowl and place it in a warm place for 15 minutes.

Roll out the dough eight or nine times, folding it in thirds after each rolling. Finally roll it out ¼ inch [6 mm.] thick. Stamp it into crackers with a biscuit cutter; prick them well with a fork, and bake them on baking sheets in a preheated 350° F. [180° C.] oven until the crackers are lightly browned—about 30 minutes.

W. T. FERNIE, M.D.
MEALS MEDICINAL: WITH "HERBAL SIMPLES"

Cracknel Crackers

Craquelins

This pastry is one of the oldest and most popular in Brittany.

To make about 60

9 cups	flour	2¼ liters
8	eggs	8
	salt	
¼ oz.	package active dry yeast, or ⅗ oz. [18 g.] cake fresh yeast, mixed with ½ cup [125 ml.] tepid water	7½ g.

Mound 6 cups [1½ liters] of the flour on a work surface, make a well in the center and into it put the eggs, a pinch of salt and the yeast mixture. Knead with your hands, then gather the dough into a ball and let it rest and rise in a warm place for one hour.

With a rolling pin, incorporate the remaining flour into the dough. Roll out the dough to a thickness of ¼ inch [6 mm.] and cut it into 4-inch [10-cm.] squares. Bring the four points of each square together, turn the square over and flatten the top. Smooth the edges of each square by patting them with the side of a knife blade.

Bring a large saucepan of water to a simmer. Add the squares—a small batch at a time; they will rise to the surface one after another. As soon as this happens, lift them out with a slotted spoon. The squares will be concave on one side and bulging on the other.

Let the squares cool briefly, then drop them into a large bowl of cold water to chill for 30 minutes. Drain the squares, concave sides down, on wire racks. Then set the crackers on baking sheets and bake them in a preheated 325° F. [160° C.] oven for 10 minutes until they are delicately browned.

LA CUISINE BRETONNE

Crackers with Cracklings and White Wine

Pogaćice Sa Ćvarcima I Belim Vinom

To make the cracklings called for in this recipe, first dice ¾ pound [350 g.] of fresh pork belly—including the skin. Place it in a large pan, add ½ cup [125 ml.] of water and fry over low heat for 10 minutes, until the pork has rendered most of its fat and the bits of skin and tissue—the cracklings—are crisp and golden. Drain them on paper towels.

To make about 80

6 oz.	pork cracklings, finely chopped (about ½ cup [125 ml.])	175 g.
2 cups	flour	½ liter
3	egg yolks	3
¼ oz.	package active dry yeast, mixed with ½ cup [125 ml.] tepid milk	7½ g.
½ cup	dry white wine	125 ml.
	salt and pepper	
4 tbsp.	lard, melted	60 ml.

Mix the cracklings with the flour. Add the egg yolks, yeast, white wine, and a little salt and pepper. Knead the dough well. Let it stand in a cool place for 30 minutes. Roll the dough out to form a rectangle about ½ inch [1 cm.] thick. Brush with the melted lard, fold like a book and roll out again. Repeat this three times, each time allowing the dough to rest for 30 minutes. Finally, roll out the dough until it is less than 1 inch [2½ cm.] thick. Cut it into rounds using a glass or biscuit cutter about 3 inches [8 cm.] in diameter. With a knife, score small squares on top of each cracker. Bake the crackers in a preheated 450° F. [230° C.] oven for 25 minutes. Serve hot.

INGE KRAMARZ
THE BALKAN COOKBOOK

Savory Crackers

Matthi

Lovage seeds are the pungent, highly aromatic seeds of a large, celery-like herb. The seeds are available whole in specialty food shops and—under the name of carom seeds—in stores specializing in Indian foods.

To make about 50

2½ cups	flour	625 ml.
3 tbsp.	vegetable shortening, melted	45 ml.
¾ tsp.	lovage seeds, crushed to a powder	4 ml.
2¼ tsp.	coarse salt	11 ml.
⅛ tsp.	baking soda	½ ml.
2 tbsp.	yogurt	30 ml.
⅔ cup	tepid water	150 ml.
	peanut or corn oil for deep frying	

Place the flour in a large bowl and make a well in the center. Pour the melted shortening into it, and rub the flour and shortening together between the palms of your hands until the flour is evenly coated with the shortening. Stir in the lovage seeds, salt and baking soda. Blend the yogurt with the water and pour the mixture over the flour in a thin stream. Gather the dough into a mass.

Place the dough on marble or a floured board. Coat your fingers and palms with shortening and knead the dough for 10 minutes, or until it is firm but pliable. Place the dough in a greased bowl, cover with a towel or plastic wrap, and let the dough rest at room temperature for at least 30 minutes.

Knead the dough again for a minute. Divide it into eight equal portions and shape them into balls. Place one ball at a time on the board. (Keep the remaining balls covered with plastic wrap to prevent a crust from forming.) Dust the ball generously with flour and roll it into a 10-inch [25-cm.] disk. Cut round crackers with a plain 2-inch [5-cm.] biscuit cutter. With a sharp knife make four to six ¼-inch [6-mm.] slashes in the center of each cracker to prevent it from puffing up during frying. Roll and cut the rest of the balls. The crackers may be set aside for an hour if they are kept loosely covered with plastic wrap to keep them from drying out.

When ready to fry the crackers, heat the peanut or corn oil in a deep skillet until it is moderately hot—325° F. [160° C.] on a deep-frying thermometer.

Drop six to eight crackers at a time into the oil. The crackers will first sink to the bottom of the pan and then—after half a minute—rise, sizzling, to the surface. Fry, turning often, until they are cooked through and barely pink—about three minutes.

Take the crackers out with a slotted spoon and place them on paper towels to drain. Fry the remaining crackers in the same way. When cool, store the crackers in airtight containers; they will keep for eight to 10 weeks.

JULIE SAHNI
CLASSIC INDIAN COOKING

Sesame Seed Wafers

To make about 30

½ cup	sesame seeds	125 ml.
2 cups	sifted flour	½ liter
½ tsp.	salt	2 ml.
12 tbsp.	butter, 10 tbsp. [150 ml.] cut into pieces, the rest softened	180 ml.
1 tsp.	caraway seeds, crushed to a powder	5 ml.
4 tsp.	ice water	20 ml.

Sprinkle the sesame seeds on a baking sheet and toast them in a preheated 350° F. [180° C.] oven until they are golden brown—five to 10 minutes. Let them cool.

Mix the flour, salt and butter pieces. Chop with two knives or a pastry blender until the pieces are the size of small beans. Add the caraway seeds and mix well. Add the water, a few drops at a time, and toss with a fork. Gather the dough up with your hands and shape it into a ball. Roll it ½ inch [1 cm.] thick on a lightly floured board. Spread the dough with the softened butter. Fold the dough in thirds and press the ends together. Chill for at least 30 minutes.

Roll out the dough again ½ inch thick. Sprinkle it with the sesame seeds and roll them in lightly. Cut with a biscuit cutter about 2 inches [5 cm.] in diameter. Place the wafers on an ungreased baking sheet. Bake in a preheated 350° F. [180° C.] oven for 15 to 20 minutes, or until golden.

ANTHONY MILLER (EDITOR)
GOOD FOOD FROM SINGAPORE

Chive Wafers

To make about 50

1 cup	whole-wheat flour	¼ liter
½ cup	wheat germ	125 ml.
¼ tsp.	salt	1 ml.
4 tbsp.	butter, cut into pieces	60 ml.
¼ cup	finely cut fresh chives	50 ml.
1	egg	1
3 to 4 tbsp.	cold milk	45 to 60 ml.

Place the flour, wheat germ and salt in a bowl. With your finger tips or a pastry blender, cut in the butter until the mixture resembles coarse meal. Stir in the chives, egg and enough milk—added a spoonful at a time—to make a stiff, cohesive dough. On a lightly floured board, roll the dough to a thickness of ⅛ inch [3 mm.]. Cut it into 1-inch [2½-cm.] rounds, and place them on lightly buttered baking sheets. Bake in a preheated 400° F. [200° C.] oven for 10 minutes, or until lightly browned. Cool the wafers on a rack.

NANCY ALBRIGHT
RODALE'S NATURALLY GREAT FOODS COOKBOOK

Poppy Seed Crackers

To make about 100

⅓ cup	boiling water	75 ml.
⅓ cup	poppy seeds	75 ml.
2 cups	whole-wheat pastry flour	½ liter
½ tsp.	baking soda	2 ml.
1 ½ tsp.	salt	7 ml.
⅓ tsp.	freshly ground black pepper	1 ml.
⅓ cup	oil	75 ml.
1 tsp.	honey	5 ml.
1	egg, lightly beaten	1
¼ cup	finely chopped onion	50 ml.

In a small bowl, add the boiling water to the poppy seeds; let the mixture stand until cool. Sift together the flour, baking soda, salt and pepper. Add the oil, honey, egg, onion and finally the poppy-seed mixture. Stir until a stiff dough forms. Knead this lightly until it is smooth and shape it into two balls.

On a lightly floured board, roll each ball of the dough ⅛ inch [3 mm.] thick and cut it into rounds with a 1½-inch [4-cm.] biscuit cutter. Place the crackers on ungreased baking sheets and prick each one with a fork. Bake the crackers in a preheated 425° F. [220° C.] oven for 10 to 12 minutes, or until lightly browned. Store them in an airtight container.

FAYE MARTIN
RODALE'S NATURALLY DELICIOUS DESSERTS AND SNACKS

Indian Fenugreek Crackers

Kasoori Mathari

Dried fenugreek leaves and Indian vegetable fat are obtainable at Asian and Indian food stores.

These crackers should rest for several days before being served, for the full-bodied aroma of fenugreek to penetrate.

To make about 80

¼ cup	dried fenugreek leaves	50 ml.
2 ½ cups	flour	625 ml.
2 tsp.	coarse salt	10 ml.
4 tbsp.	butter, chilled and cut into tiny cubes	60 ml.
4 tbsp.	Indian vegetable fat, chilled	60 ml.
about ½ cup	cold water	about 125 ml.

In a large bowl, crumble the fenugreek leaves to a rough powder. Add the flour and salt and mix thoroughly. Add the butter and fat, and mix them in with your finger tips until they are evenly distributed in the flour.

Pour the cold water, about 1 tablespoon [15 ml.] at a time, over the flour mixture until it can be gathered into a mass. Place the dough on a floured marble surface or wooden board, and knead briefly (about one minute) to make a soft, smooth ball. Divide the dough into four equal portions and shape each one into a ball. Place one on the work board, and keep the remaining ones covered with plastic wrap or a moist cloth to prevent a crust forming. Dust each ball in turn lightly with flour and roll it into a 10-inch [25-cm.] circle.

Cut the crackers out with a 1½-inch [4-cm.] round or fancy-shaped cookie cutter. Prick the crackers all over with a fork to prevent them from puffing up during baking. Line two large baking sheets with aluminum foil and place the crackers on them ¾ inch [2 cm.] apart.

Bake them in the middle of a preheated 375° F. [190° C.] oven for 10 minutes, until a few light brown spots appear on the underside. Gently turn the crackers over with a spatula and bake them for another five minutes, or until they are lightly browned on the edges.

Transfer the crackers to wire racks, and cool them thoroughly before storing them in airtight containers.

JULIE SAHNI
CLASSIC INDIAN COOKING

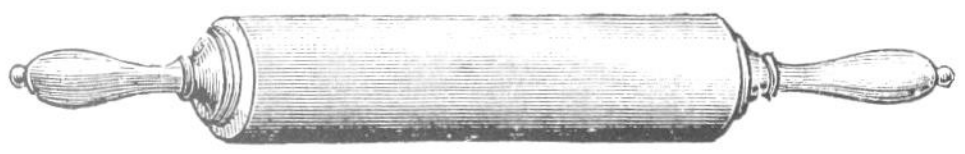

Homemade Graham Crackers

Graham flour is another name for whole-wheat flour. The name comes from Sylvester Graham, an early-19th Century American dietician, who pioneered the use of flour made from the whole grain. To sour 1 cup [¼ liter] of heavy cream, add 1 tablespoon [15 ml.] of vinegar or lemon juice, and let the mixture stand for five minutes.

To make about 40

1 cup	sour heavy cream	¼ liter
½ cup	sugar	125 ml.
1 tbsp.	butter, melted	15 ml.
1 tsp.	baking soda	5 ml.
½ tsp.	salt	2 ml.
about 4 cups	graham flour	about 1 liter

Mix the cream, sugar, butter, soda and salt thoroughly. Add enough graham flour to produce a stiff dough. On a lightly floured board, roll the dough ¼ inch [6 mm.] thick and cut it into 2-inch [5-cm.] squares, ovals or circles. Place on buttered baking sheets and bake in a preheated 450° F. [230° C.] oven for 10 to 12 minutes, or until crisp and brown.

LOUIS P. DE GOUY
THE BREAD TRAY

Graham Crackers

These crackers have a grainy texture and a full wheat-rye flavor. Keep them for at least 24 hours before serving.

To make 24 to 28

1 cup	all-purpose flour	¼ liter
¾ cup	whole-wheat flour	175 ml.
½ cup	rye flour	125 ml.
5 tbsp.	sugar	75 ml.
½ tsp.	salt	2 ml.
½ tsp.	baking soda	2 ml.
1 tsp.	baking powder	5 ml.
¼ tsp.	ground cinnamon	1 ml.
3 tbsp.	unsalted butter, chilled and cut into small pieces	45 ml.
¼ cup	solid vegetable shortening	50 ml.
2 tbsp.	honey	30 ml.
1 tbsp.	molasses	15 ml.
¼ cup	cold water	50 ml.
1 tsp.	vanilla extract	5 ml.

Blend the all-purpose flour, whole-wheat flour, rye flour, sugar, salt, baking soda, baking powder and cinnamon in a bowl. With a pastry blender or your finger tips, work in the butter and shortening until small, even particles are formed.

Mix together the honey, molasses, water and vanilla extract in a small bowl. Sprinkle this mixture gradually into the dry ingredients, tossing with a fork until the liquid is evenly incorporated. Press the dough together into a ball. It may be crumbly, but do not add water. Wrap in plastic wrap and chill for several hours or overnight.

Halve the dough. Let it soften for about 15 minutes. Sprinkle a sheet of wax paper sparingly with rye flour, place one piece of the dough on top and flatten it with a rolling pin. Sprinkle it lightly with rye flour and top with another sheet of wax paper. Roll the dough out to form a rectangle roughly 7 by 15 inches [18 by 38 cm.], rolling slowly and with even pressure so the crumbly dough does not break.

Peel off the top sheet of wax paper and prick the dough all over at ½- to 1-inch [1- to 2½-cm.] intervals, using a skewer or sharp-tined fork. Cut into squares approximately 2½ inches [6 cm.] wide. Transfer the squares to a large baking sheet with a spatula, placing them very close together—almost touching. Repeat the process with the remaining piece of dough. Reroll and cut the scraps.

Bake the crackers on the middle shelf of a preheated 350° F. [180° C.] oven for about 15 minutes, or until they brown lightly on the edges. Transfer to a rack and let cool completely, then store in an airtight container.

HELEN WITTY AND ELIZABETH SCHNEIDER COLCHIE
BETTER THAN STORE-BOUGHT

Homemade Nut and Date Crackers

To make about 40

1 cup	flour, sifted with ⅓ tsp. [1 ½ ml.] salt	¼ liter
1 cup	nuts, ground	¼ liter
1 cup	dates, pitted and ground	¼ liter
1 cup	sugar	¼ liter
3	eggs, beaten	3

Sift the flour over the nuts and dates, and stir to coat the dates evenly. Stir the sugar into the eggs, then add the flour mixture. On a lightly floured board, roll the dough ¼ inch [6 mm.] thick and cut it into two squares. Place the squares on ungreased baking sheets and bake in a preheated 350° F. [180° C.] oven for 12 to 15 minutes, until the squares are firm to the touch. When cold, break the squares into pieces and store the crackers in a cool, dry place.

LOUIS P. DE GOUY
THE BREAD TRAY

Caraway, Salt or Cheese Straws

Kümmel, Salz und Käsestangen

To make about 70

2 cups	flour	½ liter
	salt	
8 tbsp.	butter, cut into pieces	120 ml.
5 tbsp.	sour cream	75 ml.
1	egg yolk, beaten	1
	caraway seeds	
	coarse salt	
	paprika	
	freshly grated well-aged Cheddar or Gruyère cheese	

Place the flour in a bowl with a pinch of salt, then cut in the butter until the mixture has the texture of coarse meal. Stir in the sour cream to make a soft, crumbly dough. Refrigerate the dough for about half an hour. Roll the dough ¼ inch [6 mm.] thick and coat it with the beaten egg yolk.

For caraway straws, sprinkle the dough with 1 tablespoon [15 ml.] of caraway seeds and 2 teaspoons [10 ml.] of coarse salt; for salt straws, sprinkle the dough with 1 tablespoon of coarse salt and 2 teaspoons of paprika; for cheese straws, sprinkle the dough with 1 cup [¼ liter] of grated cheese and 2 teaspoons of paprika.

Cut the dough into narrow strips about ¼ inch wide and 3 inches [8 cm.] long, and arrange them on buttered baking sheets. Bake in a preheated 400° F. [200° C.] oven for 12 minutes, or until the straws are golden.

HEDWIG MARIA STUBER
ICH HELF DIR KOCHEN

Cheese Straws

Brins de Paille

To make about 20

½ cup	Gruyère cheese, grated	125 ml.
½ cup	flour	125 ml.
4 tbsp.	butter	60 ml.
	salt	
2 tbsp.	milk	30 ml.

Place the cheese, flour, butter and a pinch of salt in a bowl, and stir in the milk. Knead the mixture with your hands until it forms a smooth dough; finish by kneading it lightly on a pastry board. Roll the dough into long strips the thickness of pencils. Cut the strips into 3-inch [8-cm.] sections and place them on a buttered and floured baking sheet. Bake in a preheated 425° F. [220° C.] oven for five minutes. The straws will be golden brown and are delicious eaten hot.

PIERRE HUGUENIN
LES MEILLEURES RECETTES DE MA PAUVRE MÈRE

Hot Cheese Crackers

Sajtos Izelitö

To make about 30

¾ cup	flour	175 ml.
½ lb.	butter, half cut into pieces, half softened	¼ kg.
½ lb.	Gruyère cheese, grated (about 2 cups [½ liter])	¼ kg.
3 tbsp.	sour cream	45 ml.
½ tsp.	paprika	2 ml.
	salt	

Mix the flour and the butter pieces until the mixture forms crumbs. Add half of the cheese, 2 tablespoons [30 ml.] of the sour cream, the paprika and a little salt. Knead the dough well, then let it rest in the refrigerator for about two hours.

Roll the dough into a sheet ¼ inch [6 mm.] thick. Cut the sheet into rounds with a small biscuit cutter. Place on baking sheets and bake in a preheated 350° F. [180° C.] oven for 12 to 15 minutes, or until delicately browned. Let the crackers cool just until they can be handled easily.

Mix together the softened butter, remaining cheese and sour cream, and spread a ¼-inch layer of the mixture on half of the crackers. Place a second cracker on top of each one, making little sandwiches, and serve them while still warm.

GEORGE LANG
THE CUISINE OF HUNGARY

Thick Parmesan Crackers

This is a little-known recipe from *The Cookery Book of Lady Clark of Tillypronie,* compiled from a treasure house of note-books left by Lady Clark and published in 1909, nine years after her death. The recipe is an exceptionally good one. Lady Clark makes the point that it is the *thickness* of these crackers that gives them their character. The Parmesan cheese is also essential. The crackers can be stored in an airtight container and heated up when wanted.

To make 12

4 tbsp.	butter, cut into pieces	60 ml.
1 cup	flour	¼ liter
⅔ cup	freshly grated Parmesan cheese	150 ml.
1	egg yolk	1
	salt	
	cayenne pepper	

Rub the butter into the flour. Add the Parmesan cheese, egg yolk, and a pinch each of salt and cayenne pepper, and work well. Moisten with a little water if necessary. Roll the dough to a thickness of ½ inch [1 cm.]. Cut it into 1-inch [2½-cm.] rounds. Arrange the rounds on a lightly buttered baking sheet. Bake in the center of a preheated 325° F. [160° C.] oven for just 20 minutes, or until delicately browned. Serve the crackers hot.

ELIZABETH DAVID
SPICES, SALT AND AROMATICS IN THE ENGLISH KITCHEN

Sefton Fancies
Ramekins à l'Ude

To make about 30

½ lb.	rough puff dough *(recipe, page 166)*	¼ kg.
1 cup	grated well-aged Cheddar or Gruyère cheese	¼ liter
1	egg yolk, mixed with 2 tbsp. [30 ml.] milk	1

Roll out the dough about ¼ inch [6 mm.] thick. Sprinkle the cheese evenly over half of the dough, fold the dough over the cheese, roll it out very lightly and continue thus until the dough and cheese are well mixed. Finally, roll the dough about ¼ inch [6 mm.] thick. Cut it into rounds with a 2-inch [5-cm.] biscuit cutter. Brush the rounds with the egg yolk and milk, and place them on a buttered and floured baking sheet. Bake for about 15 minutes in a preheated 400° F. [200° C.] oven, or until the crackers are lightly browned. Serve them very hot.

SHEILA HUTCHINS
ENGLISH RECIPES AND OTHERS FROM SCOTLAND, WALES AND IRELAND

Stiltonettes

To make about 25

6 oz.	Stilton cheese, crumbled	175 g.
8 tbsp.	butter, softened	120 ml.
2 cups	flour, sifted	½ liter
2 tbsp.	yogurt	30 ml.
⅓ cup	finely chopped pimiento	75 ml.
4 tsp.	finely cut fresh chives	20 ml.

Rub the cheese and butter into the flour and add the yogurt to make a firm dough. Knead it well with floured hands; form the dough into a log, cover the log with plastic wrap, and chill it for one hour in the refrigerator or for 10 minutes in the freezer.

Roll out the chilled dough on a lightly floured board into a rectangle about ¼ inch [6 mm.] thick. Sprinkle it with the pimiento and chives and lightly pat them in with your hand. Roll up the dough lengthwise, as you would a jelly roll. Tightly wrap the roll in plastic wrap and chill it again.

When the roll is chilled, unwrap it and cut slices approximately ¼ inch thick. Set the slices about 1 inch [2½ cm.] apart on ungreased baking sheets and bake in a preheated 425° F. [220° C.] oven for 15 minutes, or until golden.

ANITA MAY PEARL
COMPLETELY CHEESE: THE CHEESELOVER'S COMPANION

Cheddar Chips

To make about 50

1 cup	whole-wheat flour	¼ liter
¼ cup	wheat germ	50 ml.
½ tsp.	salt	2 ml.
4 tbsp.	butter, cut into pieces	60 ml.
1 cup	grated sharp Cheddar cheese	¼ liter
¼ cup	very finely ground walnuts	50 ml.
1	egg yolk	1
2 to 3 tbsp.	ice water	30 to 45 ml.

Place the flour, wheat germ and salt in a bowl and mix well. Work in the butter with your finger tips or a pastry blender until the mixture is like coarse meal. Stir in the cheese, walnuts, egg yolk and blend in enough water—a spoonful at a time—to make a cohesive dough. Knead the dough briefly. Roll the dough on a lightly floured board to a thickness of ⅛ inch [3 mm.] and cut it into 2-inch [5-cm.] triangles. Place on a lightly buttered baking sheet and bake in a preheated 375° F. [190° C.] oven for 12 to 15 minutes, or until lightly browned. Cool on a rack and store in an airtight container.

NANCY ALBRIGHT
RODALE'S NATURALLY GREAT FOODS COOKBOOK

Standard Preparations

Confectioners' Sugar Glaze

This glaze may be flavored to taste with vanilla, almond or peppermint extract, or with rum, brandy or a liqueur. Because spirits must be added in larger amounts than extracts, for each tablespoon of spirits reduce the amount of water used in the glaze by 1 tablespoon [15 ml.]. For a fruit-flavored glaze, replace the water with strained fresh fruit juice. To make a coffee-flavored glaze, replace the water with strong black coffee. For a chocolate-flavored glaze, melt 2 ounces [60 g.] of semisweet baking chocolate in a heavy pan set over hot water; let the chocolate cool slightly, then stir it into the finished glaze.

To make about 1 cup [¼ liter]

1½ cups	confectioners' sugar	375 ml.
3 to 4 tbsp.	water	45 to 60 ml.

Sift the confectioners' sugar into a bowl. Stir in the water—a spoonful at a time—until the glaze reaches the desired consistency and is smooth. Use the glaze at once.

Caramel-colored Egg Glaze

The quantities called for in this recipe will produce about 1 cup [¼ liter] of caramel syrup—the smallest amount that can be made without burning the caramel, but more than is necessary for the glaze. The remaining syrup can be used as a dessert sauce.

To make about ½ cup [125 ml.]

1 cup	sugar	¼ liter
1 cup	water, ½ cup [125 ml.] hot	¼ liter
3	egg yolks	3

Combine the sugar and ½ cup [125 ml.] of cold water in a heavy saucepan. Stir until the sugar dissolves, place the pan over medium heat and continue to stir until the syrup comes to a boil. With a brush dipped in water, brush down any sugar crystals sticking to the side of the pan. Cook the syrup undisturbed over medium-high heat until it becomes reddish brown in color—about 350° F. [180° C.] on a candy thermometer. Take the pan off the heat immediately and stir ½ cup [125 ml.] of hot water into the caramel to thin it and prevent it from setting. If necessary, return the pan to the heat, stirring to thin any solidified caramel at the bottom of the pan. Let the caramel cool to room temperature. To make the glaze, beat the egg yolks until smooth. Whisking constantly, gradually pour ⅓ cup [75 ml.] of the cooled caramel syrup into the yolks.

Royal Icing

To make about 2 cups [½ liter]

2½ cups	confectioners' sugar	625 ml.
3	egg whites	3
1½ tsp.	strained fresh lemon juice	7 ml.

Using a wooden spoon, stir about half of the sugar into the egg whites. Add the lemon juice and beat the mixture with the spoon until it is thoroughly blended, then add the remaining sugar—a little at a time—beating well after each addition. Continue to beat the mixture for 15 minutes, or until it is smooth and creamy. The icing can be used immediately or kept for up to 30 minutes if covered with a damp cloth. If kept longer, the icing will begin to set.

Thick royal icing. Increase the amount of confectioners' sugar to 4 cups [1 liter] and use only two egg whites.

Uncooked Butter Icing

To make about 4 cups [1 liter]

4 tbsp.	butter, softened	60 ml.
1 lb.	confectioners' sugar, sifted	½ kg.
¼ cup	heavy cream	50 ml.
1 tsp.	vanilla extract	5 ml.

Cream the butter until light and fluffy. Beat in the sugar—a little at a time—then add the cream. Stir in the vanilla. The icing can be used immediately or kept tightly covered and refrigerated for up to a week. Soften refrigerated icing at room temperature for about two hours before using it.

Chocolate butter icing. Melt 2 ounces [60 g.] of semisweet chocolate in a bowl set over hot water. Cool before adding it.

Coffee butter icing. Add 1 tablespoon [15 ml.] of cooled, strong black coffee to the icing and stir until blended.

Lemon Filling

Orange filling can be made by substituting orange peel and juice for the lemon peel and juice.

To make about 2 cups [½ liter]

2 cups	confectioners' sugar	½ liter
4 tsp.	freshly grated lemon peel	20 ml.
¼ cup	strained fresh lemon juice	50 ml.
1 tbsp.	unsalted butter, melted and cooled	15 ml.

In a heatproof bowl, mix the confectioners' sugar and lemon peel together. Stir in the lemon juice, then add the melted butter. Place the bowl over a pan of hot water set over low heat and stir the mixture until all of the ingredients are blended smoothly. Remove the pan from the heat and let the mixture rest over the water for 10 minutes, stirring it from time to time to prevent a film from forming on the top.

Remove the bowl from the pan and beat the mixture with a whisk for about five minutes, until the paste becomes light in color and is thick enough to spread easily.

Praline Butter Filling

To make about 4 cups [1 liter]

½ lb.	almonds, blanched and peeled (about 2 cups [½ liter])	¼ kg.
1 cup	sugar	¼ liter
½ lb.	butter, softened	¼ kg.

In a heavy saucepan, cook the almonds and sugar over low heat, stirring constantly, until the sugar caramelizes and turns a light golden brown. Immediately pour this praline onto a buttered baking sheet.

When it is cool and hard, break the praline into pieces, put them in a plastic bag and crush them to a powder with a mallet or rolling pin. Sift the praline through a sieve set over a bowl; return any large pieces to the plastic bag and repeat until all of the praline is powdered.

Alternatively, drop the pieces of praline—a small batch at a time—into a food processor equipped with a metal blade. Turn the machine on and off in short bursts to grind each batch to a fine powder.

In a heavy bowl, cream the butter by beating it with a wooden spoon until it is light-colored and fluffy. Beat in the praline powder, a little at a time, and continue beating the mixture until it is smooth and thick.

Coffee butter filling. Cream the butter and gradually beat in 2½ cups [625 ml.] of sifted confectioners' sugar. Add 2 tablespoons [30 ml.] of cold, strong black coffee.

Chocolate butter filling. Cream the butter and gradually beat in 2½ cups of sifted confectioners' sugar. Then beat in 4 ounces [125 g.] of semisweet baking chocolate that has been melted in a heatproof bowl set over hot water, then cooled to room temperature.

Nut Filling

Any kind of unsalted nut—walnut, pecan, hazelnut or cashew, for example—or a mixture of several kinds of nuts, may be used for this filling.

To make 3 cups [¾ liter]

½ lb.	nuts, coarsely chopped (about 2 cups [½ liter])	¼ kg.
1 cup	sugar	¼ liter
1 tbsp.	rose water or orange-flower water, or 1 tsp. [5 ml.] vanilla or almond extract mixed with 2 tsp. [10 ml.] water	15 ml.

Place the nuts and sugar in a bowl and mix together thoroughly. Add the liquid flavoring and stir until the mixture is evenly moistened and resembles coarse bread crumbs.

Fig Filling

To make 1 to 1 ½ cups [250 to 375 ml.]

½ lb.	dried figs	¼ liter
1 cup	water	¼ liter
1 cup	sugar	¼ liter

Combine the figs and water in a saucepan and bring to a boil over high heat. Reduce the heat to low, cover, and simmer until the figs are soft—10 to 20 minutes. Drain the figs—reserving the liquid—and let them cool. Remove the stems and chop the figs into small pieces. Then return them to the saucepan with the sugar and reserved liquid. Stirring constantly, bring the mixture to a simmer over medium heat and cook until it forms a thick paste—about 10 minutes.

Nut Paste

Nut paste can be made from most kinds of nuts: almonds, beechnuts, Brazil nuts, hazelnuts, hickory nuts, pistachios, pecans, walnuts, peanuts or a mixture of these. The ratio of granulated sugar to nuts can be as high as two parts of sugar to one part of nuts. One variation is to use equal parts of ground nuts and dark brown sugar. To make an even finer-textured paste, substitute 1 pound [½ kg.] of confectioners' sugar for the granulated sugar.

Nut paste bound with whole eggs is rich, thick and dark in color, but can be stored in the refrigerator for no longer than one week. A softer and lighter-colored paste can be produced by binding the nuts with four lightly beaten egg whites instead of two whole eggs; it will keep safely in the refrigerator for three weeks.

Suitable flavorings for nut pastes include vanilla, brandy, rum, liqueur or finely grated citrus peel. To flavor and color the paste, dust a cool surface with sugar and put the paste on it. Knead in a few drops of the desired coloring and flavoring. If the mixture becomes too moist, knead in a little more sugar; if the mixture dries out during kneading, add a little lightly beaten egg.

To make about 2 pounds [1 kg.]

1 lb.	almonds, blanched, peeled and ground (about 4 cups [1 liter])	½ kg.
2 cups	sugar	½ liter
2 tsp.	finely grated lemon peel	10 ml.
2	eggs, lightly beaten	2

In a large bowl, mix together the ground almonds, sugar and lemon peel. Stirring constantly with a fork or knife, gradually add the beaten eggs, a little at a time. As soon as the nut mixture is thoroughly moistened, begin to knead the mixture gently with your hands while you continue to add the remaining eggs. Gather the mixture into a ball and knead it briefly until it forms a smooth paste.

Meringues

The technique of making meringue is demonstrated on pages 60-61. For the hazelnut-based meringues shown, add ¾ pound [375 g.]—about 3 cups [¾ liter]—of ground blanched hazelnuts to two thirds of the meringue mixture.

To make about 30

6	egg whites	6
1 cup	superfine sugar	¼ liter

Beat the egg whites until they form soft peaks. Sprinkle a few spoonfuls of the sugar over the beaten egg whites and whisk it in. Whisking constantly, continue to add the sugar, a spoonful at a time, until all of it is incorporated and the mixture is firm enough to hold stiff and glossy peaks.

Pipe or spoon small mounds of the mixture onto baking sheets lined with parchment paper, spacing the mounds about an inch [2½ cm.] apart. Place the baking sheets on a low shelf in a 200° F. [100° C.] oven and bake the meringues for about three hours, or until they are completely dry to the touch. Allow the meringues to cool before removing them from the paper.

Basic Creamed Dough

This firm creamed dough is ideal for rolled cookies. It may be further flavored with up to 1 cup [¼ liter] of chopped nuts or candied fruit. Rolled ¼ inch [6 mm.] thick and cut into 2-inch [5-cm.] rounds, the dough will yield about 40 cookies.

To make a rich creamed dough, suitable for pressed or refrigerator cookies, increase the butter by 2 tablespoons [30 ml.] to ½ pound [¼ kg.], and add an egg yolk. This version will also yield about 40 cookies.

To turn either version into chocolate cookie dough, substitute ½ cup [125 ml.] of cocoa powder for ¼ cup [50 ml.] of the flour called for in this recipe.

To make about 1½ pounds [¾ kg.]

14 tbsp.	butter, softened	210 ml.
1 cup	sugar	¼ liter
1	egg	1
1 tsp.	vanilla or almond extract, or a combination of the two	5 ml.
2 cups	flour	½ liter
½ tsp.	salt	2 ml.

Cream the butter and sugar together until pale and fluffy. Beat in the egg and flavoring extract. Sift together the flour and salt. Stir the flour gradually into the creamed mixture. When the dough becomes too stiff to stir, mix in the remaining flour by hand. Wrap the dough and refrigerate it for about 30 minutes before rolling it. The dough can safely be kept refrigerated for about seven days.

Short-Crust Dough

The proportion of fat to flour in short-crust dough can be varied according to the result required. For a light and tender pastry, use the smaller quantity of butter; for a richer and crisper pastry, use the larger quantity of butter.

To make about 1 pound [½ kg.]

2 cups	flour	½ liter
	salt	
8 to 12 tbsp.	butter, cut into pieces and chilled	120 to 180 ml.
4 to 6 tbsp.	cold water	60 to 90 ml.

Sift the flour with a pinch of salt into a bowl. Add the butter. Rub the butter and flour together with your finger tips until the mixture has a coarse, mealy texture, or cut the butter into the flour with two knives. Add 4 tablespoons [60 ml.] of the water and, with a knife or fork, quickly blend it into the flour mixture. Add just enough of the rest of the water to form a cohesive dough. Gather the dough into a ball and wrap it in plastic wrap. Refrigerate the dough for at least one hour or put it into the freezer for half that time, before rolling it out.

Rough Puff Dough

The liquid used for this recipe can be varied according to how rich a dough is required. Water, milk, cream or egg yolk thinned with water are all suitable; for an especially rich, sweet dough, the liquid may be a combination of egg yolk, cream and rum.

To make about 2½ pounds [1¼ kg.]

4 cups	flour	1 liter
	salt	
2 tbsp.	confectioners' sugar (optional)	30 ml.
1 lb.	butter, cut into cubes and chilled	½ kg.
about 1 cup	liquid	about ¼ liter

Sift the flour, a pinch of salt and the confectioners' sugar, if using, into a bowl. Add the butter and cut it rapidly into the flour with two knives, keeping the pieces of butter quite large. Quickly stir in just enough liquid to make the mixture cohere, then gather the dough together with your hands and form it into a ball. Wrap the dough in plastic wrap and refrigerate it for 45 minutes to an hour, or freeze it for about 20 minutes, until the surface is slightly frozen.

Place the dough on a cool, floured surface and beat it flat with a rolling pin. Turn the dough over to make sure that both sides are lightly floured. Roll the dough out rapidly into a rectangle about three times as long as it is wide. Fold the two ends to meet each other in the center, then fold again to align the folded edges with each other. Following the direction of the fold lines, roll the dough into a rectangle again. Fold it again in the same way, wrap the dough and refrigerate it for at least 30 minutes. Repeat this process two or three more times before using the dough. Always let the dough rest in the refrigerator between rollings.

─────────◆─────────

Basic Syrup Dough

To prepare the mixed spices called for in this recipe, mix any combination desired of ground cinnamon, ginger, cloves, coriander and black pepper; grated nutmeg; whole or ground fennel seeds and anise seeds. Rolled ¼ inch [6 mm.] thick, this dough will yield about thirty 3-inch [8-cm.] round or 1-by-3-inch [2½-by-8-cm.] rectangular cookies.

To make about 2 to 2½ pounds [1 kg.]

1⅓ cups	syrup (honey or molasses)	325 ml.
1⅓ cups	firmly packed light brown sugar	325 ml.
2 tbsp.	butter	30 ml.
2 tbsp.	water	30 ml.
3½ cups	flour	875 ml.
½ tsp.	baking soda	2 ml.
	salt	
1 to 2 tsp.	mixed spices	5 to 10 ml.
1 cup	chopped almonds or hazelnuts (optional)	¼ liter
1 cup	chopped candied lemon or orange peel (optional)	¼ liter

Place the syrup, sugar, butter and water in a saucepan and stir over low heat until the sugar has dissolved and the ingredients are blended together. Then increase the heat to bring the mixture to a boil. Remove the pan from the heat and let the mixture cool to room temperature.

Sift together the flour, baking soda, a pinch of salt and the spices. Gradually add these to the cooled syrup, stirring well after each addition. When all of the sifted ingredients have been incorporated, add the chopped nuts and candied peel, if using, and stir them in well.

Turn the dough onto a floured board. Flour your hands and knead the dough lightly for a few minutes until it is smooth. The dough is now ready to be rolled. Tightly wrapped, the dough can safely be kept in the refrigerator for a half day; in this case, bring it to room temperature before rolling it.

Soda Crackers

To make the sour milk called for in this recipe, add 1 teaspoon [5 ml.] of fresh lemon juice or vinegar to ¼ cup [50 ml.] of milk. Let the mixture stand five minutes before using it.

To make about 250

1½ tsp.	active dry yeast or one half of a ⅗ oz. [18 g.] cake fresh yeast	7 ml.
2 cups plus 1 tbsp.	tepid water	½ liter plus 15 ml.
8 cups	flour, sifted	2 liters
6 tbsp.	lard, softened	90 ml.
1 tbsp.	salt	15 ml.
1 tsp.	baking soda	5 ml.
¼ cup	buttermilk or sour milk	50 ml.

In a large bowl, mix the yeast with 2 cups [½ liter] of the tepid water and let the mixture stand for 10 minutes. Add 6 cups [1½ liters] of the flour to the yeast mixture and stir to combine the ingredients. When the dough becomes too stiff to stir, incorporate the flour with your hands. Cover the bowl with plastic wrap and set the dough in a warm, draft-free place for at least 20—but no more than 30—hours.

When the dough has doubled in volume, blend in the lard. Dissolve the salt and baking soda in 1 tablespoon [15 ml.] of tepid water. Make a well on one side of the dough and pour in the buttermilk or sour milk. Pour the soda mixture into a well on the opposite side. Mix the dough quickly with your hands. Turn the dough out onto a floured board and gradually knead in the remaining 2 cups of flour to form a very stiff but silky dough—about 10 minutes. Place the dough in a clean bowl and cover it with plastic wrap. Allow the dough to rest for four hours.

Place the dough on a lightly floured board. Pound the dough flat with a rolling pin and then roll the dough into an 18-by-28-inch [46-by-70-cm.] rectangle about ¼ inch [6 mm.] thick. Fold the dough crosswise into thirds and use a pastry brush dipped in flour to dust the folded sides very lightly. Repeat the rolling and folding two more times, until the dough is smooth. Then divide the dough into four equal portions. Cover three of the portions with plastic wrap and roll the fourth into a sheet about ¹⁄₁₆ inch [1½ mm.] thick. Trim the sheet into an 18-inch [46-cm.] square, prick it all over with a fork and cut it into 2-inch [5-cm.] squares.

Place a baking sheet in a preheated 550° F. [290° C.] oven for a few minutes to heat it, and then quickly place about 25 of the squares on the hot baking sheet and bake on the top shelf of the oven for three minutes until golden. Roll, cut and bake the remaining portions of dough similarly. Cool the crackers, then store them in an airtight container.

─────────◆─────────

Recipe Index

All recipes in the index that follows are listed by the English title except in cases where cookies or crackers of foreign origin, such as langues-de-chat, are widely recognized by their source name. Entries are organized in separate categories by major ingredients specified in the recipe titles. Foreign recipes are listed under the country or region of origin. Recipe credits appear on pages 173-176.

Algerian recipes:
 date lozenges, 154
 walnut cigars, 141
Almond:
 bites, 138
 bitter-, macaroons, 151
 cats' tongues with, 147
 Chinese, cookies, 127
 chocolate, wreaths, 140
 -coconut cookies, 138
 cookies, 137
 crescents from Provence, 137
 -date bars, 109
 and date topping, 109
 Moroccan, cookies, 138
 -paste cookies, 101
 petits fours, 148
 puff-pastry slices with, topping, 124
 sponge slices, 108
 toast, 129
 topping, 109.
 See also Macaroons
Anise:
 caps, 101
 seed shells, 118
Apple: spicy, bars, 107
Applesauce gems, 95
Apricot:
 bars, 106
 topping, 106
Austrian recipes:
 Linzer cookies, 139
 Linz nut cookies, 109
 snowballs, 154
Ayrshire shortbread, 126

Baked "potato chips," 155
Bar cookies, 103-112
Basic creamed dough, 166
Basic syrup dough, 167
Bath Oliver crackers, 158
Bear's paws, 124-125
Best peanut butter and chocolate
 cookies, 98
Best peanut butter cookies, 136
Biscuits:
 English rout, 124
 Orford's water, 157.
 See also Crackers; Wafers
Bitter-almond macaroons, 151
Black walnut and coconut bars, 111

Black and white cookies, 128
Brandy:
 brown sugar, snaps, 132
 cookie twists, 137
 snaps, 131
Brazil-nut crisps, 139
Bride's cookies, 139
Brown butter frosting, 104
Brown sugar brandy snaps, 132
Brownies:
 butterscotch, 104
 Cockaigne, 103
 marbled, 104
 peanut butter, 104
Butter:
 cardamom, cookies, 117
 chocolate, filling, 165
 chocolate, icing, 164
 coffee, filling, 165
 coffee, icing, 164
 praline, filling, 165
 rum, cookies, 113
 uncooked, icing, 164
Butterscotch brownies, 104

Cakes:
 Derbyshire wakes, 121
 Easter, 117
 original Moravian Christmas, 120
 Shrewsbury, 120.
 See also Shortbread
Calais cookies, 116
Candlemas cookies from St. Victor,
 135
Cannoli all'arancia, 146
Caramel-colored egg glaze, 164
Caraway straws, 162
Cardamom butter cookies, 117
Carrot cookies, 103
Cats' tongues, 147;
 with almonds, 147
Cheddar chips, 163
Cheese:
 cream, filling, 106
 cream, press cookies, 144
 hot, crackers, 162
 straws, 162.
 See also Cheddar; Cottage cheese;
 Cream cheese; Parmesan
Cheesecake cookies, 106
Cherokee date rocks, 97
Cherry:
 cookies, 122
 horns, 124
Chick-pea flour squares, 107
Chinese recipes:
 almond cookies, 127
 sesame roundels, 128
Chive wafers, 160
Chocolate:
 almond wreaths, 140
 best peanut butter and, cookies, 98
 butter filling, 165
 butter icing, 164
 chip cookies, 98
 confectioners' sugar cookies, 140
 crackled, drops, 98
 fleck rings, 125
 icing, 145
 oatmeal cookies, 100
 shells, 124

snaps, 98
 spritz, 145
 sticks, 124
 Toll House crunch cookies, 99
 walnut wheels, 99
Chrust, Polish, 152
Cigarettes, Russian, 133
Cinnamon:
 cookies, 109
 Czechoslovakian, cookies, 118
 Dutch, cookies, 118
 stars, 149
Citron sponge cookies, 105
Coating, honey, 143
Coconut:
 almond-, cookies, 138
 black walnut and, bars, 111
 shortbread, 113
 walnut and, topping, 111
Coffee:
 bars, 105
 butter filling, 165
 butter icing, 164
Cold-dough yeast cookies, 126
Confectioners' sugar:
 chocolate, cookies, 140
 glaze, 164
Cornets, small, 134
Cornmeal: fruited, cookies, 96
Cottage cheese cookies, 100
Country cookies, 100
Crackers, 155-163
Crackers:
 with cracklings and white wine, 159
 honey, 116
 soda, 167
 tea, 94
Crackled chocolate drops, 98
Cracklings: crackers with, and white
 wine, 159
Cracknel crackers, 158
Cream:
 filling, 151
 horns, 133
Cream cheese:
 filling, 106
 press cookies, 144
Creamed dough, basic, 166
Crescents: almond, from Provence,
 137
Crisp Chartres cookies, 147
Crisp nut cookies, 123
Crispy meringue drops, 148
Currant cookies, 121;
 small, 121
Czechoslovakian recipes:
 cinnamon cookies, 118
 original Moravian Christmas cakes,
 120

Danish recipe: vanilla wafers, 94
Date:
 almond-, bars, 109
 almond and, topping, 109
 Cherokee, rocks, 97
 cookies, 149
 homemade nut and, crackers, 162
 lozenges, 154
Dead men's bones, 127
Deep-fried pretzel-shaped sweets,
 155

Derbyshire wakes cakes, 121
Donegal oatcake, 157
Dorset shortbread, 135
Dough:
 basic creamed, 166
 basic syrup, 167
 rough puff, 166
 short-crust, 166
 wine, 108
Drop cookies, 94-103
Dutch recipes:
 cinnamon cookies, 118
 macaroons, 150
 meringue cookies, 149
 sand rosettes, 144
 "shell bark" macaroons, 125
 spicy Speculaas, 108
 spritz cookies, 144
 sweet thumbs, 144

Easter cakes, 117
Easter cookies, 140
Easter milk cookies, 142
Egg glaze, caramel-colored, 164
English rout biscuits, 124
Eulalia cookies, 102
Exquisite cookies, 115

Fenugreek crackers, Indian, 160
Fig:
 filling, 165
 newtons, 120
Filling:
 chocolate butter, 165
 coffee butter, 165
 cream, 151
 cream cheese, 106
 fig, 165
 hazelnut, 123
 lemon, 164
 nut, 165
 praline butter, 165
Flapjacks, 112
Flatbread, Norwegian, 156
Florentines, 95
Flour:
 chick-pea, squares, 107
 rice, cookies, 153
Frazer's cheaters (nut squares), 110
French recipes:
 almond crescents from Provence,
 137
 almond-paste cookies, 101
 almond petits fours, 148
 anise seed shells, 118
 bitter-almond macaroons, 151
 Candlemas cookies from St. Victor,
 135
 cats' tongues, 147
 cats' tongues with almonds, 147
 cheese straws, 162
 cracknel crackers, 158
 crisp Chartres cookies, 147
 crisp nut cookies, 123
 Easter cakes, 117
 exquisite cookies, 115
 florentines, 95
 fried cookies from Lyons, 152
 hazelnut cookies, 129
 jawbreakers, 130
 ladies' wafers, 145

ladyfingers, 145
langues-de-chat, 147
langues-de-chat aux amandes, 147
macaroons, 151
macaroons, in the style of Nice, 150
madeleines, 131
Mariette's cookies, 94
meringue fingers, 149
mirrors, 151
palets de dame, 145
pine nut cookies, 123
puff-pastry slices with almond
   topping, 124
puffs, 148
rum cookies, 146
sablés, 114
Salers' squares, 114
sand cookies, 114
sand cookies from Caen, 114
small cornets, 134
wood shavings, 133
ried cookies, 152-155
ried cookies from Lyons, 152
ried pastries, 152
ried ribbon cookies, 153
rosting:
   brown butter, 104.
    See also Icing
ruit. *See* Apple; Apricot; Cherry;
   Currant; Date; Fig; Lemon;
   Orange; Raisin
ruited cornmeal cookies, 96

Genoese cookies, 107
German recipes:
   almond toast, 129
   anise caps, 101
   bear's paws, 124
   black and white cookies, 128
   caraway straws, 162
   cheese straws, 162
   chocolate shells, 124
   cinnamon stars, 149
   cream horns, 133
   little Alberts, 113
   millennial cookies, 102
   parson's hats, 123
   peppernuts, 142
   pfeffernüsse, 142
   salt straws, 162
   small currant cookies, 121
   spoon cookies, 146
   springerle, 117
   white Nuremberg peppercakes,
    122
Ginger:
   bread, 119
   Mrs. Gurney's, snaps, 119
   Swedish, nuts, 119
Gipsy creams, 135
Glaze:
   for almond petits fours, 148
   caramel-colored egg, 164
   confectioners' sugar, 164
Graham crackers, 161;
   homemade, 161
Greek recipes:
   brandy cookie twists, 137
   chocolate confectioners' sugar
    cookies, 140
   Venetian honey cookies, 143

Hazelnut:
   cookies, 129
   filling, 123
Homemade graham crackers,
   161
Homemade nut and date crackers,
   162
Honey:
   coating, 143
   crackers, 116
   kisses, 115
   topping, 154
   Venetian, cookies, 143
Horns:
   cream, 133
   little, 136
   small cornets, 134
Hot cheese crackers, 162
Hungarian recipes:
   hot cheese crackers, 162
   hussar's kisses, 136
   rum butter cookies, 113
Hunting nuts, 142
Hussar's kisses, 136

Ice cream wafers, 113
Icebox cookies, 126
Icing:
   chocolate, 145
   chocolate butter, 164
   coffee butter, 164
   royal, 164
   uncooked butter, 164.
    See also Frosting
Indian recipes:
   deep-fried pretzel-shaped sweets,
    155
   fenugreek crackers, 160
   rice flour cookies, 153
   savory crackers, 159
Iranian recipe: chick-pea flour
   squares, 107
Italian recipes:
   almond bites, 138
   almond cookies, 137
   almond sponge slices, 108
   cannoli all'arancia, 146
   citron sponge cookies, 105
   fried ribbon cookies, 153
   fruited cornmeal cookies, 96
   Genoese cookies, 107
   jam cookies, 96
   lady's kisses, 136
   nut-filled pastries, 111
   orange pipes, 146
   pistachio cookies, 101
   roof tiles, 132
   spilamberto macaroons, 150
   Venetian "bean" cookies, 141
   Vercelli spice sticks, 146
   wine sipping cookies, 141

Jam cookies, 96
Jamaican squares, 112
Jawbreakers, 130
Juice: orange, cookies, 97

Karen's oat cookies, 122

Lace molasses wafers, 131
Ladies' wafers, 145

Ladyfingers, 145
Lady's kisses, 136
Langues-de-chat, 147;
   aux amandes, 147
Lebanese recipes:
   Easter cookies, 140
   Easter milk cookies, 142
Lemon:
   bars, 106
   filling, 164
   praline cookies, 138
Light cookies, 95
Linzer cookies, 139
Linz nut cookies, 109
Little Alberts, 113
Little horns, 136
Little loaves, 124
Lozenges, date, 154

Macaroons, 150-151
Macaroons, Dutch "shell bark," 125
Madeleines, 131
Maple sugar:
   bars, 115
   cookies, 115
Marbled brownies, 104
Mariette's cookies, 94
Meringues, 148-149, 166
Mexican recipe: bride's cookies, 139
Milk: Easter, cookies, 142
Millennial cookies, 102
Mirrors, 151
Molasses: lace, wafers, 131
**Molded and hand-shaped
  cookies,** 129-143
Moroccan recipes:
   almond cookies, 138
   sesame seed cookies, 143
Mrs. Gurney's ginger snaps, 119

Norwegian recipes:
   flatbread, 156
   Karen's oat cookies, 122
Nut:
   crisp, cookies, 123
   -filled pastries, 111
   filling, 165
   homemade, and date crackers, 162
   Linz, cookies, 109
   paste, 165
   squares (Frazer's cheaters), 110.
    See also Almond; Brazil nut;
    Coconut; Hazelnut; Linz nut;
    Peanut; Pecan; Pine nut;
    Pistachio; Walnut

Oatcake:
   Donegal, 159
   Scotch, 157
Oat crackers, 156
Oatmeal:
   chocolate, cookies, 100
   country cookies, 100
   gipsy creams, 135
   Karen's oat cookies, 122
   pecan, cookies, 99
   raisin cookies, 100
Orange:
   juice cookies, 97
   jumbles, 96
   pecan cookies, 127

pipes, 146
Orford's water biscuits, 157
Original Moravian Christmas cakes,
   120

Palets de dame, 145
Parmesan: thick, crackers, 163
Parson's hats, 123
Paste:
   nut, 165
   walnut, 141
Pastry:
   fried, 152
   nut-filled, 111
   puff-, slices with almond topping,
    124
Peanut butter:
   best, and chocolate cookies, 98
   best, cookies, 136
   brownies, 104
   cookies, 97
   rolled, cookies, 125
Peanut crackers, 158
Pecan:
   cookies, 110
   oatmeal cookies, 99
   orange, cookies, 127
   squares, 111
   topping, 110
Peppercakes, white Nuremberg, 122
Peppernuts, 142
Peruvian recipe: little horns, 136
Petits fours, almond, 148
Pfeffernüsse, 142
Pine nut cookies, 123
Pistachio cookies, 101
Pitcaithly bannock, 112
Polish recipes:
   chocolate almond wreaths, 140
   chrust, 152
   cold-dough yeast cookies, 126
   honey kisses, 115
   poppy seed cookies, 118
Poppy seed:
   cookies, 118
   crackers, 160
"Potato chips," baked, 155
Praline:
   butter filling, 165
   lemon, cookies, 138
Pressed and piped cookies,
   144-148
Pressed sour-cream cookies, 144
Pressed spice cookies, 144
Puff dough, rough, 166
Puff-pastry slices with almond
   topping, 124
Puffs, French, 148
Pumpkin cookies, 102

Raisin:
   cookies, 97
   oatmeal cookies, 100
Refrigerator cookies, 126-129
Rice flour cookies, 153
Rolled cookies, 112-126
Rolled peanut butter cookies, 125
Roof tiles, 132;
   Italian, 132
Rough puff dough, 166
Rout biscuits, English, 124

Rout rings, 124
Royal icing, 164
Rum:
    butter cookies, 113
    cookies, 146
Russian recipes:
    almond-date bars, 109
    cigarettes, 133
    cookies, 131
    sugar cookies, 116
Rye:
    crackers, 158
    drops, 154
    Uncle Max's, crackers, 156

Sablés, 114;
    de Caen, 114
Salers' squares, 114
Salt straws, 162
Sand:
    cookies, 114
    cookies from Caen, 114
    rosettes, 144
Savory crackers, 159
Scotch oatcakes, 157
Sefton fancies, 163
Sesame roundels, 128
Sesame seed:
    Moroccan, cookies, 143
    wafers, 160
Shells:
    anise seed, 118
    chocolate, 124
Short-crust dough, 166
Shortbread, 134;
    Ayrshire, 126
    coconut, 113
    Dorset, 135
    walnut, 134

Shrewsbury cakes, 120
Sighs from Cudillero, 135
Singaporean recipe: sesame seed
    wafers, 160
Small cornets, 134
Small currant cookies, 121
Snowballs, 154
Soda crackers, 167
Sour cream:
    cookies, 116
    pressed, cookies, 144
Spanish recipes:
    almond-coconut cookies, 138
    country cookies, 100
    Eulalia, 102
    fried pastries, 152
    light cookies, 95
    raisin cookies, 97
    roof tiles, 132
    sighs from Cudillero, 135
    wine cookies, 153
Speculaas, spicy, 108
Spice:
    pressed, cookies, 144
    Vercelli, sticks, 146.
    See also Anise; Caraway;
        Cardamom; Cinnamon; Ginger;
        Poppy seed; Sesame seed
Spicy apple bars, 107
Spicy Speculaas, 108
Spilamberto macaroons, 150
Spoon cookies, 146
Springerle, 117
Spritz cookies, 144-145
Standard preparations, 164-167
Stiltonettes, 163
Straws:
    caraway, 162
    cheese, 162

salt, 162
Sugar. See Brown sugar;
    Confectioners' sugar; Maple sugar
Sugar cookies, Russian, 116
Swedish recipes:
    gingernuts, 119
    pressed spice cookies, 144
Sweet-potato cookies, 103
Sweet thumbs, 144
Swiss recipes:
    cinnamon cookies, 109
    dead men's bones, 127
Syrup, 154;
    basic, dough, 167

Tea crackers, 94
Thick Parmesan crackers, 163
Toast:
    almond, 129
    zwieback, 130
Toffee:
    squares, 110
    treats, 110
Toll House chocolate crunch cookies,
99
Topping:
    almond, 109
    almond and date, 109
    apricot, 106
    honey, 154
    pecan, 110
    puff-pastry slices with almond, 124
    walnut and coconut, 111

Uncle Max's rye crackers, 156
Uncooked butter icing, 164

Vanilla wafers, 94
Vegetables. See Carrot; Potato;

Sweet potato; Pumpkin
Venetian "bean" cookies, 141
Venetian honey cookies, 143
Vercelli spice sticks, 146

Wafers:
    chive, 160
    ice cream, 113
    lace molasses, 131
    ladies', 145
    palets de dame, 145
    sesame seed, 160
    vanilla, 94.
    See also Biscuits; Crackers
Walnut:
    black, and coconut bars, 111
    bonbons, 124
    chocolate, wheels, 99
    cigars, 141
    and coconut topping, 111
    paste, 141
    shortbread, 134
Water biscuits, Orford's, 157
White Nuremberg peppercakes, 122
White wine, crackers with cracklings
    and, 159
Wine:
    cookies, 153
    dough, 108
    sipping cookies, 141
    white, crackers with cracklings and,
    159
Wood shavings, 133

Yeast: cold-dough, cookies, 126
Yugoslavian recipe: crackers with
    cracklings and white wine, 159

Zwieback, 130

General Index/ Glossary

Included in this index to the cooking demonstrations are definitions, in italics, of special culinary terms not explained elsewhere in this volume. The Recipe Index begins on page 168.

Allspice, 5; in almond toast, 30
Almond butter: as replacement for
peanut butter, 28
Almond extract: in almond toast,
30; in creamed dough, 16, 17; in
macaroons, 56; in meringue, 60; in
pastry dough, 38
Almonds: bitter, 56; blanched and
peeled, 6, 58; crescents, 55, 58-59; in
florentines, 81; on gingerbread, 79;
grinding, 6, 56, 58; in lebkuchen, 75;
in macaroons, 56; paste, 37, 42-43;
on pastry dough, 37, 38, 42-43, 50; in
praline butter, 12; on pressed
cookies, 23; on roof tiles, 34; toasts,
30

Angelica: *a native European herb
cultivated mostly for its roots, which are
used in producing cordials and liqueurs
such as chartreuse, and for its stalks,
which are candied in sugar syrup when
they are green and are available at
specialty food stores;* 6, 79
Anise: caps, 66; -liqueur-flavored
springerle, 66, 67; seeds, 5, 89; in
syrup dough, 74
Apricots: dried, as garnish, 6; filling,
10; jam in nut crescents, 58; jam glaze
on ladies' wafers, 14, 15, 31
Baking powder, 28; in crackers,
88; in creamed-dough drop cookies,
28; in rubbed dough, 42; in syrup
dough, 76, 82
Baking sheets: parchment paper
covering for, 13, 30, 56, 63; selection
and preparation, 13
Baking soda, 28; in crackers, 89,
90-91; in creamed-dough drop
cookies, 28, 29; in syrup dough, 74,
76, 82
Bar cookies: brownies, 73, 82-83;
pastry dough, 37, 38-39; shortbread,
37, 38-39; syrup dough, 73, 82-83

Barley flour: crackers, 85, 86
Beaten-egg dough, 5, 64-71;
anise caps, 66; butter in, 66, 69;
confectioners' sugar in, 66, 68; eggs
and sugar beaten in, 65, 66, 68, 70;
flour in, 65, 66, 67, 68, 70; ladyfingers,
65, 70-71; lemon peel grated in, 66,
67, 68; madeleines, 5, 64, 65, 68-69;
molded, 64, 65, 68-69; orange-flower
water in, 70; piped, 65, 70-71; ribbon
stage, 66, 70; rolled, 65, 66-67;
springerle, 5, 65, 66-67; trapped air
as leavening agent in, 65, 66; vanilla
extract in, 68
Biscuits: cheese straws, 92;
historical uses of, 5, 85; water, 84, 85,
88. See also Crackers; Wafers
Blanching: nuts, 6, 56, 58
Bowls: copper, for beating egg
whites, 55, 60, 70
Bran: in cracker dough, 85
Brazil nuts: peeling, 6; in toast, 30
Brown sugar: melted, in syrup
dough, 73, 74, 82, 83
Brownies: butterscotch, 73, 82, 83;
chocolate, 73, 82
Buckwheat flour: crackers, 85, 90

Buckwheat grits: as replacement
for rolled oats, 28
Butter: almond, 28; in beaten-egg
dough, 66, 69; cashew, 28; and
confectioners' sugar filling, 10, 11; in
creamed dough, 15, 16, 32; for
greasing baking sheets, 13; icing,
uncooked, 8, 20, 21; melted with
sugar in syrup doughs, 73-83; in
pastry dough, 37, 38, 40, 44, 52;
praline, filling, 10, 12, 34, 35; in rough
puff dough, 46; in short-crust dough,
44
Butterflies, 5, 36, 37, 50
Buttermilk: in fried pastry dough,
37, 52; in soda crackers, 90
Butterscotch brownies, 73, 82,
83
Candied citrus peel, 6;
preparation of, 7; in syrup dough, 74,
75, 80, 81
Candied fruit, 6; in creamed
dough, 15, 16, 17; on gingerbread
house, 78, 79; preparation of, 7; in
syrup dough, 74, 80, 81, 82
Candy thermometer, 9, 62, 63
Caramel: colored egg glaze, 8, 9,

41; praline butter, 10, 12, 34, 35
Caraway seeds: on crackers, 44, 85, 86, 88, 92
Cardamom: *an East Indian spice consisting of a fibrous oval pod containing hard, brownish black seeds with a powerful, faintly lemon-like flavor. When dried in kilns, the pod remains green; when sun-dried, the pod bleaches to a cream color. The varieties are interchangeable. Obtainable where fine spices are sold;* 5, 66
Cashew butter: as replacement for peanut butter, 28
Cashews: on roof tiles, 34
Cats' tongues, 5, 32-33
Cayenne: in crackers, 85, 90, 92
Celery seeds: on crackers, 44, 85
Cheddar cheese: crackers, 44, 85, 92
Cheese: as cracker filling, 44; crackers, 6, 44, 85, 92; as garnish, 6; straws, 92. *See also individual cheeses*
Cherry: jam glaze, 31
Chocolate, 6; brownies, 73, 82; cats' tongues dipped in, 32; chip creamed-dough drop cookies, 28-29; chips, preparation of, 6; as cigarette filling, 34; in creamed dough, 15, 22, 24, 26, 27, 28-29; on florentines, 80, 81; as garnish, 6, 20, 32, 34, 71, 80, 81; icing, melted, 8, 31; on ladies' wafers, 31; on ladyfingers, 32, 71; melted, in syrup dough, 73, 82-83; pretzels, creamed dough, 27. *See also* Cocoa powder
Chocolate sprinkles: *tiny chocolate-flavored candy pellets used as decorations for cakes, cookies and candy.*
Cigarettes, 34-35; fillings for, 10, 34, 35
Cinnamon, 5; in almond toast, 30; in meringue, 60; in pastry dough, 42, 44, 50; in springerle, 66; in syrup dough, 73, 74, 76
Cloves, 5; in almond toast, 30; in syrup dough, 73, 74, 76
Coarse salt, 6; on crackers, 86, 88, 90
Coarse sugar: *a specially refined, large crystalline form of sugar designed for use in decorations. Obtainable from baking-supply stores and gourmet-food specialty stores;* 27
Cocoa powder: creamed dough colored with, 22, 24, 26, 27. *See also* Chocolate
Coconuts: shelling, 6
Coffee: in caramel-colored egg glaze, 41; in fillings, 10; in icings, 8; in meringue, 62
Confectioners' sugar: in beaten-egg doughs, 66, 68; and butter filling, 10, 11; in cats' tongues, 32; as dusting on baked cookies, 19, 22, 27, 52, 56, 69; in egg-white cookies, 58, 60, 61; glaze, 8, 20, 74, 75; glaze with rum, 8, 14, 15, 31, 53; in icings, 8, 9, 14, 15, 31, 53; on ladyfingers, 70; in pastry dough, 40

Cookie press: creamed dough shaped with, 15, 22, 23
Cookies: historical uses of, 5, 73
Coriander seeds, 89
Corn syrup, 76
Cracked wheat: as replacement for rolled oats, 28
Crackers, 5, 84-92; all-purpose flour, 85, 86, 90; barley, 85, 86; bran in, 85; buckwheat, 85, 90; cheese, 6, 44, 85, 92; cheese straws, 92; coarse salt on, 86, 88, 90; deep-fried *matthi*, 89; filled, 44; flatbread, 85, 86-87; garnishes for, 6, 44, 85, 90; gluten in dough, 85, 86, 88, 89, 90; herb, 44, 85, 90; historical uses of, 5, 84; kneading dough for, 86, 87, 89, 90, 91; lard in, 85, 88, 89, 90, 91; leavening agents in, 85, 88, 89, 90; millet, 85; nuts in, 92; oat, 85, 90; Parmesan, 44, 85, 92; pastry-dough, 44, 84, 85, 92; rolled, 84-92; rough puff dough, 46, 85, 92; rye, 85, 90; seeds on, 44, 85, 86, 88, 89, 90, 92; short-crust dough, 44, 84, 85; soda, 85, 90-91; spices in, 44, 85, 90, 92; water biscuits, 84, 85, 88; whole-wheat, 85, 86, 90. *See also* Biscuits; Wafers
Cream: egg yolk beaten with, on pastry dough, 53; in rough puff dough, 46; in syrup dough, 73, 80. *See also* Sour cream; Whipped cream
Creamed dough, 5, 15-35; almond toasts, 30; candied fruit in, 15, 16, 17; cats' tongues, 32-33; chocolate in, 15, 22, 24, 26, 27, 28-29; chocolate pretzels, 27; cigarettes, 34-35; cocoa-powder-colored, 22, 24, 26, 27; consistency of, 15, 16, 18, 24, 28, 31; decorated cookies, 20-21; dried currants in, 15; drop cookies, 15, 28-29; egg whites in, 15, 32-35; fillings for, 10-11, 12, 15, 18-19, 32, 34-35; garnishes in, 14, 15, 16, 17, 18; glazes on, 8-9, 14, 15, 18, 20, 27, 31; gluten in, 15, 16, 32; heart-shaped sandwiches with lemon cream, 19; icings on, 8-9, 15, 18, 20, 21, 31; ingredient proportions in, 15, 16, 24, 31; ladies' wafers, 14, 15, 31; liquid flavorings for, 16, 17; nuts in, 15, 16, 18; open-ring cookies, 18; orange peel in, 16, 32; overworked, 15, 16; piped and painted, 20-21, 22, 31, 32, 34; pressed, 22-23; raisins in, 14, 15; refrigerated, 15, 24-27; rich, 16, 30, 31; rolled, 15, 16-21, 24-26; roof tiles, 34-35; rusks, 30; sandwiched cookies, 18, 19, 32; spices in, 16, 30; wafers, 15, 34-35
Crescents: nut, 55, 58-59; turnovers, deep fried, 52-53
Currants, dried. *See* Dried currants
Dates: chopped, on shortbread, 38; filling, 42
Decorated cookies: creamed dough, 20-21; dyed egg white and icing painted on, 20-21; springerle, 66-67

Deep-fried cookies: bowknots, 52-53; oil for, 52, 53; pastry-dough, 37, 52-53; rum-flavored confectioners' sugar glaze on, 53; thermometer for, 52; turnovers, 52, 53
Deep-fried crackers: *matthi,* 89
Dill seeds: on crackers, 44
Dough: beaten-egg, 5, 64-71; cracker, 44, 84-92; creamed, 5, 15-35; deep-fried pastry, 37, 52-53; egg-white, 5, 54-63; historical uses of, 5, 85; pastry, 5, 36-53; rough puff, 36, 37, 37, 46-51, 92; rubbed, 38-43; shortbread, 37, 38-39, 44; short-crust, 37, 44-45; syrup, 5, 72-83
Dried currants: in creamed dough, 15; as garnish, 6
Dried fruit, 6; filling, 10-11, 18, 42, 52; as garnish, 6; grinding of, 10; paste, 10, 11; on pastry-dough cookies, 37, 38, 42, 44; on refrigerator cookies, 24. *See also individual fruits*
Drop cookies: chocolate chip, 28-29; creamed-dough, 15, 28-29; decorating, 29; florentines, 73, 80-81; leavening agents in, 28, 29; mixing dough for, 28-29; nuts in, 28, 29; oatmeal, 28; peanut butter, 28, 29; raisins in, 28
Eggs: beaten, as adhesive, 18, 42; in beaten-egg dough, 64-71; in creamed dough, 15, 16, 17, 28, 31; glaze, beaten, 8, 18, 27, 42; glaze, caramel-colored, 8, 9, 41; in pastry dough, 37, 40; proteins in, 55, 65; in syrup dough, 76, 82, 83; yolk, beaten with cream, on pastry dough, 53; yolk, beaten with water, on rough puff dough, 50, 51; yolk, separated from white, 60
Egg white: batter, creamed, 32-35; beaten into foam, 55, 60; beaten for meringue, 60; as binder for dry ingredients, 55; in cats' tongues, 32-33; in cigarettes, 34-35; in creamed dough, 15, 32-33; dyed, for painted decoration, 20, 21; equipment for beating, 55, 60, 70; glaze, beaten, 8, 24, 25, 26, 27, 28; in ladyfingers, 65, 70-71; proteins in, 55; in refrigerator cookies, 24, 25, 26, 27; in roof tiles, 34-35; in royal icing, 8, 9
Egg-white cookies, 5, 54-63; confectioners' sugar in, 58, 60, 61; liquid flavorings in, 55, 56, 58, 60, 62-63; macaroons, 55-57; meringues, 5, 13, 54, 55, 60-63; nut crescents, 55, 58-59; nuts in, 55, 56-61; pastry bag shaping of, 56, 63; piped, 56, 63; sugar in, 55, 56, 57, 58, 60, 61, 62
Extracts. *See* Liquid flavorings
Fats. *See* Butter; Lard; Oil; Vegetable shortening
Fennel seeds, 89; in springerle, 66; in syrup dough, 74
Fenugreek seed: *a brownish yellow seed from an herb belonging to the bean family. An essential curry spice because of its musty aroma and bitter taste. Sold at Indian markets.*
Figs: chopped, on shortbread, 38;

filling, 10, 18, 42, 52
Filled cookies, 10-13; adhesive for, 18, 42; cigarettes, 10, 34-35; creamed dough, 10-11, 12, 15, 18-19, 32, 34-35; hollow, 10, 18; open-ring, 18; pastry-dough, 36, 37, 42-43, 44, 50, 51, 52; sandwiched, 10, 18, 19, 32; short-crust dough, 44
Fillings, 10-13; almond paste, 42-43; apricot, 10; cheese, 44; confectioners' sugar and butter, 10; cracker, 44; date, 42; fig, 10, 18, 42, 52; fruit, 10-11, 18, 19, 42, 51, 52; jam, 10, 18, 32, 34, 36, 37, 50, 51; lemon, 10, 11, 18, 19; liquid flavorings in, 10, 11; marzipan, 42-43; nut, 10, 11, 18, 42-43, 52; praline butter, 10, 12, 34, 35; raspberry jam, 51; walnut, 10, 18; whipped cream, 34
Flatbread, 85, 86-87
Florentines, 73, 80-81
Flour, 5; all-purpose, 85, 86, 90; barley, 85, 86; in beaten-egg dough, 65, 66, 67, 68, 70; buckwheat, 85, 90; in crackers, 85, 86, 90; in creamed dough, 15, 16, 17, 24, 32; millet, 85; oat, 85, 90; paste, use in early cracker making, 5; in pastry dough, 37, 38, 44, 52; quantity in creamed egg-white batter, 32-35; rice, in shortbread, 38; in rough puff dough, 46; rye, 85, 90; in shortbread, 38; in syrup dough, 73, 74, 75, 76, 80, 82; whole-wheat, 85, 86, 90. *See also* Gluten
Food coloring: egg white dyed with, 20, 21; glaze dyed with, 20; icing dyed with, 8, 20, 21
Food processor: dried fruit ground in, 10; nuts ground in, 6, 11, 12, 56, 58, 60; praline ground in, 10, 12
Fried cookies. *See* Deep-fried cookies
Fruit: fillings, 10-11, 18, 19, 42, 51, 52; glazes, 14, 15, 31; liqueur icing, 8; purée, in meringue, 55, 62-63; on syrup-dough cookies, 74, 78, 79. *See also* Candied citrus peel; Candied fruit; Dried fruit; *individual fruits;* Jam
Garnishes: for crackers, 6, 44, 85, 90; for creamed-dough cookies, 14, 15, 16, 17, 18; for pastry-dough cookies, 37, 38, 42, 44, 50; preparation of, 6-7; for short-crust cookies, 44; for syrup-dough cookies, 74, 75, 76, 78, 79, 80, 81. *See also* Candied fruit; Cheese; Chocolate; Dried fruit; Herbs; Nuts; Raisins; Spices
Ginger, 5; in syrup dough, 73, 74, 76
Gingerbread, 5, 72, 73, 76-79; garnishes for, 76, 78, 79; house, 73, 78-79; men, 72, 73, 76-77; molasses in, 76-77; royal icing, 8, 76, 78-79. *See also* Lebkuchen
Glazes, 8-9; apricot jam, on ladies' wafers, 14, 15, 31; on baked or unbaked cookies, 8; caramel-colored egg, 8, 9, 41; confectioners' sugar, 8, 20, 74, 75; confectioners' sugar with rum, 8, 14, 15, 31, 53; on creamed-

dough cookies, 8-9, 14, 15, 18, 20, 27, 31; dyed, 20; egg, beaten, 8, 27, 42; egg white, beaten, 8, 24, 25, 26, 27, 58; fruit, 14, 15, 31; on pastry-dough cookies, 8-9, 36, 37, 40, 41, 42, 53; piped application of, 15, 20-21; sweetened milk, 58, 59; on syrup-dough cookies, 74, 75. *See also* Icing

Gluten: in all-purpose flour, 85; in cracker doughs, 85, 86, 88, 89, 90; in creamed dough, 15, 16, 32; in fried pastry dough, 52; in pastry dough, 37, 40, 44, 46, 52; in soda crackers, 90; in syrup dough, 74, 76; in whole-wheat flour, 85, 86; yogurt for development of, in crackers, 89

Golden syrup: *a mild molasses syrup imported from England and obtainable at some specialty food stores;* 76

Grinding: dried fruit, 10; nuts, 6, 11, 12, 55, 56-57, 58, 60; praline, 11, 12; spices, 74. *See also* Food processor; Mortar

Ground mace: in almond toast, 30

Gruyère cheese: crackers, 85, 92

Hazelnuts: filling, 10; in macaroons, 56; meringue, 60-61; peeling, 6, 7; on pressed cookies, 23; on roof tiles, 34; in toast, 30

Herbs, 6; crackers, 44, 85, 90; as garnish, 6. *See also individual herbs*

Honey, 5; heated, in syrup-dough cookies, 73, 74, 76, 80; in lebkuchen, 73, 74

Icebox cookies. *See* Refrigerator cookies

Icings, 8-9; butter, uncooked, 8, 20, 21; coffee in, 8; confectioners' sugar, 8, 9, 14, 15, 31, 53; on creamed-dough cookies, 8-9, 15, 18, 20, 21, 31; dyed, 8, 20, 21; on ladies' wafers, 14, 15, 31; lemon juice in, 8, 9; liqueur in, 8, 14, 15, 31, 53; liquid flavorings in, 8; melted chocolate, 8, 31; piped, 8, 15, 20-21, 76, 78, 79; preparation of, 8-9; royal, 8, 9, 20, 21, 74, 76, 78-79, 80; rum-flavored confectioners' sugar, 8, 14, 15, 31, 53; spreading, 8; on syrup-dough cookies, 8, 74, 76, 78-79, 80. *See also* Glazes

Italian meringue, 55, 62-63

Jam: apricot, in nut crescents, 58; fillings, 10, 18, 32, 34, 36, 37, 50, 51; glazes, 14, 15, 31

Kneading: cracker dough, 86, 87, 89, 90, 91; rubbed dough, 40

Ladies' wafers, 14, 15, 31

Ladyfingers, 32, 65, 70-71; garnishes on, 32, 70, 71

Lard: in crackers, 85, 88, 89, 90, 91

Leavening agents: in crackers, 85, 88, 89, 90; in creamed-dough drop cookies, 28, 29; in syrup dough, 74, 76, 82; trapped air, in beaten-egg dough, 65, 66; yeast, in soda crackers, 85, 90-91. *See also* Baking powder; Baking soda

Lebkuchen, 5, 73, 74-75; ingredient proportions in, 73, 74; royal icing on, 74. *See also* Gingerbread

Lemon: cream filling, heart shapes sandwiched with, 19; filling, 10, 11, 18, 19; juice, in icing, 8, 9; peel, grated, in beaten-egg doughs, 66, 67, 68; peel, grated, in cats' tongues, 32; peel, grated, in pastry dough, 40, 50

Liqueur: anise, in springerle, 66, 67; in fillings, 10; in icings, 8, 14, 15, 31, 53; in meringue, 62

Liquid flavorings: in creamed dough, 16, 17; in egg-white cookies, 55, 56, 58, 60, 62-63; in fillings, 10, 11; in icing, 8, 14, 15; in pastry dough, 37, 38, 40; strawberry purée, in meringue, 55, 62-63; sugar syrup, in meringue, 62-63. *See also* Almond extract; Coffee; Liqueur; Orange-flower water; Peppermint extract; Rose water; Vanilla extract; Wine

Lovage seeds: in crackers, 89, 92

Macaroons, 55-57; almond extract in, 56; nuts in, 56-57; pastry-bag shaping of, 56

Madeleines, 5, 64, 65, 68-69; confectioners' sugar coating on, 69; molds for, 68-69

Maple syrup: in filling, 10

Marzipan: filling, in pastry dough, 42-43

Meringues, 5, 13, 54, 55, 60-63; cinnamon-and-nut, 60; egg whites beaten for, 60; hazelnut, 60-61; Italian, 55, 62-63; layered, 60, 61; liquid flavorings in, 55, 60, 62-63; pastry-bag shaping of, 63; spices in, 60; strawberry purée in, 55, 62-63; syrup method, 62-63

Milk: sour, in soda crackers, 90, 91; sweetened, glaze, 58, 59. *See also* Buttermilk; Cream

Millet flour: crackers, 85

Molasses: melted, in syrup dough, 73, 74, 76-77

Molded and shaped cookies: beaten-egg dough, 64, 65, 68-69; cigarettes, 10, 34-35; countries of origin of, 5; creamed-dough, 15, 22-23, 27, 34-35; curved wafers, 34-35; implements for, 34, 35; madeleines, 5, 64, 65, 68-69; moss, 22-23; pastry dough, 36, 37-39; pretzels, chocolate, 5, 15, 27; roof tiles, 34-35; shortbread, 38-39; strainer for, 15, 22; swirls, 22

Mortar, 10; nuts ground in, 6, 55, 56-57; spices ground in, 74

Moss cookies, 22-23

Nut cracker, 6

Nut grinder, 58, 60

Nutmeg, 5; in almond toast, 30; in meringue, 60; in pastry dough, 44, 50; in syrup dough, 74

Nuts: baking, 6, 7; chopping by hand, 6, 7; as cigarette filling, 34; in crackers, 92; in creamed dough, 15, 16, 18; crescents, 55, 58-59; in drop cookies, 28, 29; in egg-white cookies, 55, 56-61; fillings, 10, 11, 18, 42-43, 52; as garnish, 6-7, 34; on gingerbread house, 78, 79; grinding, 6, 11, 12, 55, 56-57, 58, 60; in

macaroons, 56-57; in meringue, 60, 61; paste, 10, 11, 12, 55, 56-57, 58-59; in pastry dough, 36, 37, 38, 39, 42, 44, 50; peeling, 6, 7, 56, 58; in praline butter, 10, 12, 34, 35; on pressed cookies, 23; on refrigerator cookies, 24, 27; on roof tiles, 34; in rough puff dough, 50; on shortbread, 38, 39; in syrup dough, 74, 75, 80, 81, 82, 83; in toast, 30. *See also individual nuts*

Oat flour: crackers, 85, 90

Oatmeal: creamed-dough drop cookies, 28; replacements for, 28

Oil: for deep-fried cookies, 52, 53; for greasing baking sheets, 13

Orange: -flavored liqueur, in cats' tongues, 32; juice, in filling, 10; peel, grated, in creamed dough, 16, 32

Orange-flower water: *a flavoring made by distilling the oil of orange-blossom petals. Produced in the Middle East, it is available at pharmacies and specialty food stores;* 70

Painted cookies: creamed-dough, 20, 21

Palmiers, 36, 37, 46, 48-49

Parchment paper: baking sheet covered with, 13, 30, 56, 63

Parmesan cheese: crackers, 44, 85, 92

Paste: almond, in pastry dough, 37, 42-43; dried fruit, 10, 11; flour, use in early cracker making, 5; nut, 10, 11, 12, 55, 56-57, 58-59

Pastry bag: creamed dough shaped with, 15, 20-21, 22, 31, 32, 34; ladyfingers shaped with, 32, 70-71; macaroons shaped with, 56; meringues shaped with, 63; for piped icing, 8, 15, 20-21. *See also* Piped cookies

Pastry brush, 58, 63, 69

Pastry dough, 5, 36-53; almond paste in, 37, 42-43; baking powder in, 42; bar cookies, 37, 38-39; bowknots, 52-53; butterflies, 36, 37, 50; buttermilk, 37, 52; cool ingredients for, 37; crackers, 44, 84, 85, 92; crescent turnovers, 52, 53; deep-fried, 37, 52-53; dried fruit on, 37, 38, 42, 44; fillings for, 36, 37, 42-43, 44, 50, 51, 52; flour in, 37, 38, 44, 52; garnishes for, 37, 38, 42, 44, 50; glazes on, 8-9, 36, 37, 40, 41, 42, 53; gluten in, 37, 40, 44, 46, 52; grated citrus peel in, 40, 50; ingredient proportions in, 37, 38, 40, 44, 52; liquid flavorings in, 37, 38, 40; mixing, 37, 38, 41, 44-45; nuts in, 36, 37, 38, 39, 42, 44, 50; *palmiers,* 36, 37, 46, 48-49; rolled, 37, 40-53; rough puff, 36, 37, 46-51, 92; rubbed, 38-43; sablés, 40-41; shaped cookies, 36, 37-39; short-crust, 37, 44-45; shortbread, 5, 37, 38-39, 44; sour cream and rum, for deep-fried cookies, 52; spices in, 37, 40, 42, 44, 50; wrapped for marzipan filling, 42-43; yogurt in, 37

Peanut butter: replacements for,

28; creamed-dough drop cookies, 28, 29

Pecans: in brownies, 83; crescents, 58; in macaroons, 56; on roof tiles, 34; in toast, 30

Peeling: nuts, 6, 7, 56, 58

Peppermint extract: in meringue, 60

Pine nuts: *the small, cream-colored, mild-flavored kernels from the cones of the stone pine. They are often marketed under their Italian name, pignola, and are available at specialty food stores.*

Piped cookies: beaten-egg dough, 65, 70-71; cats' tongues, 32-33; confectioners' sugar glaze as base for, 20; creamed-dough, 20, 22, 31, 32, 34; dyed egg white and icing as decoration, 20-21; egg-white, 56, 63; ladies' wafers, 31; ladyfingers, 32, 65, 70-71; macaroons, 56; meringues, 63; pastry bag for, 15, 20-21, 22, 31, 32, 34, 56, 63; royal icing as base for, 20, 21. *See also* Pressed cookies

Pistachios, 6; chopping by hand, 7; filling, 10; on pressed cookies, 23

Poppy seeds: on crackers, 44, 85, 86, 88

Praline butter: filling, 10, 12, 34, 35; preparation of, 10, 12

Pressed cookies: confectioners' sugar dusting on, 22; cookie press for, 15, 22, 23; creamed-dough, 22-23; moss 22-23; nuts on, 23; rosettes, 23; strainer for, 15, 22; swirls, 22. *See also* Piped cookies

Pretzel cookies, 5; chocolate creamed dough, 27; creamed-dough, 15, 27

Purée: fruit, in meringue, 55, 62-63

Raisins, 6; in brownies, 82; in creamed dough, 14, 15; as garnish, 6, 76; on gingerbread, 76; in ladies' wafers, 31; in oatmeal drop cookies, 28

Raspberry: jam filling, 51; jam glaze, 31; purée, in meringue, 62

Refrigerator cookies: checkerboard, 24, 26; creamed-dough, 15, 24-27; dried fruit on, 24; log, 24, 26; nuts on, 24, 27; refrigeration time for, 24; rolled, 24-27; shaped, 27; spirals, 24-25

Render: *to refine fat by melting pure fat out of fleshy tissues.*

Rice flour: in shortbread, 38

Rolled cookies: beaten-egg dough, 65, 66-67; checkerboard, 24, 26; creamed-dough, 15, 16-21, 24-26; daisies, 20-21; fried pastry dough, 52; gingerbread, 72, 73, 76-79; heart, sandwiched with lemon cream, 19; lebkuchen, 74; log, 24, 26; open-ring, 18; pastry-dough, 37, 40-53; refrigerated, 24-27; rubbed dough with marzipan filling, 42-43; sablés, 40-41; short-crust, 37, 44-45; spirals, 24-25, 44-45; springerle, 65, 66-67

Rolled crackers, 84-92. *See also* Crackers

Rolling pin: carved, for springerle, 55, 66, 67

Romano cheese: crackers, 85

Roof tiles, 5, 34-35

Rose water: a flavoring produced in the Balkans, the Middle East and India by distilling the oil of rose petals. Available at pharmacies and specialty food stores; 5, 10, 18

Rough puff dough, 36, 37, 46-51; butterflies, 36, 37, 50; chilled, 46, 47, 48, 50, 51, 92; crackers, 46, 85, 92; egg yolk beaten with water on, 50, 51; folded, 46, 47, 49, 92; ingredient proportions in, 46; jam filling for, 50, 51; nuts in, 50; palmiers, 36, 37, 46, 48-49; placement during baking, 50; rolled, 46, 47, 50, 92; shaping, 49-51, 92; shells, filled, 50; short-crust transformed into, 37, 46; sugar-coated, 46, 48, 50; turned, 47; twists, 50

Royal icing, 8, 9; as base for piped decoration, 20, 21; egg whites in, 8, 9; on florentines, 80; on gingerbread, 8, 76, 78-79; on lebkuchen, 74

Rubbed dough: baking powder in, 42; cookies with amber glaze, 40-41; ingredient proportions in, 40; kneading, 40; with marzipan filling, 42-43; mixing, 41; shortbread, 38-39

Rum: in cats' tongues, 32; confectioners' sugar glaze with, 8, 14, 15, 31, 53; in fillings, 10; in rough puff dough, 46; and sour cream, in deep-fried pastry-dough cookies, 52

Rusks, 30

Rye flour: crackers, 85, 90

Sablés, 40-41

Saffron: the dried stigmas of a species of crocus. Used to impart a distinctive aroma and yellow color to certain foods. Sold in thread or ground forms.

Sage: in crackers, 85, 90

Salt, coarse. See Coarse salt

Sandwiched cookies, 10; cats' tongues, 32; creamed-dough, 18, 19, 32; hearts sandwiched with lemon cream, 19

Scald: a cooking term—usually applied to milk—that means to heat liquid to just below the boiling point or until small bubbles appear around the edge of the pan.

Seeds: on crackers, 44, 85, 86, 88, 89, 90, 92; as garnish, 6. See also types of seeds

Semolina: coarse cream-colored granules, milled from the hearts of durum-wheat berries. Similar to farina, which is made from the hearts of other hard-wheat berries; 38

Sesame seeds: on crackers, 85, 92

Shaped cookies. See Molded and shaped cookies

Shelling: nuts, 6

Short-crust dough, 37; chilled, 44, 45, 46; with cinnamon-and-sugar filling, 44-45; crackers, 44, 84, 85; garnishes for, 44; ingredient proportions in, 44; mixing, 44-45; rolled, 37, 44-45, 46; rough puff dough made from, 37, 46

Shortbread, 5; bar cookies, 38-39; disk, 38-39; dough, 37, 38-39, 44; garnishes for, 38, 39; topping for, 37, 38-39

Soda crackers, 85, 90-91

Sour cream: and rum, in deep-fried pastry-dough cookies, 52

Speculaas spice, 42; in almond paste, 42

Spices: in almond toast, 30; in crackers, 44, 85, 90, 92; in creamed dough, 16, 30; grinding, 74; historical uses of, 5, 73; in meringue, 60; in pastry dough, 37, 40, 42, 44, 50; Speculaas, in almond paste, 42; in springerle, 66; storage of, 74; in syrup-dough cookies, 73, 74, 76. See also individual spices

Sponge base. See Beaten-egg dough

Springerle, 5, 65, 66-67; anise in, 66, 67; carved rolling pin for, 65, 66, 67; dried before baking for crust, 65, 66-67; lemon peel grated in, 66, 67; spices in, 66

Strainer: for pressed creamed-dough cookies, 15, 22

Strawberry: jam glaze, 31; purée, in Italian meringue, 62-63

Sugar, 5; in beaten-egg dough, 65, 66, 68, 70; coarse, 27; cookies, 16-17; in creamed dough, 15, 16; as decoration for creamed dough, 20, 22, 27; in egg-white cookies, 55, 56, 57, 58, 60, 61, 62; melted, in syrup dough, 73-83; in pastry dough, 37, 40, 44; rough puff dough coated with, 46, 48, 50; short-crust cookies sprinkled with, 44; syrup, in Italian meringue, 62-63. See also Brown sugar; Confectioners' sugar; Honey; Syrup; Vanilla-flavored sugar

Syrup: corn, 76; golden, 76; maple, in filling, 10; sugar, in Italian meringue, 62-63

Syrup dough, 5, 72-83; bar cookies, 73, 82-83; brown sugar melted in, 73, 74, 82, 83; brownies, 73, 82-83; candied fruit in, 74, 80, 81, 82; chocolate melted in, 73, 82-83; cream in, 73, 80; egg in, 76, 82, 83; florentines, 73, 80-81; flour in, 73, 74, 75, 76, 80, 82; garnishes for, 74, 75, 76, 78, 79, 80, 81; gingerbread, 5, 8, 72, 73, 76-79; glazes on, 74, 75; gluten development in, 74, 76; historical uses of, 73; honey in, 73, 74, 76, 80; icings on, 8, 74, 76, 78-79, 80; ingredient proportions in, 73, 74, 76, 80; leavening agents in, 74, 76, 82; lebkuchen, 5, 73, 74-75; molasses melted in, 73, 74, 76-77; nuts in, 74, 75, 80, 81, 82, 83; rolling, 74, 77; spices in, 73, 74, 76

Thermometers: candy, 9, 62, 63; deep-frying, 52, 89

Toast: almond, 30

Toll House cookies, 28-29

Toppings. See Garnishes; Glazes; Icings

Treacle: a dark, heavy syrup produced from molasses; it is rarely obtainable in the United States. Molasses makes a suitable substitute.

Turnovers: deep-fried pastry dough, 52, 53

Vanilla bean: scraped into beaten-egg dough, 68. See also Vanilla-flavored sugar

Vanilla extract: in almond toast, 30; in beaten-egg dough, 68; in brownies, 82, 83; in cats' tongues, 32; in creamed dough, 16, 17; in meringue, 60; in nut crescents, 58; in pastry dough, 38; in uncooked butter icing, 8

Vanilla-flavored sugar: to make vanilla-flavored sugar, place a whole vanilla bean in a tightly closed canister of sugar for about one week; 38

Vegetable shortening: in matthi crackers, 89

Wafers, 84-92; cigarettes, 34-35; creamed dough, 15, 34-35; florentines, 73, 80-81; historical uses of, 5, 85; ladies', 14, 15, 31; roof tiles, 34-35; water, 84, 85, 88. See also Biscuits; Crackers

Walnuts: crescents, 58; in drop cookies, 29; filling, 10, 18; in macaroons, 56; in toast, 30

Water biscuits, 84, 85, 88

Whipped cream: filling, 34

Whole-wheat flour: crackers, 85, 86, 90; gluten in, 85, 86

Wine: in filling, 10; in fried pastry dough, 52

Wire whisk: for beating egg whites, 60, 70; for beating sponge batter, 66-67, 70

Yeast: in soda crackers, 85, 90-91

Yogurt: for gluten development in crackers, 89; in pastry dough, deep fried, 37

Recipe Credits

The sources for the recipes in this volume are shown below. Page references in parentheses indicate where the recipes appear in the Anthology.

Adam, Hans Karl, Das Kochbuch aus Schwaben. © copyright 1976 by Verlagsteam Wolfgang Hölker. Published by Wolfgang Hölker, Münster. Translated by permission of Verlag Wolfgang Hölker(113, 124).

Albright, Nancy, Rodale's Naturally Great Foods Cookbook. Copyright © 1977 Rodale Press, Inc. Permission granted by Rodale Press, Inc., Emmaus, Pa. 18049(160, 163).

Amicale des Cuisiniers et Pâtissiers Auvergnats de Paris, Cuisine d'Auvergne (Cuisines du Terroir). © 1979 Denoël, Paris. Published by Éditions Denoël. Translated by permission of Éditions Denoël(114, 129).

Aoun, Fayez, 280 Recettes de Cuisine Familiale Libanaise. © 1980, Jacques Grancher, Éditeur. Published by Jacques Grancher, Éditeur, Paris. Translated by permission of Jacques Grancher, Éditeur(140, 142).

Artocchini, Carmen, 400 Ricette della Cucina Piacentina. Published by Stabilimento Tipografica Piacentino, Piacenza, 1977. Translated by permission of the author, Piacenza(108).

Autumn, Violeta, A Russian Jew Cooks in Perú. Copyright © 1973 Violeta Autumn. Published by 101 Productions, San Francisco. By permission of 101 Productions(116, 136).

Barker, William, The Modern Pâtissier: A Complete Guide to Pastry Cookery. © William Barker and Northwood Publications Ltd., 1974 and 1978. Published by Northwood Publications Ltd., London. By permission of Northwood Publications Ltd.(134).

Bates, Margaret, Talking about Cakes with an Irish and Scottish Accent. Copyright © 1964 Pergamon Press Ltd.

Published by Pergamon Press Ltd., Oxford. By permission of Pergamon Press Ltd.(124, 134, 150).

Besson, Joséphine, La Mère Besson "Ma Cuisine Provençale." © Editions Albin Michel, 1977. Published by Éditions Albin Michel, Paris. Translated by permission of Éditions Albin Michel(150).

Blanquet, Mme. Rosalie, Le Pâtissier des Ménages. Published by Librairie de Théodore Lefèvre et Cie/Émile Guérin, Éditeur, Paris, 1878(124, 146, 148).

Borer, Eva Maria, Tante Heidi's Swiss Kitchen. English text copyright © 1965 by Nicholas Kaye Ltd. Copyright © 1981 Kaye & Ward Ltd. Published by Kaye & Ward Ltd., London. First published as Die Echte Schweizer Kuche by Mary Hahns Kochbuchverlag, Berlin W., 1963. By permission of Kaye & Ward Ltd.(109, 127).

Bouayed, Fatima-Zohra, La Cuisine Algérienne. Published by S.N.E.D. (Société Nationale d'Édition et de Diffusion), Algiers, 1978. Translated by permission of the author, Algiers(141, 155).

Boyd, Lizzie (Editor), British Cookery. © 1976 by British

Tourist Authority and British Farm Produce Council. Published by Croom Helm Ltd., London. By permission of the British Tourist Authority, London(135).

Břízová, Joza and Maryna Klimentová *Tschechische Küche*. © by Verlag PRÁCE, Praha/CSSR, and Verlag für die Frau, Leipzig/DDR. Published by PRÁCE, Prague and Verlag für die Frau, Leipzig, 1977. Translated by permission of DILIA, Theatrical and Literary Agency, Prague, for the authors(118).

Brobeck, Florence and Monika B. Kjellberg, *Smörgåsbord and Scandinavian Cookery*. Published in 1948 by Little, Brown and Company(94).

Brown, Catherine, *Scottish Regional Recipes*. Published by The Molendinar Press, Glasgow 1981. By permission of Richard Drew Publishing Limited, Glasgow(112, 126).

Brown, Marion, *The Southern Cook Book*. © 1968 The University of North Carolina Press. Published by The University of North Carolina Press, Chapel Hill. By permission of The University of North Carolina Press(120—Mrs. Don E. Scott).

Brownstone, Cecily, *Cecily Brownstone's Associated Press Cook Book*. © Copyright 1972 by The Associated Press. Published by David McKay Company, Inc., New York. By permission of David McKay Company, Inc.(98).

Byron, May, *Pot-Luck*. Copyright by Hodder and Stoughton Limited. Seventh Edition published by Hodder and Stoughton Limited, London 1926. By permission of Hodder and Stoughton Limited, Kent(119).

Carême, Antonin, *Le Pâtissier Royal Parisien*. First published in Paris, 1841. Published by Laffitte Reprints, Marseille 1980. Translated by permission of Laffitte Reprints(148, 151).

Cascante, Maria del Carmen, *Manual Moderno de Pasteleria Casera*. © Editorial De Vecchi, S.A., Barcelona, 1978. Published by Editorial De Vecchi, S.A. Translated by permission of Editorial De Vecchi, S.A.(100, 132). *150 Recetas de Dulces de Fácil Preparación*. © Editorial De Vecchi, S.A., 1975. Published by Editorial De Vecchi, S.A., Barcelona. Translated by permission of Editorial De Vecchi, S.A.(95).

Casella, Dolores, *A World of Baking*. Copyright © 1968 by Dolores Casella. Used by permission of David White, Inc.(144).

Cavalcanti, Ippolito, Duca di Buonvicino, *Cucina Teorico-Pratica*. Tipografia di G. Palma, Naples. Second edition, 1839(96, 101).

Ceccaldi, Marie, *Cuisine de Corse (Cuisines du Terroir)*. © 1980, by Éditions Denoël, Paris. Published by Éditions Denoël. Translated by permission of Éditions Denoël(117).

Cobbett, Anne, *The English Housekeeper*. Originally published by A. Cobbett, Strand, sixth edition, 1851. Reprinted in facsimile by EP Publishing Limited. Copyright © 1973 by EP Publishing Limited, Wakefield, Yorkshire(120).

Colquitt, Harriet Ross (Editor), *The Savannah Cook Book*. © 1933 by Harriet Ross Colquitt. © 1960 by Harriet Ross Colquitt. Eighth edition 1974 published by Colonial Publishers, Charleston, S.C. By permission of Colonial Publishers(111).

Comelade, Éliane Thibaut, *La Cuisine Catalane*. © Éditions J. Lanore CLT. Published by Éditions Jacques Lanore, CLT, Paris 1978. Translated by permission of Éditions Jacques Lanore, CLT, Malakoff(97).

Craig, Elizabeth, *Scandinavian Cooking*. © Elizabeth Craig 1958. Published by André Deutsch Limited, London. By permission of André Deutsch Limited(122).

La Cuisine Bretonne (L'Encyclopédie de la Cuisine Régionale). © Presses Pocket, 1979. Published by Presses Pocket, Paris. Translated by permission of Les Presses de la Cité, Paris(158).

La Cuisine d'Ève et Olympe, © Éditions Mengès. Published by Éditions Mengès, Paris 1980. Translated by permission of Éditions Mengès(131).

La Cuisine du Périgord (L'Encyclopédie de la Cuisine Régionale). © Presses Pocket, 1979. Published by Presses Pocket, Paris. Translated by permission of Les Presses de la Cité, Paris(123).

Cutler, Carol, *The Six-Minute Soufflé and Other Culinary Delights*. Copyright © 1976 by Carol Cutler. By permission of Clarkson N. Potter, Inc.(112).

Czerny, Zofia and Maria Strasburger, *Żywienie Rodziny*. Copyright by Zofia Czerny and Maria Strasburger. Published by Czytelnik Spoldzielnia Wydawnicza 1948. Translated by permission of Agencja Autorska, Warsaw, for the heiress to the authors(115, 118).

David, Elizabeth, *English Bread and Yeast Cookery*. Copyright © Elizabeth David, 1977. First published by Allen Lane. Published by Penguin Books Ltd., London 1979. By permission of Penguin Books Ltd.(157). *Spices, Salt and Aromatics in the English Kitchen*. Copyright © Elizabeth David, 1970. Published by Penguin Books Ltd., London. By permission of Penguin Books Ltd.(163).

Davidis, Henriette, *Praktisches Kochbuch*. Newly revised by Luise Holle. Published in Bielefeld and Leipzig, 1898(149).

Davis, Irving, *A Catalan Cookery Book*. Lucien Scheler, Paris, 1969. By permission of Lucien Scheler, Libraire(138).

De Andreis, Florence, *La Cuisine Provençale d'Aujourd'hui*. © Rivages 1980. Published by Éditions Rivages, Marseille. Translated by permission of Éditions Rivages(135).

De Gouy, Louis P., *The Bread Tray*. Copyright © 1974 by Jacqueline D. Dooner. Reprinted by permission of Dover Publications, Inc., New York(161, 162).

Deschamps, B. and J.Cl. Deschaintre, *Pâtisserie, Confiserie, Glacerie: Travaux Pratiques*. © Éditions J. Lanore CLT-1979. Published by Éditions Jacques Lanore CLT, Paris. Translated by permission of Éditions Jacques Lanore CLT, Malakoff(114).

Disslowa, Marja, *Jak Gotować*. Published by Wydawnictwo Polskie R. Wegnera, Poznań, 1938. Translated by permission of Agencja Autorska, Warsaw, for the author(140).

Dorset Federation of Women's Institutes, *What's Cooking in Dorset*. Published by the Dorset Federation of Women's Institutes, 1972. By permission of the Dorset Federation of Women's Institutes(135).

Dowson, Mrs. Aubrey (Editor), *The Women's Suffrage Cookery Book*. Published by Women's Printing Society Limited, London(121).

Dworkin, Stan and Floss, *Natural Snacks and Sweets: The Good Goodies*. Copyright © 1974 by Stan and Floss Dworkin. Published by Rodale Press, Inc., Book Division, Emmaus, Pa. By permission of Rodale Press, Inc.(158).

Elkon, Juliette, *The Chocolate Cookbook*. Copyright © 1973 by Juliette Elkon. Published by The Bobbs-Merrill Co., Inc., Indianapolis/New York. By permission of The Bobbs-Merrill Co., Inc., Indianapolis(98, 100, 125).

Fance, Wilfred J. (Editor), *The New International Confectioner*. © Copyright English language editions Virtue and Company Limited, London and Coulsdon. © Copyright international editions Rone Kramer publisher, Lugano-Castagnola, Switzerland. Fourth edition with revisions published in 1979 by Virtue and Company Limited. By permission of Virtue and Company Limited(108).

The Fannie Farmer Cookbook. Eleventh edition, revised by Wilma Lord Perkins. Copyright 1896, 1900, 1901, 1902, 1903, 1904, 1905, 1906, 1912, 1914 by Fannie Merritt Farmer. Copyright 1915, 1918, 1923, 1924, 1928, 1929 by Cora D. Perkins. Copyright 1930, 1931, 1932, 1933, 1934, 1936, 1941, 1942, 1946, 1951 by Dexter Perkins. Copyright © 1959, 1965 by Dexter and Wilma Lord Perkins. Published by Little, Brown & Company, Boston. By permission of The Fannie Farmer Cookbook Corporation(97, 104).

Fernie, M.D., W. T., *Meals Medicinal: with "Herbal Simples."* Published by John Wright & Co., Bristol 1905. By permission of John Wright and Sons Limited, Bristol(158).

Filippini, Maria Nunzia, *La Cuisine Corse*. Published by Société d'Éditions-Serena, Ajaccio, 1978. Translated by permission of Société d'Éditions-Serena(130).

Flexner, Marion, *Out of Kentucky Kitchens*. Copyright, 1949 by Marion Flexner. Published by Franklin Watts, Inc., New York. By permission of Franklin Watts, Inc.(97, 110).

Foods of the World. *American Cooking: The Great West*. Copyright © 1971 by Time Inc. *The Cooking of India*. Copyright © 1969, 1975 by Time Inc.(106; 154).

Francatelli's The Modern Cook (1846). Copyright © 1973 by Dover Publications, Inc. Published by Dover Publications, Inc., New York(131).

Frank, Dorothy C., *Cooking with Nuts*. © 1979 by Dorothy C. Frank. Published by Clarkson N. Potter, Inc./Publishers, New York. By permission of Clarkson N. Potter, Inc.(128).

Frederick, J. George, *Pennsylvania Dutch Cookery*. Copyright 1935 by The Business Bourse. Published by The Business Bourse Publishers. A reprint of the Original © Favorite Recipes Press, Inc., 1966. By permission of Favorite Recipes Press/Nashville Educational Marketing Services, Inc., Nashville, Tennessee(125).

García, Maria Luisa, *El Arte de Cocinar*. Copyright © M. Luisa García. Eighth edition published by Edival Ediciones, Valladolid 1977. Translated by permission of the author, Mieres, Asturias(135).

Gaspero, Josh (Editor), *Hershey's 1934 Cookbook*. © Copyright 1971 by Hershey Foods Corporation. Published by Hershey Foods Corporation, Hershey, Pa. By permission of Hershey Foods Corporation(99).

Gavotti, Erina (Editor), *Millericette*. © Copyright 1965 by Garzanti Editore. Published by Garzanti Editore, Milan. Translated by permission of Garzanti Editore s.p.a.(107).

Gérard, Jacqueline, *Bonnes Recettes d'Autrefois*. © Librairie Larousse, 1980. Published by Librairie Larousse, Paris. Translated by permission of Société Encyclopédique Universelle, Paris(147, 151).

The Girl Guides' Association of Fiji (Editors), *South Sea Islands Recipes*. Published by The Girl Guides' Association of Fiji 1958. By permission of Fiji Girl Guides' Association(113).

Giusti, Giorgio (Editor), *Centonovantadue Ricette dell'800 Padano*. Published in Modena 1970. Translated by permission of the author, Modena(150).

The Good Housekeeping Institute, *Good Housekeeping Cookery Book*. © The Hearst Corporation 1944, 1966, 1972, 1976. First published in Great Britain 1948. Reprinted by Ebury Press, London 1977. By permission of National Magazine Co., Ltd., London(112).

Gosetti, Fernanda, *In Cucina con Fernanda Gosetti*. © 1978 Fabbri Editori, Milano. Published by Fabbri Editori. Translated by permission of Gruppo Editoriale Fabbri Bompiani Sonzogno Etas, Milano(132, 146).

The Great Cooks' Guide to Cookies. Copyright © 1977 by Albert Lowenthal Sr.(126—Carol Cutler).

Haitsma Mulier-van Beusekom, C. A. H. (Editor), *Culinaire Encyclopédie*. Copyright © 1957/1971 by Elsevier Nederland, Amsterdam. Published by Elsevier 1957. Revised edition 1971 by Elsevier Nederland B.V. and E.H.A. Nakken-Rovekamp. Translated by permission of Elsevier Nederland B.V.(149).

Hartley, Dorothy, *Food in England*. © Copyright 1954 by Dorothy Hartley. Published by Macdonald and Jane's, London, 1954. Adapted by permission of Macdonald Futura Publishers Ltd., London(132).

Hazelton, Nika, *The Regional Italian Kitchen*. Copyright © 1978 by Nika Hazelton. Published by M. Evans and Company, Inc., New York. Used by permission of Curtis Brown Ltd., New York, and M. Evans and Co., Inc., New York(96, 137, 153).

The Hellenic Woman's Club, *Come Cook With Us*. Copyright © 1967, 1971 by The Hellenic Woman's Club, Norfolk, Virginia. Published by the Bobbs-Merrill Company, Inc. Used by permission of The Hellenic Woman's Club, Norfolk, Virginia(137, 140).

Henderson, H. H. F., H. Toors, and H. M. Callenbach, *Het Nieuwe Kookboek*. © 1948/1972 Zomer & Keuning-Wageningen. Published by Zomer & Keuning-Wageningen. Translated by permission of Zomer & Keuning Boeken B. V. Ede, the Netherlands(118).

Hérissé, Émile, *The Art of Pastry Making*. Published by Ward, Lock, Bowden and Co., London, 1893(101).

Hewitt, Jean, *The New York Times New England Heritage Cookbook*. Copyright © 1972 and 1977 by The New York Times Company. Published by G. P. Putnam's Sons, New York. By permission of Curtis Brown Ltd., New York(110).

Huguenin, Pierre, *Les Meilleures Recettes de ma Pauvre Mère*. Published by Comité de la Foire Gastronomique de Dijon, Dijon, 1936. Translated by permission of Maitre Patrice Huguenin, heir to the author, Begune(162).

Hutchins, Sheila, *English Recipes and Others from Scot-*

d, Wales and Ireland. © 1967 by Sheila Hutchins. First ublished by Methuen & Co., Ltd. Published by The Cook-y Book Club, 1970. By permission of the author(163).

ck, Florence B., Cookery for Every Household. Published by Thomas Nelson and Sons, Ltd., London and Edinburgh 1934. By permission of Thomas Nelson and Sons ., Walton-on-Thames, Surrey(134, 157).

kyll, Lady, Kitchen Essays. © Lady Freyberg. Published Collins Publishers, London and Glasgow 1969. By permission of Collins Publishers. London(96).

e Jekyll Island Garden Club, Golden Isles Cuisine: Collection of Culinary Gems from the Golden Isles of orgia. Copyright © 1978 by Dot Gibson Publications, 03 Rainbow Drive, Waycross, Ga. 31501(105—Dorothy Donovan).

wry, Mary (Editor), Warne's Model Cookery. © Copyright F. Warne (Publishers) Limited. Published by Frederick arne and Co., London and New York 1872. By permission of Frederick Warne (Publishers) Limited(142).

hnson, Alice B., The Complete Scandinavian Cook-ok. Copyright © 1964 by Alice B. Johnson. Reprinted by rmission of Macmillan Publishing Co., Inc.(144).

e Junior Charity League of Monroe, Louisi-a, The Cotton Country Collection. Copyright 1972 Junior harity League, Monroe, Louisiana. Published by The Junior Charity League of Monroe. By permission of The Cotton Country Collection, Junior Charity League, Inc.(99, 0, 136).

e Junior League of Charleston, West Virginia, Inc. ountain Measures. Copyright © 1974 by The Junior ague of Charleston, West Virginia, Inc. Published by The nior League of Charleston, West Virginia, Inc., P.O. Box 24, Charleston, W.V., 25327(106—Mrs. William E. amb).

nior League of Houston, Inc., Houston Junior ague Cookbook: Favorite Recipes. Copyright © 1968 by e Junior League of Houston. Reprinted by permission of e Junior League of Houston, 1626 Post Oak Park Drive, ouston, Tex. 77027(104, 144).

nior League of Memphis, Inc. The Memphis Cook ok. Copyright 1952 the Junior League of Memphis, Inc. blished by Memphis Junior League Publications of the nior League of Memphis, Inc., Memphis, Tennessee. By rmission of Memphis Junior League Publications of the nior League of Memphis, Inc.(110—Mrs. J. N. Beley).

e Junior League of Pine Bluff, Inc., Southern Ac-nt. Copyright © 1976 by The Junior League of Pine ff, Inc., Pine Bluff, Arkansas. Used by permission of e Junior League of Pine Bluff, Inc.(106—Mrs. John E. aruthers Sr.).

nior League of Spartanburg, Inc., Spartanburg crets II. Published by the Junior League of Spartanburg, ., Spartanburg, South Carolina 1964. By permission of Junior League of Spartanburg, Inc.(126—Jane hitaker).

aplan, Janet, Crackers and Snackers. Copyright © 76 by Janet Kaplan. Reprinted by permission of Janet aplan, 46 Rodeo Avenue, Sausalito, Calif. 94965(155, 6, 158).

aufman, William I. and Sister Mary Ursula ooper, O.P., The Art of Creole Cookery. Copyright © 62 by William I. Kaufman and Emelda Marie Cooper. ed by permission of William I. Kaufman(127, 138).

amarz, Inge, The Balkan Cookbook. © 1972 by own Publishers, Inc. Published by Crown Publishers, Inc., w York. By permission of Crown Publishers, Inc.(113, 6, 163).

üger, Arne and Annette Wolter, Kochen Heute. © Gräfe und Unzer Verlag München. Published by Gräfe d Unzer GmbH. Translated by permission of Gräfe und zer GmbH(146).

asri, Ahmed, 240 Recettes de Cuisine Marocaine. © 78 Jacques Grancher, Éditeur. Published by Jacques rancher, Éditeur, Paris. Translated by permission of cques Grancher, Éditeur(138, 143).

ng, George, The Cuisine of Hungary. Copyright © 71 by George Lang. Published by Atheneum Publishers, ., New York. By permission of Atheneum Publishers, .(162).

Levy, Faye, La Varenne Tour Book. © 1979 La Varenne U.S.A., Inc. Published by Peanut Butter Publishing, Seattle, Wash. By permission of Latoque International Ltd., Gladwyne, Pa.(95, 148).

The McCormick Spices of the World Cookbook. Copyright © 1979 by McCormick & Co., Inc. Published by McGraw-Hill Book Company, New York. By permission of McGraw-Hill Book Company(117).

MacMiadhacháin, Anna, Spanish Regional Cookery. Copyright © Anna MacMiadhacháin, 1976. Published by Penguin Books Ltd., London. By permission of Penguin Books Ltd.(152).

Maffioli, Giuseppe, Cucina e Vini delle Tre Venezie. © Copyright 1972 U. Mursia & C. Published by U. Mursia & C., Milan. Translated by permission of Ugo Mursia Editore(111).

Magyar, Elek, Kochbuch für Feinschmecker. © Dr. Magyar Bálint. © Dr. Magyar Pál. Originally published in 1967 under the title Az Ínyesmester Szakácskönyve by Corvina Verlag, Budapest. Translated by permission of Artisjus, Agence Litteraire Theatrale et de Musique, Budapest, on behalf of the legal successors of Elek Magyar(109).

Manning, Elise W., Country Fair Cookbook: Every Recipe a Blue Ribbon Winner. Copyright © 1975 by Farm Journal, Inc. Reprinted by permission of Farm Journal, Inc.(104).

Le Manuel de la Friandise (ou les Talents de ma Cuisinière Isabeau Mis en Lumière). Attributed to author of Le Petit Cuisinier Économe. Published by Janet, Libraire, Rue Saint-Jacques, Paris, in 1796 and 1797(115).

Manuel Pratique de Cuisine Provençale. © Pierre Belfond, 1980. Published by Pierre Belfond, Paris(133, 151).

Martin, Faye, Rodale's Naturally Delicious Desserts and Snacks. Copyright © 1978 Rodale Press, Inc. Published by Rodale Press Inc., Emmaus, Pa. By permission of Rodale Press Inc.(156, 160).

Mathiot, Ginette, Je Sais Faire la Pâtisserie. © 1938 Albin Michel, Éditeur, Paris. Published by Éditions Albin Michel. Translated by permission of Éditions Albin Michel(145).

Mestayer de Echagüe, María (Marquesa de Parabere), Confitería y Repostería (Enciclopedia Culinaria). Seventh Edition published by Espasa-Calpe, S.A., Madrid 1950. Translated by permission of Editorial Espasa-Calpe S.A.(153).

Miller, Anthony (Editor), Good Food from Singapore. Second edition 1960. Published by J. Ay-Buch & Co., Ltd.(160).

Mosto, Ranieri da, Il Veneto in Cucina. © Di Aldo Martello Editore-Milano. Published by Aldo Martello Editore, 1974. Translated by permission of Giunti Publishing Group, Florence(141).

New Jersey Recipes, Olde & New. Published by Jersey Central Power & Light Company. By permission of Jersey Central Power & Light Company, Morristown, N.J.(97, 103).

Nichols, Nell B., Editor, Farm Journal's Country Cookbook. Copyright © 1959, 1972 by Farm Journal, Inc. Reprinted by permission of Farm Journal, Inc.(107, 113).

Norberg, Inga (Editor), Good Food from Sweden. Published by Chatto & Windus, London 1935. By permission of Curtis Brown Ltd., London, Agents for the editor(119).

Norman, Hope J. and Louise A. Simon (Editors), Louisiana Entertains. Menus and Recipes from The Rapides Symphony Guild, Alexandria, La. Copyright © 1978 by Rapides Symphony Guild, Alexandria, La. Published by Rapides Symphony Guild. By permission of Rapides Symphony Guild(131—Judy M. Heyman).

Ortiz, Elisabeth Lambert, The Complete Book of Mexican Cooking. Copyright © 1967 by Elisabeth Lambert Ortiz. Published by M. Evans and Company, Inc., New York. By permission of the author(139).

Pappas, Lou Seibert, Cookies. Copyright © 1980 by Nitty Gritty Productions. Used by permission of Nitty Gritty Productions(102, 145).

Pasley, Virginia, The Christmas Cookie Book. Copyright 1949 by Virginia Pasley. Published by Atlantic Little, Brown and Co. By permission of the author, Westwood,

Calif.(139).

Pearl, Anita May, Completely Cheese: The Cheeselover's Companion. Co-authors Constance Cuttle and Barbara B. Deskins. Edited by David Kolatch. Copyright © 1978 by Jonathan David Publishers, Inc. Published by Warner Books by arrangement with Jonathan David Publishers, Inc., New York. By permission of Jonathan David Publishers, Inc.(163).

Peck, Paula, The Art of Fine Baking. Copyright © 1961 by Paula Peck. Reprinted by permission of Simon & Schuster, a division of Gulf & Western Corporation(98, 152).

Perry, Josephine, Cookies from Many Lands. Reprinted by permission of Dover Publications, 1972(100).

Piotrowski, Joyce, The Christmas Cookie Collection. Copyright © 1978 by The Peppercorn(139).

Portinari, Laura Gras, Cucina e Vini del Piemonte e della Valle D'Aosta. © Copyright 1971 U. Mursia & C. Published by U. Mursia & C., Milan. Translated by permission of Ugo Mursia Editore(136, 138, 146).

Ramazani, Nesta, Persian Cooking. Copyright © 1974 by Nesta Ramazani. Published by Quadrangle/The New York Times Book Company, New York. By permission of the author(107).

Rao, Nguyen Ngoc, La Cuisine Chinoise à l'Usage des Français. © 1980, by Éditions Denoël, Paris. Published by Éditions Denoël. Translated by permission of Éditions Denoël(127, 128).

Reich, Lilly Joss, The Viennese Pastry Cookbook. Copyright © 1970 by Lilly Joss Reich. Reprinted with permission of Macmillan Publishing Co., Inc.(154).

Rey-Billeton, Lucette, Les Bonnes Recettes du Soleil. © by Éditions Aubanel 1980. Published by Éditions Aubanel, Avignon. Translated by permission of Éditions Aubanel(118).

Richardson, Mrs. Don (Editor), Carolina Low Country Cook Book of Georgetown, South Carolina. © 1947 Mrs. Don Richardson, Georgetown, S.C. Printed by Walker, Evans & Cogswell Co., Charleston, S.C., 1963, 1975 for Women's Auxiliary, Prince George, Winyah, Protestant Episcopal Church, Georgetown, S.C. By permission of Mrs. Don Richardson(149—Bess Ellis).

Rivoyre, Éliane and Jacquette de, La Cuisine Landaise (Cuisines du Terroir). © 1980, by Éditions Denoël, Paris. Published by Éditions Denoël. Translated by permission of Éditions Denoël(94, 123).

Romagnoli, Margaret and G. Franco, The New Italian Cooking. Copyright © 1980 by Margaret and G. Franco Romagnoli. Reprinted by permission of Atlantic-Little, Brown(141).

Rombauer, Irma S. and Marion Rombauer Becker, The Joy of Cooking. Copyright © 1931, 1936, 1941, 1942, 1943, 1946, 1951, 1952, 1953, 1962, 1963, 1964, 1975 by Irma S. Rombauer and Marion Rombauer Becker. Reprinted by permission of the publisher, The Bobbs-Merrill Company, Inc.(103).

Ross, Annette Laslett and Jean Adams Disney, The Art of Making Good Cookies Plain and Fancy. Copyright © 1963 by Annette Laslett Ross and Jean Adams Disney. Published in America by Doubleday & Co. Inc., New York. Published in England as Good Cookies by Faber and Faber Limited, London 1963. By permission of Doubleday & Co. Inc.(95, 98, 142, 154).

Sahni, Julie, Classic Indian Cooking. Copyright © 1980 by Julie Sahni. Published by William Morrow and Company, Inc., New York. By permission of Jill Norman & Hobhouse Ltd., London and William Morrow and Company(159, 160).

St. Clair, Lady Harriet (Editor), Dainty Dishes. Eleventh edition published c. 1880 by John Hogg, London(133).

Santa Maria, Jack, Indian Sweet Cookery. © Jack Santa Maria 1979. Published by Rider and Company, London. By permission of Rider and Company(153).

Scheibler, Sophie Wilhelmine, Allgemeines Deutsches Kochbuch für Alle Stände. Published by C. F. Amelangs Verlag, Leipzig 1896(101, 102, 121, 122).

Schuler, Elizabeth, Mein Kochbuch. © Copyright 1948 by Schuler-Verlag, Stuttgart-N, Lenzhalde 28. Published by Schuler Verlagsgesellschaft mbH, Herrsching. Translated by permission of Schuler Verlagsgesellschaft mbH(123).

Serra, Victoria, *Tía Victoria's Spanish Kitchen.* English text copyright © by Elizabeth Gili, 1963. Published by Kaye & Ward Ltd., London, 1963. Translated by Elizabeth Gili from the original Spanish entitled *Sabores: Cocina del Hogar* by Victoria Serra Sunol. By permission of Kaye & Ward Ltd.(102).

The Settlement Cook Book. Copyright © 1965, 1976 by the Settlement Cookbook Co. Reprinted by permission of Simon & Schuster, a division of Gulf & Western Corporation(111).

Showalter, Mary Emma, *Mennonite Community Cookbook.* Copyright © 1950, 1957, renewed 1978 by Mary Emma Showalter. Reprinted by permission of Herald Press, Scottsdale, Pa. 15683(103—Mrs. M. A. Benner; 115—Mrs. Silas Beachy).

Smith, E., *The Compleat Housewife: or, Accomplish'd Gentlewoman's Companion.* Fifteenth edition, London 1753. Facsimile edition first published 1968 by Literary Services and Production Limited, London(94).

Spry, Constance and Rosemary Hume, *The Constance Spry Cookery Book.* Copyright © 1957 by Constance Spry. Reprinted by permission of E. P. Dutton, Inc., New York, and J. M. Dent & Sons, Ltd., London(157).

Stechishin, Savella, *Traditional Ukrainian Cookery.* Copyright, 1957, 1959 by Savella Stechishin. Published by Trident Press Ltd., Winnipeg, Canada 1979. By permission of Trident Press Ltd.(109).

Stoll, F. M. and W. H. de Groot, *Het Haagse Kookboek.* © 1973 Van Goor Zonen. © 1979 Elsevier Nederland B.V., Amsterdam/Brussels. Published by Gebroeders van Cleef, den Haag. Translated by permission of Elsevier Nederland B.V.(144).

Stuber, Hedwig Maria, *Ich Helf Dir Kochen.* © BLV Verlagsgesellschaft mbH, Munchen, 1955. Published by BLV Verlagsgesellschaft mbH, Munich. Translated by permission of BLV Verlagsgesellschaft mbH(117, 128, 162).

Sumption, Lois Lintner and Marguerite Lintner Ashbrook, *Around-the-World Cooky Book.* Published by Dover Publications, Inc., New York 1979. Originally published under the title *Cookies and More Cookies* by Chas. A. Bennett Co., Peoria, Ill., 1948(94, 116).

Thuilier, Raymond and Michel Lemonnier, *Les Recettes de Baumanière.* © 1980, Éditions Stock. Published by Éditions Stock, Paris. Translated by permission of Éditions Stock(152).

Vaughan, Beatrice, *Yankee Hill-Country Cooking.* Copyright © 1963 by Beatrice Vaughan. Published by The Stephen Greene Press, Brattleboro, Vt. 05301(100, 105).

Vence, Céline, *Encyclopédie Hachette de la Cuisine Régionale.* © Hachette 1979. Published by Librairie Hachette, Paris. Translated by permission of Librairie Hachette(114).

Vialardi, Giovanni, *Trattato di Cucina, Pasticceria Moderna*(105).

Vitalis, M., *Les Bases de la Pâtisserie, Confiserie, Glacerie.* © Éditions CLT J. Lanore. Published by Éditions Jacques Lanore CLT, Paris 1980. Translated by permission of Éditions Jacques Lanore CLT, Malakoff(145, 147, 149).

Wade, Margaret, *Cakes and Biscuits.* © 1977 Phoebus Publishing Company/BPC Publishing Limited, London. Published by The Hamlyn Publishing Group Limited, London. Adapted by permission of Macdonald Educational Limited, London(119).

Wakefield, Ruth Graves, *Toll House Tried and True Recipes.* Published by Dover Publications, Inc.(99).

Walker, Lorna and Joyce Hughes, *The Complete Bread Book.* © Copyright The Hamlyn Publishing Group Limited 1977. Published by The Hamlyn Publishing Group Limited, London. By permission of The Hamlyn Publishing Group Limited(156).

Weaver, Louise Bennett and Helen Cowles Le-Cron, *A Thousand Ways to Please a Husband.* Copyright, 1917 by Britton Publishing Company, Inc. Copyright, 1932 by A. L. Burt Company. Published by Blue Ribbon Books, Inc., New York(116).

Weber, Dominique, *Les Bonnes Recettes des Provinces de France.* © Bordas, Paris, 1979. Published by Éditions Bordas, Paris. Translated by permission of Éditions Bordas(137, 147).

White, Florence, *Good English Food.* First published by Jonathan Cape Ltd., London, 1952. By permission of Jonathan Cape Ltd.(122).

Willan, Anne, *French Cookery School.* Copyright © 1980 by Anne Willan and Jane Grigson. Reprinted by permission of Harold Ober Associates, Inc.(133).

Witty, Helen and Elizabeth Schneider Colchie, *Better Than Store-Bought.* Copyright © 1979 by Helen Witty and Elizabeth Schneider Colchie. Published by Harper & Row Publishers, Inc., New York. By permission of Harper & Row Publishers, Inc.(120, 129, 130, 161).

Wolcott, Imogene (Editor), *The Yankee Cook Book.* Copyright 1939, © 1963 by Imogene Wolcott. Published by Ives Washburn, Inc., New York(116—Gretchen McMullen 131—Marjorie Mills).

Yianilos, Theresa Karas, *The Complete Greek Cookbook.* Copyright © 1971 by Theresa Karas Yianilos (Funk & Wagnall). Reprinted by permission of Harper & Row Publishers, Inc.(143).

Acknowledgments

The indexes for this book were prepared by Karla J. Knight. The editors are particularly indebted to Don Dubois, American Institute of Baking, Manhattan, Kansas; Gail Duff, Kent, England; Temple R. Mayhall, Biscuit and Cracker Manufacturers' Association, Washington, D.C.; Bob Mills, The Vermont Country Store, Rockingham, Vermont; John C. Morris, Ekco Products, Inc., Chicago; Lyman Orton, The Vermont Country Store, Weston, Vermont; Ann O'Sullivan, Majorca, Spain; Nancy Pollard, La Cuisine, Alexandria, Virginia; Dr. R. H. Smith, Aberdeen, Scotland.

The editors also wish to thank: Danielle Adkinson, London; Bagpuss Antiques, Grays Antique Market, London; Baker Smith (Cake Decorators) Ltd., Surrey, England; Maggie Black, London; Nora Carey, Paris; Marisa Centis, London; Carol Charlton, London; Josephine Christian, Somerset, England; Lesley Coates, Essex, England; Emma Codrington, Surrey, England; Dr. W. F. Collins, Virginia Polytechnic Institute and State University, Blacksburg; June Dowding, Essex, England; Maurice DuFour, Ridgewells, Bethesda, Maryland; Mimi Errington, Nottinghamshire, England; Jay Ferguson, London; Nayla Freeman, London; Julian Hale, London; Annie Hall, London; Margaret Happel, Nabisco Brands USA, East Hanover, New Jersey; Evan K. Heaton, Kay McWatters, Department of Food Science, University of Georgia, Experiment; Maggi Heinz, London; Maria Johnson, Kent, England; Rebecca Johnson, Publications South, Inc., Atlanta, Georgia; Sarah Kelly, London; Wanda Kemp-Welch, Nottinghamshire, England; Elisabeth Lamers, Accokeek, Maryland; Philippa Millard, London; Sonya Mills, Oxford, England; Wendy Morris, London; Dilys Naylor, Surrey, England; Winona O'Connor, Essex, England; Dr. Richard E. Pyler, Department of Cereal Chemistry and Technology, North Dakota State University, Fargo; Sylvia Robertson, Surrey, England; Julie Sahni, Brooklyn; Eloise Sanchez, Washington, D.C.; Peggy Simon, The Sugar Association, Inc., Washington, D.C.; Melvin Sjerven, Milling and Baking News, Kansas City, Missouri; Bruce Stillings, Nabisco Brands USA, Fairlawn, New Jersey; James H. Sullivan, Grocery Products Division, McCormick & Company, Inc., Baltimore, Maryland; Ray Thelen, San Diego, California; Stephanie Thompson, London; Fiona Tillett, London; Tina Walker, London; Rita Walters, Essex, England; Jolene Worthington, Chicago.

Picture Credits

The sources for the pictures in this book are listed below. Credits for each of the photographers and illustrators are listed by page number in sequence with successive pages indicated by hyphens; where necessary, the locations of pictures within pages are also indicated—separated from page numbers by dashes.

Photographs by John Elliott: 7—bottom center, bottom right, 8—bottom, 9—top, 10-12, 16-17—bottom, 18, 19—top left, bottom left and center, 22—center and right, 23-26, 32-33, 74-75, 76—bottom, 80-81, 86-87.
Photographs by Tom Belshaw: 6, 7—top and bottom left, 9—bottom, 14, 19—bottom right, 27, 30-31, 36-38, 39—top, 40-41, 42—center and right, 43—bottom left, 44—top, 46-51, 78-79, 88, 92.
Other photographs (alphabetically): John Cook, 34-35—top, 66-67, 70—left, center and top right, 71—top. Alan Duns, 34-35—bottom, 39—bottom, 44—bottom, 45, 70—bottom right, 71—bottom. Louis Klein, 2. Bob Komar, 4, 6—bottom, 42—bottom left, 43—top and bottom right, 54-59, 60—top, 61-64, 68-69, 72, 76—top, 77. Aldo Tutino, cover, 8—top, 13, 16-17—top, 19—top right, 20-21, 22—bottom left, 28-29, 52-53, 60—bottom, 82-84, 89-91.
Illustrations: From The Mary Evans Picture Library and private sources and *Food & Drink: A Pictorial Archive from Nineteenth Century Sources* by Jim Harter, published by Dover Publications, Inc., 1979, 94-161.

Library of Congress Cataloguing in Publication Data
Main entry under title:
Cookies & crackers.
  (The Good cook, techniques and recipes)
  Includes index.
  1. Cookies. 2. Crackers. I. Crackers. I. Time-Life Books.
II. Title: Cookies and crackers. III. Series.
TX772.C64 1982   641.8'654   82-5839
ISBN 0-8094-2939-X   AACR2
ISBN 0-8094-2938-1 (lib. bdg.)
ISBN 0-8094-2937-3 (retail ed.)